Bodie
ON THE ROAD

DRIVING THE PACIFIC COAST HIGHWAY
WITH MY RESCUE DOG

BELINDA JONES

summersdale

BODIE ON THE ROAD

Summersdale Publishers Ltd
46 West Street
Chichester
West Sussex
PO19 1RP
UK

www.summersdale.com

Printed and bound by CPI Group (UK) Ltd, Croydon, CR0 4YY

ISBN: 978-1-78685-074-4

Substantial discounts on bulk quantities of Summersdale books are available to corporations, professional associations and other organisations. For details contact general enquiries: telephone: +44 (0) 1243 771107, fax: +44 (0) 1243 786300 or email: enquiries@summersdale.com.

For Winnie
Bodie's First & Biggest Dog Love
2007–2017

Contents

PACIFIC
OCEAN

OREGON

Portland
Mount Tabor
Lincoln City
Newport   Silverton
Oregon Dunes
Bandon   Eugene
Port Orford
Gold Beach
Klamath Falls
Tour Thru Tree
Weed
Eureka
Mount Shasta
Benbow Inn

IDAHO

NEVADA

Santa Rosa   Napa Valley
San Francisco
Sunol
Salinas
Carmel
Big Sur   CALIFORNIA
Cambria
Pismo Beach
Solvang
Santa Barbara   San Ysidro Ranch
Los Angeles

He loves to ride in cars!
PRYOR'S PLANET ON BODIE

Prologue

Before Bodie, I would have sworn I was a cat person to my very core. With a minor sideline in shrews around the age of five. And only then because my tabby Tibbles had scared them rigid, excavating them from the flower bed, and I was trying to resuscitate their dainty rodent selves by giving them mouth-to-mouth.

My mother was horrified – she wasn't even keen on the idea of a muddy-pawed cat in the house.

'Have you seen Tibbles?' she would ask every night as she came to tuck me in.

'He looked like he was heading out...' I'd reply vaguely, as if I'd caught him streaking his whiskers with cologne and adjusting his fedora when, in reality, he was wedged hot and stifled down by my feet.

The second my mum closed the bedroom door, I'd raise the top of the duvet and he'd tunnel towards the light, take a moment to inhale the cooler air, then settle his head on my pillow where we'd sleep nose to nose, exchanging breath for breath until morning.

I was rarely parted from him. When my parents divorced, I insisted on transporting him to and from my dad's every single weekend and even brought him house-hunting with us on the grounds that 'he had to like the new home too'.

Moving away to London at age 19 to study journalism, I was forced to get my fixes on street corners: there wasn't a cat secreted under a parked car that I couldn't coax out for a nuzzle. Ten years on, when my magazine freelancing took me to Los Angeles, I began volunteering as a 'Cat Socialiser' at the Glendale Humane Society. The American kitties were just as lovely as the British ones, but I would avert my eyes every time I walked past the dog enclosures, flinching like a prison newbie as those hardened convicts rattled the iron doors and bashed tin cups against the bars, taunting and whooping and howling.

Why did they always make such a racket? It felt so threatening to me, all that lunging and flashing of teeth. Such a relief to get to the cat room where my feline sisterhood would slink and splay in the sunlight – just another day at the spa. I'd scoop up the neediest furball, relish its purring and look out of the window at the dogs: all that pent-up energy, all that walking and running they were longing to do. But I was no use to them. Aside from being scared and skill-less, I was more on a par with the repose schedule of cats – I liked to be lying down almost all of the day.

But then, as spring unfurled its fresh greenery, I underwent The Change.

Part One

Finding Bodie

Chapter 1

Love at First Sit

It was almost eerie how it happened.

Each time I stepped outside my door, I found myself entranced by every passing dog, be it a trudgey, waddling dumpling or dainty pin-legged prancer. As we made our approach, the world would shift into slow motion and I'd feel like I'd stepped into one of those shampoo ads where the woman shakes and flips her cascading locks – only in this case it would be the golden swing and spring of a Spaniel's ears or the grasses-in-the-wind sway of a Sheepdog's coat that held me spellbound.

Drawing level, our eyes would lock and they would give me a knowing look as if to say, *'It's time...'*

At first I couldn't understand this sudden urgent pull. Typically after a relationship break-up I'm ultra-sensitive to the sight of every couple – yearning for their sense of togetherness, experiencing every public nuzzle and dreamy-eyed gaze with left-out longing – but this time all I saw was imminent pain: didn't they know that happiness was just a phase and heartbreak was lurking around the corner?

The bond that seemed to be calling to me the most was that of human and dog.

Perhaps it just seemed safer and more honest. Dogs don't leave you. You don't come home one day to find a suitcase by the door or a farewell note stuck to the fridge. Dogs don't fall out of love with their owners. And, most emphatically, dogs do not abandon you to go and fight pirates in Somalia.

As exit strategies go, I suppose Nathan's was a pretty good one. You can't really argue with the US Navy's deployment schedule. You can, however, complain about it, shake your fists at the sky and ask why-why-why after over 20 years of duds you finally meet a good one and then he's taken away.

Of course plenty of couples survive these six-month separations. And I was all set to do the same. Even when they added a second 'cruise' to Russia and permanently relocated him 3,000 miles away from me in Virginia, meaning that we would only be able to be together for two or three weeks of the coming year.

As I prepared to turn the anguish of long-distance love into an art form, he told me that he felt he couldn't make me any promises in the face of such uncertainty. He was just being realistic. Responsible even. All I heard was the rejection. He said I was the love of his life but he was letting me go.

I fell to my knees as I watched my dreams of having a happy heart and a dimply baby and someone to snug up to at night evaporate into the Los Angeles smog. I was 41 at that point and I had finally started to believe that my turn had come. Now I felt like the plain girl who can't believe her luck that the school stud has asked her out, only to find out that it was all for a bet. Humiliated by my own hope.

Yet some part of me wouldn't accept what was happening. Why would things finally line up within my grasp only to be snatched away? Was I really supposed to go back to the way I was before? Suddenly everything I had been looking forward to had gone. My life had never looked so blank. Even my writing, which had always been my salvation, offered no solace.

While I disappeared into a murky underworld of disillusionment and despair, everyone around me seemed to think I'd dodged a bullet – life as a Navy wife would have been no picnic. That I couldn't deny. The year we had been together had already been testing and I was about as far from military-compatible as a person could be. So it had to be for the best. At some point I would stop shaking and feel relief. Right? I was lucky in so many other ways. Just not romantically. Eventually this sensation of having experienced a life-changing love wouldn't even seem real. Eventually, I too would tut at the whimsical notion that it could have lasted. Eventually, I would just go back to being me.

But for now, I wanted to know, how was I supposed to get through another day?

If I knew one thing for sure it was that this time I couldn't get through this alone. I needed assistance from a metaphorical Saint Bernard, if not perhaps a real one. Preferably one equipped with a hefty cask of brandy.

It's time…

They say you shouldn't pick out a dog post-break-up because you're too needy and emotionally unhinged to make a balanced, considered decision.

It's quite true. But I only found this out *after* the fact.

All I knew at the time was that I felt like I might spontaneously combust if I didn't find an outlet for all my displaced love. I had no idea my motive would be so transparent.

'Oh I get it, she's trying to replace the boyfriend!' my landlord hooted when the local Humane Society called to check that my apartment building would in fact allow pets.

My sense of being exposed increased when I read through the application form.

Reason for adoption – please circle one of the following:

- *Playmate for family dog.*
- *Guard dog.*
- *Exercise motivator.*
- *Companion.*

My face grew hot at the last option.

They know. They know how lonely I am. They know I can't make a relationship work with a person so I'm resorting to a dog.

And then it dawned on me: if it's there in black and white on an official form then I am not alone in my aloneness – I am not the only person to have reached out in this way. Maybe there isn't even any shame in it. Certainly, in some ways, this listing was an endorsement – that emptiness I am hoping to ease... It can be done! And a dog is just the thing to do it.

But which dog? With over half a million unwanted dogs in the US to choose from, how would I know which one was meant to be mine? And would I reach him before he became another euthanasia statistic? (A chilling 60 per cent of shelter dogs don't make it.)

Eager to get started, I began my selection process online.

I knew I didn't want a handbag dog – nothing I could accidentally sit on or suck up with the vacuum. What I really wanted was something that could knock me over. The bigger and furrier the better. Basically Chewbacca on all fours.

For days I fixated on a Tibetan Mastiff named Dharma, captivated by her squinty old-soul eyes and the fountain of fluff she had for a tail. I loved the idea of being able to wrap my arms around that warm body and become entirely engulfed by nose-tickling wisps. But then I read that Tibetan Mastiffs are nocturnal barkers and I didn't think my neighbours would thank me for that.

Akitas appealed, though something about their dignified stance suggested they'd rather keep their immaculate coat just so and not have you tousling them willy-nilly. Plus I read that they have a dominant personality and need an owner who can exert control. I am not that owner.

So I moved on to Huskies.

I had always found sled dogs to be the most swoon-inducingly striking – the precision tufting of that monochromatic fur, the zing of those white-blue eyes – but they didn't seem the best match for the eternal sunshine of California and, if my people-pleasing issues translated into dog-pleasing, I could end up relocating to Siberia.

The one breed I found myself drawn to over and over again was the Chow Chow. They really do look like a cross between a teddy bear and a lion, chubby with dense fur and crowned with a back-combed ruff. I particularly liked the amber hues and the contrast of their bluey-black tongues, like they'd been sucking on a blackcurrant cough drop. I didn't mind that they were considered aloof and 'not as motivated as other dogs to please their masters' because I was used to cats and actually found their disdain endearing.

(Add that to the 'discuss in therapy' list.)

But then I found out my landlord had a 'No Chow' policy. And he used to breed them. I think it may have had something to do with their 'bite first, ask questions later' reputation. Apparently, this is due to their lack of peripheral vision (thus easily caught unawares) but I suppose that is of little consolation to the person with the fang marks in their thigh.

And so I looked at every other breed – from wiry Airedales to sleek Weimaraners – but no matter how beguiling the pose, Chows remained my guilty pleasure and I always found my way back to their online listings, falling so deeply in love with one shaggy old beast that I actually snuck along to the Pasadena Humane Society to meet him.

I was the one working the puppy-dog eyes when I got there – Kerry (the girl assigned to help me) said that Leo was not a good match for a first-time owner and insisted on parading a ramshackle array of strays before me. My gaze repeatedly returned to Leo's cage. He was nine so not exactly on the hot list as far as adoptions go. Couldn't I at least meet him? Eventually she conceded and told me to wait in the play area.

As soon as he walked in, he reared up and threw his raggedy paws around me.

'GET DOWN!' She yanked him back.

'Oh I don't mind!' I actually welcomed the affection.

'He's got a severe humping problem.'

'Oh!' I startled.

I hadn't realised he was trying to hump me; I thought he just wanted a hug. Same old story.

'Trust me, you'll soon grow tired of this,' Kerry tutted as Leo tried it on seven more times in as many minutes.

The truth is, if she hadn't been so insistent that he was a bad idea for me, he'd be home with me right now. I was not in a discerning, objective frame of mind. All I really wanted was to leave the shelter a different person to the sad, shuffling reject who had come in. I wanted to spin round three times and become a bouncy, new dog owner – laughing and skipping through fields of buttercups. I wanted to have something positive and surprising to say when people asked how I was. I wanted to jolt myself out of my malaise by doing something major, irreversible and demanding.

The last criteria may sound strange – who needs extra demands in their life? The truth was that, after a lifetime of prioritising freedom above all else, I had ended up feeling unanchored and unconnected. I wanted some responsibility. I actually wanted to be able to say, 'Oh I'd love to but I can't – I've got to get home to feed the dog.'

So I couldn't leave empty-handed, I just couldn't. I asked if I could peruse the cages by myself, see if there were any other options we might have overlooked. Another couple had just arrived so she let me wander unattended. What a relief that was

– before I felt like I was trying to humour a matchmaker but now I could let my instincts guide me. As odd as it may sound, you really do have to find your dog physically attractive. The genius thing is that everyone has wildly different tastes – some like smushed-up thug faces, others high-society bone structure and snootishly elevated jaws. There is a dog for every man or woman. But where was mine?

As I moved among the cages, I felt as if I was flicking through images on a dating site. No, no, not me… Hmmm, maybe… And then I saw this scrappy little yellow-and-white fellow who looked like the early pencil sketch for a cartoon. As our eyes met, I got the heart wrench I'd been waiting for. I knelt beside the cage and he came straight over, such a gentle presence but with a clear message, 'I am lonesome and in need of saving.' And there it was – that melting sensation. I'd been suckered!

I wanted to run and find Kerry but I was worried he'd be snatched up in my absence so for the next ten minutes I guarded his cage – periodically edging down the path, hoping to catch Kerry, only to dart back if I saw newcomers on the prowl. Finally, she appeared.

'Ta-daaaa!' I made a grand flourish.

'Oh no.'

'No?' My face fell.

'Not for a first-time owner.'

'Really?' I sighed exasperated. *'But why?'*

She looked around and then leaned close, 'Killed a cat, scaled a six-foot wall, bit a man.'

I looked back at this little tuft of a dog. 'You did all that?'

'What can I tell you?' he seemed to say. 'We all have bad days.'

'He needs a more experienced handler,' Kerry insisted.

Still, I was torn. The wall scaling could be seen as athleticism. Maybe the man in question was a burglar. But the cat... I could never forgive myself if he did that again on my watch.

'Okay,' I mumbled. 'I'll keep looking.'

And I did – every night – trawling the internet, searching for the canine love of my life. Every time I thought, 'He's the one!' I'd be knocked back. Just as with my taste in men, it seemed that I was fatally attracted to all the troubled basket cases with dark pasts and antisocial habits.

One day a friend dropped round to find my make-up tracked with tears.

'Listen to this,' I sniffed. 'Some guy who evaluates foreclosed homes goes into this dank, dark property, uses the flash to photograph the bathroom because there is no light and when he gets home and reviews the pictures he sees there is a dog huddled in the corner – he didn't even know he was there, didn't make a sound. So he returns and finds this weak little puppy, so skinny his ribcage is showing. He hasn't had any food or fresh water in a month because the owners just shut him in the bathroom when they left the house. Can you imagine?'

'That's awful.'

'It gets worse!' I continued with tale after tale of abandonment and abuse until my friend couldn't take any more and finally rallied in exasperation, '*Why don't you just get a happy dog?*'

This concept literally stopped me in my tracks.

Up until that moment I thought the whole point of getting a rescue dog was that you found yourself swamped with compassion at his tragic story and then took his trembling, fearful frame and lavished him with love until he was all better.

That had always been my approach to human relationships, after all – my (clearly flawed) theory being that if I were the one to make a sad heart happy, they would never leave me.

The idea of teaming up with a being that was already happy and didn't need fixing, just a home... Well, that was a revelation.

The very next day I was heading for the Farmers Market in Studio City when I spied a street adoption scenario. This is quite popular in California – rescue groups catching the eyes of passers-by by setting up a little pop-up shop, often outside the big pet stores, with their blessing of course. This one was outside a bank but on a busy pedestrian intersection and featured a dozen or so dog crates draped in blankets to shield the occupants from the sun. I didn't know at this point that Pryor's Planet was founded by comedian Richard Pryor, or that the attractive woman with the black pixie crop over by the small dog playpen was in fact his widow, Jennifer.

Scanning the bigger dog crates, my heart did a little leap as I spied a Chow. With one eye. Double whammy. Instantly forgetting my vow to ditch the sympathy vote, I all but fell to my knees at the base of his cage, eager to show respect for this most ancient of breeds. Naturally he ignored me. Next to him was a stocky, short-haired mutt whom, in turn, I ignored.

Another woman, Trudy, introduced me to both. The Chow promptly turned his back on me and yes there was the issue of my landlord's ban on Chows but, really, I wasn't going to let either of these minor details deter me. I could hear Trudy saying how the other dog, Bodie, would be ideal for a first-time owner, ideal for someone who lived in a small apartment, ideal for someone who liked to travel – he was always game for a car ride.

'Mmmhmmm...'

'Would you like to meet him?'

I said yes more to be polite than anything and to give the Chow a little more time to come around to me.

She led Bodie over to the low brick wall, I sat down and then he did the same, planting his furry behind on my bare flip-flopped foot.

And that was all it took. One move and he'd won me over.

'He's such an easy-going fellow,' Trudy told me as she smooshed his face until it wrinkled into a Shar Pei. 'You can do anything to him and he doesn't mind a bit.'

Sold and sold. I've never liked those irritable animals that squirm and writhe away from your touch.

'Do you know what he is, breed-wise?'

She hesitated.

'You can tell me anything and I'll believe you – I'm very new to the dog world.'

'The ears suggest Shepherd,' she ventured, inviting me to feel their thick velvet.

Large, pointy and ultra-alert. That sounded about right.

'The barrel body?'

'Pitbull,' she said, almost under her breath.

'It's okay,' I assured her. 'I watch the *Dog Whisperer*. I'm not prejudiced.'

'The truth is, everyone sees something different in him: Akita, Cattle Dog—'

And then he yawned extensively, tongue rolling out like a stretch of moist Hubba Bubba. And that's when I saw the bluey-purple stripes underneath, spots on top.

'Is there a little bit of Chow in him?'

'Most likely.'

I grinned back at her. A Chow that didn't look like one and wasn't classed as one. It was so cunning, I loved it. We had a winner!

While I took in every fleck of his fur, Trudy told me a little about his history: how he was picked up as a stray on the mean streets of South Central LA, possibly as the result of his owner losing their home – the homeless shelters don't accept animals so he may well have been turned loose to fend for himself. It doesn't bear thinking about – this smiley chap wandering around gangland LA, hot sun bearing down, barely a blade of grass to be had. Where did he sleep? What did he find to eat while foraging in the street garbage? He had a cough and a sniffle when Animal Control bundled him in their van and took him to a shelter that only allots one month for collection or adoption. No one came to claim him. No one wanted to take him home. So he was sent to death row. Literally hours before he was to be put down, Pryor's Planet swooped in and rescued him. Since then he'd been with a mix of foster families, most recently a bunch of musician guys.

'They say he loves to run.'

I looked down at him sitting so patiently in the sunshine, eyes closed now, maybe dreaming of the same buttercup field as me.

'What do you think?'

My heart was beating fast. I knew I wanted him. Pryor's Planet wanted me to have him. Was I being rash? Suddenly the magnitude of the decision hit me: this is all day every day for the next ten years or so. It was all happening so fast! I spent longer picking out my last toothbrush. And yet I heard myself say: 'Just tell me what I need to do and I'll do it.'

Chapter 2

In the Doghouse

And so the day came for the Home Visit. Pryor's Planet insist on checking out the dog's future residence before completing the adoption. I think this is an excellent policy and, in a bid to meet their standards, my apartment had never been so clean.

I paced the gleaming floorboards and rearranged the vase of fresh flowers, wondering if he'd like the place, wondering how he'd react. It had been three days since we first met – would he show any recognition?

Ding-dong!

In he bowled, sniffing fervently, not a hint of caution, which I took to be a good sign. Better yet, when I sat down by the window to fill out the rest of the paperwork, he padded over and sat diligently beside me like he knew exactly why he was there: 'So you're my new master. That's cool! I'm down with that.'

And then I began asking a million questions that had only just occurred to me.

'What time does he get up in the morning?'

'He'll fit in with your schedule.'

'And I take him straight out for a pee?'

'Absolutely. You might want to have an outfit ready so you can just pull it on and stumble out.'

I experienced a moment's unease – I never go out without my make-up on.

'And where should he sleep?'

'Wherever you are comfortable having him.'

'And while I'm working…'

'He'll probably just lie by your feet.'

Oh I liked that idea. Silent companionship.

'And what time should I feed him? How much exercise does he need? Is it all right to take him to the dog park? What about leaving him in the house alone?'

To the last question Trudy said I was probably best getting a crate.

'Really?' I found this surprising, since I presumed he would have had bad experiences with caging.

'They find it very comforting having their own space,' she assured me. 'You can drape a blanket over the top to make it feel more sheltered and snug.'

'And I just shut him in there?' I still wasn't convinced.

'He'll be fine.'

We went through the Pryor's Planet contract, basically confirming that I would have their phone number on his collar tag as well as my own and that if I ever had to give him up, they would be my first call.

Trudy then explained that he'd just been neutered so I needed to be watchful that he didn't keep 'worrying' the stitches. 'They'll fall out when they're good and ready,' she assured me.

And then she got to her feet and headed for the door.

'So…' I hesitated.

She turned back.

'Is he mine? Can he stay?'

She smiled and nodded. 'He's all yours.'

I couldn't believe it. I thought they might just come, give me the once-over and then go away and deliberate some more but I'd been approved! Oh my god!

The second the door closed, I wondered what the hell I'd done. Watching Bodie trot back and forth, toenails clicking on the varnished wood, I felt like I may as well have a wild boar running loose in the house – it just felt so alien. I was used to the subtle stealth of cats. He was just so robust and stocky. My place is compact and he seemed to be everywhere: in the bedroom, the bathroom, the kitchen pantry, back into the lounge. What exactly was I supposed to *do* with him? If he were a cat, he'd be asleep by now. But instead his brown eyes looked at me full of expectation. I looked back with undisguised inadequacy.

It's then I realised that I didn't have a single dog accoutrement – I didn't want to be presumptuous so I had held back on buying a dog bed and bowl. I didn't even have any dog food. How terrible! Like bringing a newborn into a home without a nursery or even a rattle.

And so I decided our first walk would be to the pet store.

Turns out that simply watching the *Dog Whisperer* does not infuse you with a mastery of The Walk. I knew he wasn't supposed to go ahead of me; I knew I was supposed to set the pace. I knew there wasn't meant to be any pulling. But Bodie was so hyped-up by his new environment he continually criss-crossed the path in front of me, tangling the way-too-long leash in the shrubbery, spurting ahead and then stopping abruptly. It was only a ten-minute walk but at this rate we'd be lucky if we got there before sunset. Bang went my vision of a nice, even-paced stroll.

'Oh no! Not in that flower bed!'

He started kicking up the turf for no apparent reason.

As I pulled him away he dervished around, forcing me to constantly change leash hands to un-twirl myself, then yanked me on with shoulder-dislocating force.

It was then I understood the advantage of a powder-puff-sized Pomeranian or Bichon Frise. If they're running amok, you just pick them up and put them in your bag. Bodie was just so strong! Thank goodness I didn't get anything bigger or I'd be rucked face-first over the dislodged paving slabs and unruly tree roots.

'Oh my god!'

He just peed on my foot. And I'm wearing flip-flops.

I quickened my pace towards the experts.

Set between a frozen yoghurt bar and a nail salon, Catts & Doggs had always intrigued me with its one-off style. Would you paint a pet store black? Even their logo is made from hand-curled metal. As we entered, Bodie's excitement increased – his nose twitching at the heady combination of peanut butter and (what I later discover to be) dehydrated bulls' penises, also known as Bully Sticks.

A sweet-as-can-be chap named Andy came directly to my aid, welcoming Bodie like his long-lost son and then helping me pick out a lighter, shorter leash. One that wouldn't leave my hands looking like I'd been roping cattle.

'I don't know how they got so black,' I frowned, contemplating the blue leash he came with.

But then Andy held up his sooty palms.

'I think it's coming from his fur.'

It was then I spied the full-service dog wash beyond the racks of pigs' ear chews.

'Do you have a slot open now?'

Andy checked the appointment book and we were a go.

'Just come back in an hour.' Andy reached for him.

'Oh.' I hesitated. 'Do you mind if I stick around for the first few minutes to make sure he's okay? I only got him today.'

'Of course, no problem.'

I watched as he led Bodie into the back area, all kitted out with waist-high tubs and giant dryer fans. Within minutes Bodie was wearing a mop-top of white bubbles, fully accentuating his coal-black nose. He didn't seem to be resisting the process, just looked mildly humiliated.

Deciding it was probably best to leave him to it, I headed next door to indulge in a swirl of pomegranate frozen yogurt, hold the toppings. I was glad for the breather and sat there wondering when he was going to have his first poop. Perhaps I should get some more bags. Who knew how often he'd go? I shuddered a little – it was going to be so gross. I couldn't believe I was even putting myself in a situation where that was to become a daily activity. What if it made me retch? What if I was actually sick? God, what a pair we'd be.

I looked at my watch. Ages to go.

I really hoped I'd done the right thing. I hoped I was going to be a capable dog owner. Suddenly, it felt like there was so much I didn't know. I needed to do some more reading. I wondered when I should tell people that I had officially adopted him. I'd already fibbed to my mother about this being a temporary foster scenario, all very casual. Because? Well, she just sounded so aghast. As if I hadn't thought through any of the responsibilities.

'You know dogs need walking every day?'

'Yes.'

'And feeding. Every day.'

'Yes.'

'They're a lot more work than a cat.'

'I know.'

'And what about when you go away?'

'Well, I'll leave a few meals in the freezer and he should be familiar with the neighbourhood by then.'

My dad, contrastingly, was actually all for it: 'Better that than making another bad man-decision.'

What can I say? He had a point.

Thank goodness all my LA friends thought it was a splendid idea.

'Yesssss! Do it!!!' they cheered.

That's what I love about California – so gung-ho and make-it-happen! Act now, think later!

My phone buzzed. It was the fur salon at Catts & Doggs – Bodie was ready to go!

As with all the best makeovers, the subject sashayed out with newfound confidence and self-esteem.

'Look at me!' Bodie said, all peppy and proud. 'Look how handsome I am!'

'He's a completely different colour!' I gasped at his transformation from rusty brunette to honey blonde. 'And soft! Feel him – he's like teddy-bear soft.'

Andy smiled. 'He's a good dog.'

'Really?' I looked up at him, eager for assurance.

'Trust me. You can imagine how many dogs we get in here. All different temperaments. You got a good one.'

Now it was my turn to puff up with pride.

Excitedly, I picked out the dog basics – a bed, pair of bowls, big sack of healthy food and a long orange snake with multiple squeakers. And then I realised I couldn't possibly carry them all back so I had to go home and get the car. Bodie was indeed an excellent passenger. In fact, I grew more impressed by him with every passing hour. Didn't all dogs beg and whimper at the dinner table? Bodie wouldn't even look my way as I was eating. I had no qualms about him climbing on the furniture but every time I hoicked him on to the sofa or the bed, he jumped right back down to lie dutifully beside me on the floor. Shoes were left un-chewed, doors un-scratched. He was just so zen.

And then the medication wore off.

Chapter 3

A Whole New World

The first morning I woke to Bodie's bright eyes and hyper-alert tail I thought I was dreaming and let my lids droop back closed. But then the high-pitched whining started up and it dawned on me: 'That dog is real and he needs a wee!'

I threw myself out of bed and pulled on the outfit I had set aside, just as Trudy advised. Then I made the mistake of looking in the bathroom mirror. Like so many of us, I have a 'Styled by Russell Brand' hairdo first thing. The dark purple shadows under my eyes lend my pale complexion a junkie vibe and there's always a big scar-like crease across my chin from where I have smooshed my face into the pillow during the night. Not a good look.

Bodie whined again.

I don't think I'm an especially vain person – I just don't like to actively scare people. That is why I always put on make-up before I leave the house. *Always*. But not that day.

Grimacing, I opened the back door and hurried down to the grassy verge at the front of the apartment block. Bodie sniffed around and then cocked his leg on the tree and began giving it a thorough hosing. I looked up furtively, hoping no neighbours would pass me on their way to work, and that is when I saw that I was not alone – all along the street, people were standing out in pyjama bottoms and hoodies, hair askew, bleary-eyed, some with coffee mug in hand, all waiting on their dog's bladders.

I found myself smiling. My new comrades.

Seeing as I was up and wearing matching shoes, I decided I may as well keep going and get our first morning walk underway.

Prior to this, my outings had always been destination-specific – down the hill to Trader Joe's supermarket, a few blocks to the left to Little Dom's for dinner – but today I was letting Bodie's nose lead the way.

And what a busy nose it was. His olfactory fascination for every leaf, lamp post, paving slab and bin amazed me. Everything seemed to have a giddying allure – would you look at the brass-studding on this door, surely imported from Morocco? And the spiky crest of this bird of paradise flower! Now, that's a cool vintage Mustang in the driveway here – I think I'd like to pee on its tyres. Okay, I know this road sign says it's a dead end but let's go up here anyway – who knows what we'll find?

All the while he was leading me hither and thither, I felt this niggling sense of familiarity. About forty minutes into the walk it dawned on me: I used to be like that. I used to be overly curious and wilfully enthusiastic, always straining forward, eager to the point of impatience to discover what adventure lay around the corner. Nathan even said that what first attracted him to me was my 'exuberance'. What a far-off planet that seemed now. Was it possible to regain that level of vitality, I wondered, or was I worn out for good?

Suddenly a squirrel sighting sent Bodie into warp drive – as the skittish grey taunter shot up the nearest tree, he reared up on to his hind legs and danced agitatedly at its base like Ali waiting to strike. Even as I coaxed him onward around the corner, he was still pogoing upright – boing-boing-boing – causing a morning jogger to do a stumbling double take, as if I was taking my dog for a vertical walk.

This was fun!

The only fly in the ointment was the poop. Or lack thereof. Nothing that morning or that evening or the day following that. At first I couldn't believe my luck – I had acquired the world's only non-pooping dog! But by Day Three I was starting to feel concerned. On our morning walk I left Trudy a voicemail, wondering if this was normal, and the second I clicked off the phone, he did the do. I was so relieved I performed a triumphant jig right there on Los Feliz Boulevard during rush hour traffic.

'Good boy, Bodie!'

It felt nothing short of an honour to pick up after him now and I skipped all the way home, swinging the blue plastic baggie as if he'd just presented me with a trinket from Tiffany's.

The rather more curious thing was that he seemed eager to return the favour: every time I headed for the bathroom he came tearing in after me and waited diligently while I used the facilities. I would have shooed him away but he just seemed so pleased with himself.

'See! You can count on me. I'll be there for loo!'

Perhaps his last owner had a communal bathroom and a broken lock and he was obliged to stand guard? All I know is that nothing would keep him from his post – not even when he came in at such a pace that he skidded head first into my dropped knickers and ended up looking like he was wearing a surgeon's mask.

'It's wonderful to hear you laugh again,' my mum sighed down the phone to me. 'Bodie sounds quite the tonic.'

'Oh he is,' I confirmed.

For starters, his clumsiness was pure slapstick. I had just three wooden steps at my back door and not a day went by that he didn't pratfall down them in his eagerness to get going on his walk. He would make querying Scooby-Doo noises when someone came to check the mailboxes next to my front door. He extended his front paws like Superman when he lay out on his tummy and flattened out his hindquarters like a frog or spatchcocked chicken. Perhaps it was a way of cooling his inner thighs but it never ceased to make me smile. Especially when his top lip got all lopsidedly stuck up on his gum and he looked like a cartoon baddie mid-snarl.

Time and again I would catch myself chortling out loud and think, 'By golly, I've still got it! I still have the capacity to be amused and delighted! Who knew?'

In essence, Bodie consumed my every waking thought – all I wanted to do was make his day better and try to decode his every sigh or brow furrow. I couldn't walk past him without dropping down for a cuddle. But I wouldn't say it was love at this point. It had only been two weeks and we were both cautious, seemingly wary that this new presence might be just as fleeting as the others. I could tell he was still on his best behaviour. Still wouldn't look my way while I was eating. (Even if he would monitor my every move at all other times, which I found highly disconcerting, like having a reality TV crew trailing me around the house.) Still wouldn't sleep on the bed...

But then one evening my friend Tezz was in town from Vegas, stopped in for a quick drink, and we got into such an intense conversation about his latest show that we didn't notice that Bodie was lapping at the goblet of Merlot he had set on the floor beside his chair. I know now that grapes are poisonous to dogs but at the time all I saw was a loosening of his inhibitions – he slept on the bed all night that night, only to wake up the next morning with such a startled look he all but grabbed the sheets up around his chin, gasping, 'What did I do?'

'I know, Bodie, you're not that kind of dog. We won't mention it again.'

But from then on he slept beside me. Or, more specifically, diagonally across the mattress, requiring assorted angular contortions to accommodate him.

I definitely felt closer to him after that. The yearning for Nathan weighed heavy within me but there was comfort to be found enfolding Bodie's warm body in my arms. It soothed me. Took the edge off. My tears began to trickle rather than chug and mostly I thought I'd really rather not dampen his fur, or his spirits for that matter. Not that he seemed to take my melancholy on board. He had such a steadiness to him, he just let me be. I was so grateful for that. Grateful to not have to pretend to be feeling something that I wasn't. Since Nathan and I had parted, I had been hiding myself away from most of my friends, feeling that my misery was too disquieting to be around. But during my daily walks, it became apparent that no one was paying attention to me any more – Bodie pulled focus and held it.

'He's quite the acrobat!' the owner of a Pyrenean Mountain Dog noted as Bodie flipped like a fish on a line, trying to engage her dog in play.

'Isn't he just?' I mirrored her incredulity. 'Yours seems to have a very sweet nature.'

She shrugged away the compliment. 'I just wish he didn't shed so much. I could make another dog with what I vacuum up every day.'

I appreciated this easy camaraderie between dog owners – straight into conversation, no formalities required. A brief, take-me-as-you-find-me encounter with no agenda. How refreshing.

And then I noticed that the other person didn't even have to have a dog to engage – people out running or tending their garden stopped what they were doing to ask what breed Bodie was, how old and was it okay to pet him?

This was amazing to me. LA isn't an unfriendly place – people in Los Feliz always say hello as you pass them in the street – but this was way beyond a courteous 'Morning!' The mere sight of Bodie's goofy grin and wonky walk had their faces lighting up and hearts flinging wide open. I'd never felt such instantaneous warmth from strangers. It's almost as if walking with a dog allows you to experience the very best in people – their least cynical, most loving side, typically reserved for people they've known and trusted for years.

One elderly woman asked if he was a rescue and when I told her yes she said, 'Bless you!' with such sincerity that, for the first time in a long time, I felt like I'd done something good.

And so, suitably emboldened, I accepted an invitation to a sunny poolside party in Studio City and prepared to introduce him to the clan.

'Oh you got a *dog* dog!' was the primary reaction from fellow Brit Tony.

'As opposed to…'

'I thought you were going to get something fluffy and pocket-sized. You know like Josh and Sindy have.'

Josh and Sindy have a Papillon, a breed named after the French word for butterfly on account of having ears that could get a *petit chien* airborne with a brief flutter. Little Jimmy may only be 8 pounds but he runs them ragged, like a child eternally stuck in the terrible twos phase.

That day Sindy was looking particularly haunted.

'Everything all right?' I asked.

She gulped hard. 'I just discovered that, of all the breeds, Papillons live the longest.'

'How long?'

'Twenty-four years,' she said with a gurgle of dread.

'Gosh. That is a long time.'

Tony, eavesdropping, couldn't believe it so he did a quick Google search and found out there was one Papillon in the UK that lived until he was 29.

'He's going to be with us until we retire,' Sindy confirmed and then poured herself another glass of wine.

Tony's then wife Gretchen seemed delighted by Bodie's eager explorations of the house, noting, 'He is very stocky. Like a pig.'

'Excuse me!'

'In a nice way.'

'Is there a nice way to resemble a pig?' I queried. I actually thought he looked more like a deer – particularly the light tufty fluff on his bottom and the way his outsize ears go back at a 45-degree angle.

Amy had the best reaction. She just called him Handsome Man over and over, and he had absolutely no reason to doubt her – Bodie is a confident dog, happy in his own fur. He didn't appear to be carrying any trauma from his past, whereas Jack, the Shepherd/Rhodesian Ridgeback mix peeking out from behind the sofa, had more of a mixed personality. His mum Leslie described him as, 'Alternately confident and wary. Wildly exuberant yet mellow. Protective but the sound of a firework will leave him cowering... He's a Gemini like his mama!'

I can totally see why she was drawn to this dog. There's just something about him that stirs your heart. Plus he has such attractive lines, coat and bone structure that he looks like the dog version of Hugh Jackman. (Bodie, I see more as a squat Matt Damon.)

Now I come to think of it, Jack's whole household is good-looking. His dad is a hipster musician and mum Leslie is a Pilates instructor with the figure to match. She lives walking distance from me and the day after the pool party she invited me and Bodie to join her and Jack on a hike in Griffith Park.

Following the curve of the sandy path ever upwards, Leslie chatted easily while I rasped for breath and felt my face flushing pink with exertion. But it was worth the trek to the top for the startling panorama of the City of Angels.

It's hard not to feel inspired when you look out at that view, across the cityscape and down to the sea. It made me want to ball up all my heartache and cast it off the hilltop but its grip was too tenacious. Or maybe it was *my* grip that was tight? I had thought about visiting a cord-cutter – a person who performs a scary-sounding spiritual practice severing ties with people you really shouldn't be attached to any more. But I was still reluctant to let Nathan go. I didn't want to be without the feelings I had for him. I knew it couldn't be healthy but some part of me *wanted* to cling on. I thought about discussing this with Leslie but instead sought her counsel on a more pressing issue…

'I can't leave Bodie alone in the house,' I explained. 'Not that he'd do anything destructive while I'm out – it just seems to get him so het up when I try to leave.'

The first time I tried it, he stood on his back paws, pounding at the fragile glass of the back door. I knew it to be fragile because I'd once smashed a pane with a grocery bag swinging from my wrist as I twiddled with the lock. I had this horrible vision of coming home to blood, broken glass and no Bodie, so I rounded the block and came back inside.

The next time, I put a barrier up to keep him away from the back door but was concerned about his gut-wrenching barking so I left my phone on record to assure myself it was just a few minutes' initial complaint. He barked solidly until I got home an hour later.

Finally, I relented and spent $120 on a crate from Petsmart.

'Now you have your own den!' I tried to sound enthusiastic but could only imagine how I would feel being cooped up like that – I still shudder at the memory of the human cages I saw on a school trip to the London Dungeon.

Naturally, I went about introducing him to his 'private suite' in entirely the wrong way, luring him in like the Child Catcher in *Chitty Chitty Bang Bang*, clanking the door closed and hoping for the best.

I can barely bring myself to describe what I came home to that time. Poor Bodie had pooped in distress then paced and twisted in the restricted space until he had covered himself and every inch of the crate in the stinky stuff. I was beyond mortified. It didn't bear thinking about how long he'd been in that dreadful state.

'So now I never go out,' I told Leslie. 'Unless it's somewhere I can take him.'

Leslie shook her head. She had never used crates with Jack so she didn't know what advice to give. But wait! Her neighbour Molly – coincidentally the most popular name for a female dog in the UK – was apparently quite the authority.

'Really?' My eyes gleamed with hope.

Within a few minutes, a rendezvous was arranged and, though I didn't know it at the time, my life was about to veer in a whole new direction.

Chapter 4
When Bodie Met Winnie

I had met Molly once at a dinner party and remembered her as a wickedly funny modelesque blonde with a taste for the finer things in life. What I didn't know at the time was that she had a vast slobbering English Mastiff named Winnie.

They struck me as an unlikely pairing, since owner Molly is visually more of a blonde Afghan Hound – you know, those elegantly slender dogs whose long hair looks like it's been conditioned with Pantene and then flat-ironed. By her own admission, Molly is a Type A clean-freak – every time Winnie takes a slurp of water, she has to mop away the drool and then throw the towel in the washing machine.

But oh how she loves that dog. With good reason – Winnie is about as docile and sweet-natured as can be. Wouldn't hurt a fly. Not on purpose, anyway... Talk about a dog that can knock you off your feet. She doesn't even have to give it any elbow grease, no run-up necessary – she simply has to brush past you and it's like being floored by a wrestler.

Between Bodie and Winnie there's a 70-pound weight difference. You could strap a Bulldog and a Beagle to Bodie's back, and he'd only just come up to her weight. And yet it was love at first sight.

No sooner had we entered Molly's apartment courtyard than they were at it – frolicking and rollicking and tussling with relentless panting enthusiasm. Molly invited me to take a seat at the circular patio table and that's when they began chasing each other round and round like they were magnetised to the inside of a roulette wheel – Winnie with her lumbering, lolloping gait and Bodie with his little legs going nineteen to the dozen. I actually got so dizzy watching them I had to close my eyes a few times. Apparently Bodie felt the same – more than once he concussed himself on a heavy wrought-iron chair leg only to stumble in a daze with cartoon stars twirling about his skull.

'Careful Bode-ster!' Molly would set him straight, administer a treat or add a bone or chew toy to the mix, and then encourage them to rehydrate at the outdoor tap – Winnie's great tongue flapping at the cool flow of water, Bodie elbowing his way in for a parched gulp.

And then they'd start up their track race again.

I couldn't have been more delighted. Bodie had clearly met his match. And I was enjoying the company too. Molly is such a smart wit I could feel my brain sitting up and paying extra attention as she talked. She gave great dog advice, had just begun a dog memoir called *From Dior to Drool* and was a 'military brat' – her father was high up in the Navy and she and her family used to be based out at Virginia Beach, Nathan's current base. There was just so much to talk about!

What a double-whammy new-friend day this had turned out to be!

And then she said, 'It's such a shame that we're not going to be neighbours for much longer.'

'What?'

Even Bodie screeched to a halt at this point.

'We're moving to Oregon.'

'*What?*' I repeated myself.

'Portland is a certified dog paradise. And for what I'm paying for my apartment here I can get an entire three-bedroom house with a huge backyard there.'

Even so, it seemed unfathomable to me to want to leave LA. Contrary to its smoggy, superficial reputation, it really is a wonderful place to live. Sunny and vibrant and the Los Feliz neighbourhood in particular is such a villagey delight. Plus, she had so many friends here – wasn't she going to miss them?

'Leslie may come with me for the drive – we're thinking of taking the dogs on the coastal route, all the way up.'

And that's when my feelings switched from bewilderment and loss to envy.

A road trip! They're going on a road trip *with their dogs.*

I could barely hold myself back from squeaking, 'Can we come too?' but instead settled for a less imposing, 'Maybe we'll come and visit you…'

And then Molly's next social engagement arrived at the gate and we took our leave.

Bodie was so punch-drunk by this point he could barely put one paw in front of the other but I was buzzing all the way home. Travel has always ignited a feverish passion in me. My London flatmate James used to say he'd only have to comment, 'Salzburg looks nice at this time of year…' and within minutes I'd be presenting him with four hotel options, the best flight price and a low-down on the local cuisine. I could never spend $200 on a designer handbag or a pair of shoes but I'd blow it on one night in a fancy hotel in a heartbeat. Sometimes I wondered about all the money I've spent on flights and accommodation over the past 20 years – just how much would it amount to en masse? The price of a new car or a down payment on a house? It's academic really, because if you gave me that money back now, I'd spend it on travel all over again. And I wonder why I have so little to show for my earnings. In the material realm at least. I do have a fabulous array of memories. And I could really see a trip like this adding to the collection.

The most amazing thing was just how excited and motivated I felt. Wasn't I supposed to be catatonic with misery? Could the combination of a new dog and new horizons be the ultimate antidote to heartache? Of course, I really should stay put and get on with my novel writing but it wouldn't hurt to look at a map, would it? Just out of curiosity. I mean, I wasn't even sure how far Portland is from Los Angeles…

One thousand miles, depending on the route.

If it were me, which it's not, I'd divert a little inland to visit Napa. I've always wanted to see California's winelands. And I'd definitely stop off at Redwood National Forest – isn't that where they have those giant drive-through trees? How cool would that be? Gosh, I didn't realise how close Portland was to Seattle – just a three-hour drive apart. I wonder if they are equally rainy?

And then I started to Google. And then Google some more. Along the way I discovered that Portland has been voted most dog-friendly city in America multiple times, thanks in part to its 32 leash-free dog parks, more than 20 dog bakeries and the celebrated annual Doggie Dash in which over 2,000 dog owners unite in a fundraising run/walk along the leafy waterfront. Wouldn't that be amazing? I bet you anything I've just missed it. But no – it's a perfect six weeks away on 15 May.

It's a sign! It's a sign!

I had to get up from the sofa and pace the room – I was getting so carried away. Every time I researched a new destination, another timely event presented itself: the annual Klamath Falls dog show, the Silverton Pet Parade, the Graduation Ceremony for the Guide Dogs for the Blind – all within a few doable days of each other.

I couldn't quite believe the synchronicity of it all.

Up until then, everything had felt like such a battle but this hypothetical itinerary was linking together as effortlessly as a pebble skipping the surface of a lake.

So why not follow through? Why not actually go? After all, it felt so good, so compelling. For the past six months I'd been saving up, thinking Nathan and I were going to start a life together, but now that expense has been nixed I'd have enough funds to cover the trip.

No, no, no. I'm being ridiculous. I'm emotionally unstable. I've only had Bodie a few weeks. I have to let this go.

Oh my god, there's a town just outside San Francisco where a dog was elected mayor! For real. And, just two hours on from there, an entire museum dedicated to Snoopy!

Stop! Just stop.

And so I went back to my normal life. Day after day of sitting in with my laptop, Bodie watching me with a look that said, 'Is this as good as it gets?'

'I don't know what to tell you,' I'd sigh. 'This is my job; this is my life.'

'And the tears?'

I wiped away the salty streams from my cheeks. I barely even noticed them any more – they had become something I just let flow, eager to advance to that 'all-cried-out' stage. Not that I seemed to be getting any closer to shifting the pain. It appeared to have settled in for the duration, weighing heavy within me day and night. I think some part of me was still in shock – love had been such a long time coming, could it really be gone so soon? Was there really no hope?

'Wanna play tug of war?' I offered him the soggy leg of the latest toy he'd ripped the stuffing out of.

He just sighed.

'You miss Winnie, don't you?'

He averted his eyes.

'I know you do. And, trust me, I know what it's like to have your beloved go far, far away.'

For a while I sat there, reviewing all the reasons I had given myself for not taking the trip, all valid. I knew that if I went, I'd be accused of running away from my problems but that wouldn't be the first time, or the tenth for that matter. But what if I looked at this from a different angle: as an act of faith in the name of love? We didn't *both* need to have a broken heart after all – a certain English Mastiff was but a car journey away.

I crawled down on to the floor and contemplated Bodie.

'How would you feel about going on an adventure?'

His head tilted in curiosity.

'Every day a different park or beach or forest for you to explore... Maybe the occasional professional dog massage or a canine cupcake?'

He blinked back at me, eyes filling with wonder.

'You like that?' I asked and then pulled his golden velvety ear to my lips and whispered, 'We could even go and see Winnie.'

He made an impatient sound like, 'Don't tempt me like this! You'd better mean what you say!'

To hell with it, I decided. 'I'm going to take this trip with him – *for the love of dog!*'

Part Two
Highway to Happiness

Chapter 5

The Road Trip

D-day has arrived!

Just one month after our play date with Molly and Winnie, we're ready to embark on a dog-themed road trip to the most dog-friendly city in America!

It's going to be fun and puns all the way.

I've just finished packing Bodie's case (repurposing a zebra-print cooler on wheels) and am just cross-checking the list: water for him, water for me, treats for him, treats for me... when an email pops up from my best friend Sam, excitely telling me that her new man is taking her on a lavish trip to Lake Como in Italy.

'Remember how we stood on the balcony of the Villa d'Este and said, "One day we'll be here with our true loves!"? Well, I'm going there with Marcus! It's all coming true!'

For you, I want to say. *For you.*

I slump down. Her itinerary seems to make a mockery of my plans – I have utterly convinced myself that I want nothing more than to see the rain-squelched dog parks of Oregon, but held up against this romantic ideal...

I feel my eyes swell with hot tears. I am happy for Sam, she so deserves this. I just can't seem to escape this feeling of being left behind. Everyone else I know seems to be forging forward with their lives, pairing up, creating mini-mes and here I am, going away on the trip of a lifetime *with a dog*. Has it really come to this?

Okay. Relax. This is just a knee-jerk reaction. I still want to see and do everything we have scheduled. And yet... My head falls forward into my hands. Why can't I be loved like everyone else? I get these fleeting glimpses of what it could be like to have someone of my own. And then they're gone again.

I try to catch my breath but I feel misery tugging over my head like a hood.

Bodie pads over to me.

I look up at his concerned yet steady brown eyes. I don't know what to say to him.

'Come on, you can't give up now.' He nudges me.

I let my hand roam his furry head and then fondle the velvety ears that have become my substitute security blanket.

He jerks his jaw upward.

'Let's just take off,' he seems to be saying. 'Leave all this sadness behind. Try something new.'

I sit for a moment longer, considering the alternative.

'Okay,' I nod, taking a rousing breath. 'I'll do it for you.'

We've hired a burnt orange Honda Element for our trip because it was voted dog-friendly car of the year on account of its custom canine features, including a mesh dog enclosure at the back with a built-in fan and water bowl and a pull-down ramp for more elderly or heavier dogs. Even the rubber mats have a bone motif. It's a pretty impressive ensemble and I can't wait to get behind the wheel.

New car, new destination, new me (I hope) and a chance to bond with Bodie on a whole new level – after all, they say you never really know someone until you travel with them…

As we pull out of the driveway on to broad, leafy Los Feliz Boulevard, I reflect on the ways in which Bodie has already impacted my life – not least my wardrobe. I previously owned one pair of jeans, which I'd probably worn twice. I was solely into skirts and dresses and flounces. Not too practical at the dog park. I hardly recognised my reflection in shop windows these days – all cropped jeans and check shirts. My handbags have become cross body bags to leave both hands free to corral Bodie, every pocket contains reams of doggy bags like the never-ending handkerchief trick, and my shoes are always muddy and scuffed from our excursions. I have even designated the corridor wardrobe that used to be filled with Nathan's clothes to dog-walking gear. Of course, it's sitting empty today as all my fleecey-khaki items are travelling with us. Along with a few dresses, just in case. That's the beauty of heading into the unknown – you never know what is around the corner.

We're on the 101 Freeway now, passing the exit I took to Studio City the fortuitous day I first met Bodie at the street adoption event, then cruising through Hidden Hills, Thousand Oaks and the outlet empire of Camarillo. We've just passed the hour mark when my earlier depletion is suddenly blitzed by a surge of exhilaration – look at us merging onto the Pacific Coast Highway!

The sea, the sea, the beautiful sea!

I gasp as the road begins running parallel to the ocean. It's just so glitteringly gorgeous it's impossible to feel blue. As the road curves and cliffs rise up, I feel as if my heart is being catapulted forward and we are racing to keep up.

'Here we go, Bodie!'

We ride this wave for another half an hour and then take the Montecito exit. Signs for Mimosa Lane, Bolero Drive and Laguna Blanca School hint at the lush and fragrant beauty that abounds here, in one of the wealthiest zip codes in the whole US.

We may have many motels in our future but we are beginning our journey in style at the legendary San Ysidro Ranch. It's a somewhat justifiable extravagance as it doubles as research for *California Dreamers* – the book I am supposed to be at home writing right now. I was looking for an exclusive hideaway, somewhere a celebrity might relax with her secret husband, away from prying paparazzi. (In the story the husband is a naval officer and their dog is called Bodie – quite the stretch, I know.)

I was quickly entranced by the romantic history of the ranch: Vivien Leigh and Laurence Olivier married here. John Huston wrote *The African Queen* during his three-month stay. It's even Oprah-endorsed – she lives up the road and is a regular at the hotel's Plow & Angel cellar restaurant. Plus, it's less than an hour from Port Hueneme naval base. Perfect for the story but what's in it for Bodie, you might ask?

Well. Quite a bit actually. The property backs on to 17 miles of trails, there is a dedicated dog menu and, on account of the owner being Beanie Baby creator Ty Warner, each dog-occupied room comes with a complimentary Bow Wow

Beanie, be it Stinky the Skunk, Inky the Octopus or Nuts the Squirrel.

But the biggest doggie draw in my mind is the pet massage. For $75 Bodie will have his muscles manipulated and fur fondled by expert hands. I quite envy him his appointment.

'Here we are!' I spy the hotel sign – Western-style lettering branded on weather-greyed wood. I experience a butterfly-flutter of anticipation as we turn up the long driveway, bordered with olive trees and brimming with Spanish lavender.

The gatekeeper motions us through and our tyres grind at the golden grit as we approach the main building, a white storybook cottage cascading with vivacious cerise bougainvillea.

The adjacent rose gardens have a distinctly English feel but the backdrop is pure California with the sun-steeped Santa Ynez Mountains and cobalt blue sky. Bodie whines in rapture, eager to get out and press his undulating nose up against the beauty.

'Any minute now…' I tell him.

This is the first time I've ever checked into a hotel with a dog so I'm not quite sure of the petiquette – is he allowed to come into the lobby with me? I take tentative steps but the bowl of bone-shaped treats and dedicated registration book for 'Privileged Pets' suggest *yes*.

There's just the small matter of the tabby surveying our movements from the library lounge.

'That's Bentley,' the woman on reception introduces us. 'He's the resident cat.'

'Lovely name – very refined.'

'He was actually a stray, found hiding under a Bentley car.'

'Ahhh,' I smile, looking back with even greater affection. He looks so at home on the leather-topped desk, wedged between a brass lamp base and silver planter, part of the furnishings now.

Oh, here we go, Bodie has clocked the feline presence and surges at him but Bentley's obviously seen it all before – the fur on his back doesn't even bristle.

'I won't bother you if you don't bother me,' his steady gaze implies.

'Fair play.' Bodie moves on, enticed by the freebie dog biscuits handed to him by the welcoming staff.

'You want another?'

He doesn't need asking twice.

'And another? How about some water to wash them down?'

Presented with a shiny bowl, Bodie gulps down the contents like it's Happy Hour. More biscuits, more water, oh, the excitement is just too much – with one almighty hack he throws up the whole lot right there on their priceless pale fawn Persian rug.

Oh. My. God. I can't believe my eyes. I go to speak but nothing comes out.

'And this is the reception area...'

I look up and see an impossibly glamorous couple approaching on a property tour. Nooo! I use myself, Bodie and my bag to shield the heap of goo and then try to lock eyes with them as they pass so they don't look down.

'I'm so sorry,' I whisper to the reception staff as the couple pass on to the gardens. 'He's never done this before.'

Their manners and training are so impeccable you'd think Bodie had done little more than sneeze. They tell me not to worry and to enjoy my stay but as I turn back to give one last rueful look, I see the vast rug being rolled away. I can't even imagine the cost of the dry-cleaning bill.

Instead of heading to our cottage, I decide to take Bodie for a quick walk in the woods, just to make sure any further gunk is expelled before we settle into our luxury quarters.

The sun is mellowing and it feels as though we're stepping into the pages of my Flower Fairy book from childhood as we stroll past cottages with names like Fig, Tangerine, Oak and Willow, all lovingly entwined with foliage.

This place really does have a special feel to it. No wonder Oprah, along with her man Stedman and their dogs, chose Montecito, of all the places in the world, to call home. I can't help but wonder if we're traversing some kind of ley line or 'spirit path' as the Peruvians call them. For me it's about that particular feeling when tranquillity meets radiance. It may sound a bit woo-woo but one thing I know for sure is that all traces of this morning's self-pity have left my body. Suddenly I feel like the luckiest girl in the world.

'Come on, Bodie!'

To get to the trails we lean in and climb a hill set with expansive residential homes, the first of which is marked 'Very Private Property'. As opposed to 'Moderately Private'? Talk about keeping up with the Joneses! I expect the next house to be marked, 'Even More Private' and then the one after 'The Most Private of All'.

I'm just wondering who might live here when Bodie veers off towards a grassy plateau, the kind of area designated for event tents. It's quite bare so I'm wondering about the urgent appeal when he starts chomping on something.

'Oh no you don't!' Instinctively, I prise open his jaws, reach deep down his throat and pull out a pitta triangle. 'Oh for goodness' sake!'

'What?' He looks back at me.

'A cocktail sausage I would understand but *pitta*?'

As I wipe the saliva from my hand, it dawns on me that I just experienced my first ever knee-jerk motherly reaction. It didn't even occur to me that he might bite me. I feel a strange sense of accomplishment. I didn't know I had that in me. Maybe I wouldn't have been such a bad mother after all. Maybe certain skills would have just shown up without me having to learn them first.

'Oh Bodie!' I cry out in exasperation as he goes for the discarded pitta again. Perhaps he has some Greek heritage I don't know about. Definitely some Swiss, I decide, as he responds with admirable neutrality to the frenzied barking of a Boxer rallying against the gate of one of the grander mansions. Bodie literally doesn't even bat an eye. I love this about him. Just like Bentley, he simply rises above the fray and continues to do his own thing.

Walking on, I run my hands along the roadside lavender bushes and crush a few purple buds, inhaling the soothing scent so often used in holistic calming potions. I offer my palms to Bodie but he seems more interested in sniffing his most recent pee, trickling down the rock wall. The most overwhelming smell, though, is of money. I stop at the brow of the hill and take in the priceless view – the distant ocean the palest wash against a hazy sky.

It's hard for me to look at the sea and not wonder where Nathan is right now. He's out there somewhere. Surrounded by endless blue. Or perhaps every shade of orange and gold? He could be watching the sunset now. What a panoramic vantage point that must be. I wonder if he ever thinks of me…

'Hey!' Bodie pulls me on. 'This is not what we came here for.'

He's quite right. And so I turn my back on the ocean and head for the woods.

Within minutes we find ourselves engulfed in forest, weaving around the eucalyptus trees with their fraying, peeling bark, stepping over mossy logs, inspecting bristles of thistles and feathery ferns. Bodie kicks up a flurry of fallen leaves. This is real-deal dog territory – I feel like I should be wearing tweed knickerbockers and marking each step with a knotty walking stick.

'Isn't this idyllic?' I pause to marvel at the leaf-dappled light, the glossy trickle of the creek beside us, the clarity of the cool water spilling over the rocks.

So many times I've been somewhere beautiful and wished I was sharing it with someone, and now I am. Someone who is loving every second – darting this way and that, sniffing busily, fascinatedly. He's like a street kid in nature for the first time, curiosity driving him on to new discoveries. And then we reach a clearing and the sun infuses Bodie's fur with a golden aura. My angel.

I take a deep breath, inhaling harmony.

Then Bodie lurches at a scuttling bug.

'Okay, that's far enough.' I yank him back. 'We have an appointment to get to.'

There's just the small matter of retracing our steps. I made a mental note of a big craggy boulder – it should be along here somewhere... Stream to our left, that's right. But wait a minute – the ground appears to have switched from a twig-latticed path to a 50-deep layer of leaves. It's like walking on the forest's equivalent of a pillow top mattress – crackling and crunching underfoot, yet remarkably springy.

As Bodie pulls me on, the branches start to close in around us – I'm having to duck and twist just to get around them. Of course, Bodie has no qualms about letting a bendy bush branch spring back to thwack me in the shins but I am concerned about him inadvertently jabbing himself in the eye – the prongs are coming at us from all angles now, snagging at my cardi and needling at my thighs like woodland acupuncture.

Perhaps it's best we turn back – it's obvious we've strayed from the official trail. I turn around but nothing looks familiar or indeed accessible. It's as though the forest invited us in and now has woven a prickly-pokey fence around us. It's then we hear voices from above.

'There must be a path up there!' I cheer.

I pray the people keep talking and when I identify the voices as female I am confident the chit-chat will be continuous. We move towards the voices only to be greeted by a steep, damp bank. I'd say they are about two track loops above us. All we need is to get to the first level. Bodie is game for the scramble but every step I take, I skid back two and now I'm so low to the ground my eyes are the ones in danger of getting a gauging.

I reach for my sunglasses and put them on as protective goggles. Right. We can do this.

'I just need you to lead the way, Bodie,' I say, taking hold of his leash. 'See if you can pull me up!'

He does such a heroic job of hoisting me to safety that I wonder if he has some Husky in him – he didn't seem at all fazed by the extra load.

'Praise be!'

I've never been happier to see gravel in my life. Better yet, I know exactly where we are – we have all but looped back to the start of the trail.

'Good job, Bodie!'

He gives me a confident grin. 'All part of the service!'

The hotel guide assigned to show us to our cottage is too polite to joke that we look like we've been dragged through a hedge backwards, even though we pretty much have.

Just to ram home our lack of polish, our cottage, Rose, is positioned directly adjacent to the Kennedy cottage where the former President and First Lady honeymooned in 1953. You can bet fashion icon Jackie didn't turn up with mud-scraped shins and Stig of the Dump hair. But then we are in the countryside, I remind myself, not on the Laboutin-studded Sunset Strip. Besides, this is Montecito mud – it probably has fantastic beautifying mineral properties.

'I can't believe it!' I gasp.

Our guide has opened our private gate and bid us ascend the steps to the decking, and there at the top, beside the front door, is a wooden sign branded with two words: JONES and BODIE.

I look back at him in amazement. 'H-how?'

It's only on closer inspection that I realise the sign is made up of individual letters. So clever. Just slot them in. What a lovely welcoming touch – it really feels like this is our place now. And what a place it is.

You know how rich people often have eccentric touches to their exquisite taste? So you'll have the luxuriously upholstered window seat and the antique chandelier but then you'll notice a little hand-painted porcelain pig on a side table, sleeping with its head resting upon a soft tassled pillow. That's what it's like here – classic high-end mixed with 'trinkets from my travels', as if this were a real home, right down to the worn-to-softness wine-toned rug splayed hearthside.

What Bodie is noticing is that there is a bottle of Evian water beside his bone-shaped dog bowl (giving new meaning to the term bone china). His treats come in a little gauzey bag embossed with black velvet paw prints. His dog bed looks so plush it makes me want to curl up and take a nap. His assigned Bow Wow Beanie is the Springtime Bear – white with a confetti-like sprinkle of pastel dots. Perhaps a better match for a fluffy little Bichon Frise but Bodie clamps down on it and gives a little prance-dance of joy. It always amazes me how a dog instinctively knows what gifts are meant for him.

He brings it along as we are shown the bathroom – easily long enough to play a game of fetch, especially if you open out the far door on to the patio. This may be the prettiest bathroom I've ever seen, magazine layouts included. It's all white-wood wainscoting, cinnamon-coloured beams and natural leafy sunlight gleaming through the picture-book windows. There's a clawfoot tub with a fawn-coloured Persian rug beside it and branch-woven baskets filled with scrolled white towels. The silky-smooth tiles on the floor even heat up – we might just come in here later and lie down on it, like some interior design version of a hot stone treatment.

Then again we might just sit in the hot tub. We're outside now and I can totally see Bodie, cocktail in paw, panting a little as the bubbles tickle his tummy.

The hotel guide leaves us marvelling at the rest of the patio: an outdoor shower with Bulgari cleansing products, jasmine tumbling over the walls... I've never seen Bodie's eyes look so bright. I watch him as he listens to the birds – every time they make a chirrup or a coo, his head jerks to the side and his ears prick up all the more. Just delightful.

To think a few months ago he was on his last day at a kill shelter and look at him now! Talk about the American dream.

I just need to get him cleaned up for his massage.

As tempted as I am to place him in the clawfoot tub, fill it with bubbles and hand him a back brush, I decide the outdoor shower is the more appropriate way to de-mud him. Except, of course, that I get spattered in dirty water and then, as I towel him dry, all his excess fur transfers on to me, coating me in blonde fluff. Hmmm, I wonder if the masseuse would know the difference between us...

Ding-dong!

Bodie greets the doorbell ring with a wolverine howl. Gosh, I hope she knows what she's letting herself in for.

Chapter 6
The Dog Masseuse

Glenys is an instantly likeable South African woman in her sixties, dressed head to toe in white with a mop of tousled grey hair, pink cheeks and a tea & scones hug. I go to introduce her to Bodie but she stops me in my tracks by saying, 'Oh, I already introduced myself to him an hour ago.'

I falter. Did they meet in the woods while I wasn't looking?

'I did a meditation to prepare him for our time together.'

Interesting. Perhaps this is why Bodie is being so obliging. Glenys suggests we head out to the patio and he trots along behind her. She places a white towel on the sunlounger and before I can ruefully inform her that Bodie is unlikely to hop up there or stay, he does just that.

I watch in amazement as he submits to her touch. He's typically such a fidget-bottom, all jumpy and wriggly, but within minutes he enters a deep meditative mode. His lids are heavy, his body outstretched, holding each position with perfect poise like a yoga master. I sit down on the neighbouring sunlounger and watch slack-jawed as she methodically works her way around his legs.

'How ever did you find out you had this gift?' I ask.

She gives a happy shrug. 'I've just always loved dogs. My friends call me the Dog Whisperer!'

'I have to ask – have you ever been bitten?'

'Never. All breeds love to be massaged.'

She's working on Bodie's middle back now and he is responding with some kind of 'upward dog' pose: back legs fully extended, front paws stretched way out, chest raised as he tilts his head all the way back so that his ears are touching his shoulders and his nose is reaching skyward – all the while his eyes are fixed on a cooing Glenys.

'That was wonderful,' Glenys sighs as she concludes his half-hour session. 'He's a very special dog.'

'I bet you say that to all the dog owners!' I smile.

'Really, the pleasure was mine.'

Both Bodie and I are smitten with Glenys and sorry to see her leave.

'So what now?' Bodie looks up at me.

'Now we dine.'

One of the great treats of staying in a hotel is ordering room service and now Bodie can get in on the act with a bone-shaped bowl of chicken and rice while I enjoy steak Diane and a glass of opulent red wine.

We eat fireside – one flip of a switch sends bright yellow flames reaching up the faux-blackened chimney. While I savour every flavoursome morsel, Bodie inhales his dish in two get-every-last-fleck minutes.

Afterwards he joins me on the sofa. I relish the increasing weight upon my chest as he surrenders to a full-bellied sleep. As my left hand smoothes his fur, my right holds a small anthology of dog poetry – *Doggerel* by Carmela Ciuraru. It includes works from such luminaries as William Wordsworth, Elizabeth Barrett Browning and Rudyard Kipling. And it was placed within arm's reach of me on the sofa. I don't know the last time I paused to read something purely for pleasure. It feels so calming to do so, especially in this setting.

My favourite verse is from Siegfried Sassoon's 'Man and Dog'. It muses on the experience of being out in nature together and asks:

> *What is it makes us more than dust?*
> *My trust in him, in me his trust.*

I set down the book and look back at the fire, feeling so safe and cosy, as if I have returned to my childhood home and found everything exactly as I had left it: a wooden rocking horse, a hand-knitted blanket, a benevolent nanny bearing more than a passing resemblance to Glenys. Not that I had these things but it gives me that feeling of being taken back to a time when I was oblivious to all potential harm and heartache.

I certainly didn't expect to feel so good so soon. If I was writing a novel, my character would have to overcome a multitude of obstacles to attain this depth of sated satisfaction. Can it really have been this easy? I thought maybe a couple of weeks in I might start to feel better, but a couple of hours?

What if this is as far as I need to go? If I just stayed here, would the feeling sustain? Perhaps perpetual motion isn't the answer after all – perhaps it's simply a case of knowing when you've arrived at the right place and stopping.

That being said, unless I woke up to find I'd written a best-seller in my sleep, I wouldn't have the bank balance to indefinitely extend my stay, so I'd better relish this one night.

I stand before the vast canopied bed, resting a hand on the dark wood, admiring the never-ending whiteness of the sheets. I have the feeling I am going to sleep well tonight.

But I am wrong.

No sooner am I laid out, ready for my five-star slumber, than Bodie starts to pace.

This is no late-night snooping. He's not in security surveillance mode, checking the latches on the doors and windows – he is fully agitated and anxious.

I prop myself up so I can study his thought bubbles.

'Look, it was nice to visit but I'm ready to go home now,' he seems to be saying.

'Actually, we're staying the night.' I give him a *'Aren't we the lucky ones?'* smile.

'You're kidding.' His face falls and his pacing increases in intensity. 'Oh no-no-no.'

'Bodie!' I try to break his manic routine but he ignores me.

I fall back on to the pillow and feel an uneasy chill creeping through my body – I've concocted this entire trip for him and it's not what he wants. He's all for the daily excursions but at night he wants to be home in his own bed.

'But it's so lovely here, Bodie,' I try to reason as I reach out and attempt to enfold him in my own personal bliss.

He fidgets away, panting and looking imploringly at me. 'Can't you hear all the strange noises out there?'

'That's just the countryside. No harm will come to us, I promise.'

'I don't like it. I don't like it one bit!' he frets some more.

And then his whining turns into a low growl.

There's something – or someone – in the yard.

'Would you feel better if we took a look out there?' I raise up the blind on the glass door, spooking myself with my own reflection, and then peer into the leafy darkness.

Bodie's growling escalates further. I'm presuming he's reacting to some rabbit on a moonlit hop when he erupts with the most blood-curdling howl and frightens me half to death. Talk about sleeping with the enemy. Suddenly, this idyllic picture-book cottage feels like the Hammer House of Horror. I drop the blind and scurry back to bed, heart rattling in my ribcage. That didn't quite go according to plan. Now both of us are quaking. I take some deep breaths and look at the clock – eight more hours till daylight. I can't help but wish Nathan were here. He's such a protector – professionally trained to stand watch and guard against all harm. Not to mention the fact he has biceps like silk-wrapped boulders.

I sigh.

Then again, maybe Bodie just scared off an intruder about to perform some audacious deed like putting a chocolate-dusted almond on the pillow.

So now what?

Never having been in this position before, I reach for my laptop and begin Googling everything related to dog travel and hotel anxiety.

According to Cesar Millan, I should have entered each room ahead of Bodie and thus infused it with my scent to offer something familiar and established amongst all the new fragrances. Too late for that now.

I console myself with the fact that we are only 90 minutes from home. We can of course turn back. Just pack up the car and forget the whole thing. Chalk it up to inexperience. I had no idea he would have this reaction. I thought this was the dream plan but if he's like this here, a place with all these Oprah-endorsed good vibes, what hope is there for the rest of the trip?

Crestfallen, I see all the amazing things I had planned slipping away from me. It's not just the Doris Day hotel or the reunion with Winnie and Molly, it's the thought of losing this newfound sense of purpose. Planning this itinerary has consumed me for weeks, forcing me to look forward. The idea of backtracking, of returning to all that sadness... I don't know what I'll do. I feel the shadow of despondency creeping over me again. A leadenness returning to my heart. Why didn't I see this coming?

I look over at Bodie, hoping for some clue as to my next move and find him snoring into the bedside rug.

'Oh. My. Dog,' I mouth into the low-lit room.

Is it possible that he has settled? I daren't even switch off the light for fear that the click will trigger another episode. Instead I slide my laptop on to the other side of the bed and inch down beneath the sheets, utterly in awe that I have been given a reprieve.

But not so fast – now it's my turn for the night watch. I lie awake until 3 a.m., waiting for the nerves to subside, worrying about absolutely *everything*, until sleep finally claims me.

Chapter 7
Adventures in Santa Barbara

I love a hotel breakfast. It's enough to jettison me out of bed even after a tormented night. I decide that Bodie and I adore bacon equally. I watch him chomp-chomp-chomp on the crispy strips I've added to his kibble and get a kick out of knowing that tonight we'll be cruising to a drive-in movie together, an ambition of mine since seeing *Grease*. (Though I never expected my Danny to be a dog.) Before that I've scheduled Bodie's first off-leash hike at the 70-acre Douglas Family Preserve.

According to my guidebook, this prime slice of Santa Barbara parkland – set on a scenic mesa overlooking Arroyo Burro Beach – was slated for luxury hotel development but locals stepped in and foiled the plan by raising $2 million to protect the land. The largest donation came from actor Michael Douglas, hence the name of the preserve.

'Excuse me?'

'Yes?' I look up at the waiter.

'May I remove Douglas?'

'Um…' I'm thrown by his request. Was I reading out loud? What does he mean exactly?

He repeats his request.

'Ohhhhh! *Da glass*!' I gasp as the penny drops. 'Yes, yes, of course!'

Idiot.

It's a wrench leaving paradise so soon after finding it and I catch myself lingering in each room, so grateful for all the good feelings this cottage has conjured. Optimism is such a wonderful thing and I have missed it so.

I drop into reception to thank everyone for such a dreamy stay and then pause at the end of the driveway for one last lavender-infused snap. But Bodie doesn't look back. He's ready for his next adventure.

It's a sublime 20-minute drive, past the turning for the Four Seasons hotel and along Santa Barbara's version of Cannes' Promenade de la Croisette, looking every inch the American dream with its sun-kissed cyclists and joggers in neatly co-ordinated sportswear and hi-tech trainers. Just past the pier we veer inland and merge with the promising-sounding Cliff Drive, only to have the Garmin divert us into a residential neighbourhood and assert, 'You have arrived at your destination.'

Really? It seems unlikely that there's a 70-acre wonderland tucked amid the bungalows. But then I catch sight of some beckoning branches and minutes later Bodie and I have entered another world.

The Douglas Family Preserve is vast – a broad sandy path roams through the wispy grasses, shaggy trees and prickly cacti in such a delightfully freeform 'anything goes' way that I want to run off-leash myself.

This is clearly a special place, and not just for dogs: little clusters of artists are setting up their canvas and paints amid the wild flowers and over yonder I see paragliders taking flight, the brightly coloured arcs of their chutes looking like assorted fruit peelings – red apple, banana yellow, etc. – against the blue of the sky.

As I pause to take it all in, I realise I can hear the rush-swish of the ocean and smell the nose-tickling saltiness – I just can't see it.

I edge over to our left where the land seems to abruptly end and my stomach lurches at the drop. There are no barriers, nothing to prevent you tripping to oblivion. Well, not exactly oblivion – leaning out as far as my nerve will allow, I see an alluring curve of ivory sand trimming the aquamarine. I wonder how you get down to the beach from here? There's no apparent path. I have a vision of Bodie and me rappelling down with matching hard hats. And then get queasy and scurry back to the dirt path.

Bodie is still on leash. I feel almost self-conscious about the fact, wondering if passers-by will think I'm a control freak or tormenting him by bringing him to a place where his comrades can roam freely. Of course it was my intention to let him loose but I've heard that dogs go nuts when they know a beach playtime is nigh. What if Bodie's nose tells him that nirvana lies beyond that cliff edge and his excitement overpowers reason and he plunges to his death?

Five minutes on, another voice inside me starts nagging, 'If not now, when? When will you trust him? How will you know he is ready unless you give him the chance to prove himself?'

I assure myself that a dog who follows a person so attentively from room to room would not bolt, least of all over the side of a cliff. He's going to stick with his primary bacon-supplier. Definitely.

I take a deep calming breath and attempt to infuse myself with faith and leadership.

And he's off! Running raggle-taggle amid the bushes, hopping over toppled tree stumps and scuffing up the wood chippings.

I try to look confident and casual but I'm checking his every move. I never dare call him in the dog park for fear of looking ineffectual when he ignores me but here, with no one around, I decide to try to bring him back to the path.

'Bodie! Come, Bodie!'

Wow. He actually looked up. Better yet, he came back over in my direction. Not to my side but at least we're now both taking the same route. I'm feeling borderline cocky when two dogs appear from behind the trees. I have a moment of panic, visualising a frantic encounter triggered by Bodie's overenthusiasm but instead he greets them with a cheery, 'Morning!' nod and then trots on his way. Which is kind of a shame because the owners are so darkly attractive they look like a pair of flamenco dancers.

We're nearing the corner of the bluff now. Not so close to the edge, Bodie. Bodie! *Bodie!*

Jeez. This is so nerve-wracking. I never had these concerns with my cat. He was the classic precision tightrope walker; Bodie is more the haphazard rodeo clown.

Right now he's marking so much territory that he's practically walking on just three legs, one forever cocked. Every now and again he loses his balance and falls into the undergrowth, flattening the native plant life, and for a minute my nerves give way to delight. It's clear he's having a terrific time.

And then we round the corner only to be greeted by a scene rivalling the opening credits to the *Dog Whisperer* – a guy is approaching with a pack of ten or so lively dogs, mostly Retriever types with one small black Pug leading the way. The man is gesticulating wildly, trying to warn me about something. I think he's telling me to beware of the red dog that is bounding over, smiling directly at me. He looks so friendly, what could possibly be the problem? Then comes the smell.

'He got skunked!' The man grimaces as he draws level. 'There were these two little babies, so cute, but when the dogs got close – bam! I'm going to have to wash him in baking soda when I get back.'

'Baking soda?'

'Well, some people say tomato juice is the best household remedy for removing the smell.'

'Tomato juice?!' I gasp. There is so much for me to learn about the World of Dog.

I can see he's really suffering from the stench but oddly this is a smell I find appealing. At least in terms of an al fresco waft – I suppose it could get rather more intense in an enclosed car.

'If your dog is the type to go for squirrels, you'd better watch out.'

Uh-oh. My nemesis. No call from my lips could hold Bodie back from that chase. I ready myself with the leash but he's having way too much fun with the dogs to come my way; even as I move on, he continues in the opposite direction with them. I wonder if that's ever happened – the dog walker gets back to base to find he has an extra member or three. Fortunately, this guy is on it. He stalls his pack to allow me to attempt a retrieval. I feel self-conscious, exhibiting my amateur ways in front of a pro. Especially since the dogs are weaving around each other in such a blur of golden fur I can't even figure out which one is mine.

Finally, I get the right dog on the end of the leash. We're heading on our way when the guy backtracks and hands me his card. 'If you ever need professional help.'

My brow crumples. Is it that obvious?

As I watch him continue on his way, I feel a stirring of envy. This has got to rate pretty highly in terms of job satisfaction: making ten dogs deliriously happy while inhaling fresh sea air. The setting itself does all the work – all you have to do is throw the odd stick. I don't mean to sound like I think it's easy, though, because no doubt half of my pack would end up on a canoe bound for Hawaii.

As we continue on, I must confess I am secretly hoping for a skunk sighting. They really are the most striking creatures and the thought of seeing a mewing baby one… I've seen pictures before their tufty plumage kicks in and they just look like little humbug sweets. Bodie and I have a good ole forage in the undergrowth but have no luck finding any *petit* Pepé Le Pews so I decide to un-leash him again. Only to notice a giant horse on the horizon.

I look to the woman walking beside her steed for cues. She doesn't seem concerned and I've only ever seen dogs bounding happily alongside horses so I'm sure it will be fine, if I can just get him back on the leash. I don't want to make any sudden moves and spook the horse, or Bodie for that matter. But he's progressing ever closer. Every step I take, he takes another. I can't reach his collar and I don't want to lunge.

'Wow, that's a lot closer than most dogs get.'

'He's quite fearless,' I tell her, muttering under my breath, 'in a borderline reckless way.'

To be honest, it's not Bodie I'm worried about. I'm not that good around horses, ever since I got thrown on to the frozen earth of Patagonia while out riding with helmet-less, saddle-less gauchos. But this one is a stunner, with her coat of gleaming, sheening auburn. Bodie gives her an admiring once-over and then prepares to move on. But now the horse is intrigued by him. She takes a hoof clop closer, extends her head towards Bodie and flares her giant nostrils. At which point Bodie finally twigs this is not an exceptionally large dog and freaks out, ducking every which way and barking like he's under attack in a haunted house.

I think this is going to be the worst fright of the day but I'm wrong.

We're heading downward now, on a narrow path shrouded with trees. Bodie is getting a little too far ahead for my liking and not responding to my calls. I try to speed up but the earth is too uneven for a mere two-footer. Meanwhile, he is on a roll – little legs picking up speed on the descent.

'Bodie!' I feel a creeping sense of dread. We're approaching street level – there's a bridge ahead but I can't see where it's leading. As I round the corner, my heart stops: the path opens out on to a busy road.

I call to him, trying to be firm and masterful, but he doesn't even acknowledge my cries.

Surely he wouldn't run into the open road where there's nothing to sniff but concrete and metal and exhaust fumes? And then he does the worst possible thing: runs straight into oncoming traffic.

And I do exactly the same.

Only I'm waving my arms wildly, trying to get the trucks and cars to stop, which they most graciously do. It's only now that Bodie seems to realise this wasn't such a brilliant idea and skulks back over to me. I'm shaking so much I can barely clip his leash back on the collar. I don't know if now would be the time to discipline him, to tell him a big loud NO, but I'm too shocked and relieved to do anything but collapse on the pavement, clutching him to me.

I could have lost him. I could have rounded that corner to find him lying motionless beside some swerving black tyre marks, a driver telling me he came out of nowhere.

As I sit there waiting for my heart to stop pounding in my ears, I feel like a horrible, negligent parent. This is the worst kind of reality check. Am I being irresponsible, placing us in these untried, untested situations? Could my desire to escape be putting Bodie's health and safety at risk?

It's tough to be constantly reminded of your shortcomings. I want to be a perfect companion and guardian for Bodie but I'm not. I'm still very much learning on the job. Is this how first-time mums feel? It's like that classic scene from *Sex and the City* when Steve tries to return baby Brady to Miranda, afraid that he might 'break him'. She's having none of it, reminding him that they have an arrangement: Monday to Friday she tries not to kill him, Saturday and Sunday, he tries not to.

So what now? Again I get a blast of 'Let's Call the Whole Thing Off' but then I look up and realise we are back on Cliff Drive, just minutes from one of the best dog beaches in America. I turn to Bodie.

'I'm game!'

'Really?' I query. 'You don't think we should just play it safe from now on? Maybe take things down a notch?'

Already he is pulling me onward.

Apparently near-death experiences aren't quite so traumatic for dogs.

Chapter 8

Bo Derek on a Bicycle

The sight of Hendry's beach lifts my spirits. And not just because there's a restaurant bang on the waterfront. (I always find it so reassuring to know that food is readily to hand.) This is a dazzling location, so beautiful you can't quite believe they've assigned the whole left-hand side of the beach to dogs – every one of them all but losing their mind with gratitude. In fact, the whole area is positively thronging with good vibes: everyone seems chatty and upbeat and frankly chuffed to bits with life.

I'm just wondering how long it will be before I get up the nerve to let Bodie off his leash again when something remarkable happens: a petite golden blonde passes us, deep in conversation with her friend. Her accent causes me to cock my ear and that's when I realise dog trainer Tamar Geller has joined us on the beach. Creator of The Loved Dog training method, Tamar advocates a gentler, kinder, play-based coaching philosophy – the only one endorsed by the Humane Society of the United States – and she has worked with the dogs of numerous celebrities, including Natalie Portman and Eva Mendes. Now, if that isn't a sign, I don't know what is. We have a true guardian angel in our midst and not in a namby-pamby way – the woman is also a former Intelligence Agent in the Israeli Special Forces. So grateful for such a reassuring presence at such a crucial time, I reach for Bodie's collar and dare to release him...

Instead of bounding wildly into the surf like so many of the other dogs, he tiptoes gingerly along the sand. When the frilly edges of the waves come to meet him, he dances back looking thrown, suggesting that this is a new experience for him. We're a world away from South Central now and his nose is working overtime. Marine smells are obviously very different to city or even country ones, and he seems especially entranced by the seaweed with its rubbery ribbons of bobbly brown slime. I take out my camera and capture him just as he's lifting his leg, giving new meaning to the term sea*weed*.

I suppose that is acceptable? I mean, you can't pick up pee.

Oh! Here we go! Playtime!

A black Lab invites Bodie to have a bit of rough and tumble. It may sound unusual parenting but I'm always relieved when Bodie tussles with a dog that is bigger and tougher than him – that way I don't have to worry about him doing any damage or me having to apologise for any agonising squeals. I have confidence that he's sufficiently scrappy to get out of any pickle. Except perhaps this one – in some kind of wrestling pin-down move, the black Lab is standing over Bodie, who is lying on his back trying to push him off with his Thumper legs, to no avail. He struggles; the Lab stands strong. He relaxes then gives another burst. Nothing. The Lab looks like he could hold the position all day.

His owner is the first to crack.

'Well, we've got to be getting home – come on, Brad.'

'Wow! That's the springiest dog I've ever seen!' the next person we pass marvels as Bodie expresses his delight at having regained his freedom of movement. I'm just relieved he doesn't trample her small beige fluffball into the sand. We exchange a few pleasantries and then head on our way.

'Enjoy your walk!'

'You too!'

For a stretch it's just me and Bodie. I start to breathe deeper and really relish our surroundings. Up above I can see the edge of the preserve, indeed the very spot we were peering down from not so long ago. The cliff-face is patchy with greenery but up close it resembles an oyster shell with its white-grey ridges and curves. Running along the bottom there's a tumble of rocks and an abundance of nooks and hidey-holes. As Bodie starts to inspect them, I come to a standstill.

Oh the choices we make in our lives.

To think I could be home, cooped up in my apartment right now, fretting about life and loss, painting myself as some tragic figure. Instead I get to be here. With one very happy dog… I take a memory snap and then Bodie boldly engages a Great Dane in a game of tag.

'Well, that's weird,' her owner frowns. 'She doesn't usually like to be chased!'

But there's no mistaking her wish – she's all but calling: 'Chase me! Chase me!' as she teases and double-bluffs and then takes off.

The pair of them are going like the clappers now, careering every which way.

'This is what I want!' he cheers. 'To see her run!'

The man explains that he brings her to the beach nearly every day in a desperate bid to tire those lanky legs but rarely does she go as full pelt as she is now.

At one point the two dogs bound into the waves. The water is barely lapping the Great Dane's knees but Bodie is in up to his nose and then his ears as she puts a paw on him, pressing him down.

'Oh god! She's going to drown him!'

I rush forward but Bodie rears up to the surface, drenched fur slicked to his side. He probably weighs a good 10 pounds more right now but he manages to haul himself back to land and then gives an almighty car wash brush of a shake.

Still they frolic.

I tell the man that this is Bodie's first time at the beach – I'd heard Hendry's was one of the best for dogs and came from LA to find out.

'So you got a hotel here, just so you could take your dog to the beach?'

'Something like that.'

'Where are you staying?'

'San Ysidro Ranch.'

He does a 'holy moly' spin and then shakes his head. 'You know, I have friends on the East Coast who fly their dogs here on a private jet and that's where they stay.'

'Well, I can understand why.'

He gives me a sideways glance, obviously wondering how I can possibly afford such luxuries.

'Your dog looks so clean,' I note, moving the conversation on. Her short fur seems to entirely deflect the water whereas Bodie's every strand looks as if it has been dipped in dirt and then punk-gelled for an edgier look.

'Oh dear, is that wise?' I ask as he begins lapping at the seawater.

'Might upset his stomach but,' he shrugs, 'what are you going to do?'

And with that the guy and his Great Dane move on. Bodie follows briefly and then pogoes back to me. I've never seen him so manic and, considering his personality, that's saying a lot. As I watch him bounding in circles around me, he seems to be panting out the words, 'This is the best! Just the best-*best*-BEST!'

I'm afraid I've triggered a new level of madness but after several hectic circuits, he flumps down on the sand, utterly, deliriously exhausted. He is still for approximately three seconds and then he starts digging. His bottom is high in the air, his front paws burrowing for all he's worth. Periodically, he topples into the hole he's digging but apparently there's cooler, damper sand to be had and he keeps on going with rhythmical strokes and all the intensity of a boxing bag workout. He now has sand everywhere, balancing on his eyelashes, coating his nose, edging his mouth… I shudder, recalling the gritty crunch of beach sandwiches as a child but he doesn't seem to mind. He just bumps his chin down on the edge of his pit, emits a heartfelt sigh and closes his eyes.

I'm so glad we did this. After such a harrowing blunder it's good to feel I did something right. I look around for Tamar, wishing I could thank her for her timely presence. She really does seem like an admirable woman, trying to rid the world of choke chains and harsh words. But she's nowhere in sight so I settle on a word I know will enliven Bodie.

'Lunch?'

He scrambles to his feet. 'I think it's time.'

We make our way back to the Boathouse restaurant. Up on the deck, well-to-do folk are enjoying lobster tacos and chilled

Sauvignon Blanc beneath blue parasols. Bodie and I opt for the walk-up window, order a hot dog with a side of fries and a Coke and then settle on a wooden bench to eat these classic American calories. Of course I've ruined him now. It was one thing eating separately at home with the distraction of the TV but when it's just the two of us in a café or restaurant, it seems rude not to include him. So now he expects a piece of the action. I tell myself he's doing me a favour, reducing my portion sizes and I'll be a slip of a thing in no time. I just hope I'm not supersizing him as a result.

This day has been quite the adrenalin rush so far but now we're about to hit the road again the tiredness starts to kick in. I have to give Bodie a bump up to get into the back of the car and he slumps straight down to sleep. If only I could do the same. I'm barely 20 minutes down the track when my eyelids seem intent on shutting down for a nap. I check my Garmin – it's only an hour to our next stop but if we want to get there crash-free, I'm going to need another jolt of caffeine.

Highway 154 takes us on a snakily scenic route to Los Olivos – population 1,000, all of them from Anthropologie Casting, or so it seems. The little town is blooming with flowers and all things epicurean and artisanal. There are just two commercial streets – Grand Avenue and Alamo Pintado – with an inordinate number of wine-tasting rooms and an impressive hotel named Fess Parker Wine Country Inn & Spa. (It's a clue to the true nature of the place that rooms start at $500 a night.)

Bodie and I are posing for pictures by the vintage gas pumps outside the Los Olivos General Store when I see a woman who reminds me of my mother – all slimness and prettiness and sculpted cheekbones. As she draws level, I see it is Bo Derek. I kid you not. Bo Derek on a bicycle. I feel like I'm on some kind of celebrity-tag tour.

I remember now that she has a ranch in this area with her beau, John Corbett, aka Aiden from *Sex and the City* aka the man most people wished Carrie had ended up with instead of Big. Or is that just me? I have a recollection that Bo and John once gave the *Oprah* show a tour of their ranch and, while Bodie and I enjoy our drinks on the shady porch of Corner House Coffee, I find the video clip on my phone... They are being filmed outside by the horses and John Corbett, sporting a cowboy hat, is laughing as he says that every relationship needs 100 acres per couple, so you can keep a little distance.

Bo concurs, talking about their mutual independence and how 'absence makes the heart grow fonder'.

I sit back in my chair. Perhaps this separation from Nathan isn't the end. Perhaps it's just what we need. We just don't know it yet.

I watch a little more footage, loving that Bo Derek says she'd rather clean out the horses' stalls than go to the gym. She physically recoils at the 'mindlessness' and 'mirrors everywhere'! Which is also kind of crazy, considering she's still a total ten.

And then I absently Google 'Bo Derek Dogs' and to my amazement discover that she has had her own range of organic pet shampoos and conditioners since 1999.

She says: 'A goal of mine has been to keep my dogs clean enough to sleep on the bed with me and now they can.'

One of her special ingredients is oil extracted from a plant called Meadowfoam, native to northern California and given its name because, when in bloom, it resembles white foam blowing on the ocean.

I sigh. What a dreamy place this is. I look down at Bodie, who is doing his impression of a bear rug on the wooden decking of the café, and reckon we could quite happily sit here in leafy peace all week. But the caffeine is kicking in and our next stop is calling.

Chapter 9

The Dog-Friendly Drive-In

It seems every beach town in California has its own distinctive persona. Pismo Beach is a curious one. From a distance, looking down as we are from the terrace of the Cottage Inn by the Sea, it's impressive.

We're sitting on a pair of matching Adirondack chairs beneath a Chinese juniper tree, surrounded by colourful landscaping, gazing at the almighty sweep of beach. The black stilts of the pier wade out as the water changes from Tiffany blue to moody teal and it all seems terribly Côte d'Azur glam.

Up close it's rather more cheap and cheerful, bustling with families with multiple children, all below waist-height, all clamouring for ice creams and candyfloss and a fistful of fries from a series of weather-worn food shacks with names like Mo's Smokehouse and the Cracked Crab. The beach is just a few feet away but we've both had enough exercise for one day so we find a sheltered spot amid the dunes and have a little lie-down, allowing the sea breeze to skim over us. It would be nice to stay here until the stars came out but we have other plans for our evening entertainment – a movie at the Sunset Drive-In, just ten minutes from our hotel.

I love that they allow dogs to accompany you in your car. Bodie is sitting up front now, like he's my date. Better yet, they're playing *How to Train Your Dragon* so, who knows, I could pick up a few tips.

As we roll into the giant parking lot, I feel like we're cruising right into that iconic scene from *Grease*. They even have those dancing hot dog ads! Easily suggestible, I buy our second batch of the day, get the speaker attached and settle in, though I opt out of sharing the popcorn in case there's any hacking-choking incidents and I don't know if you can Heimlich a dog.

One by one the cars pull in alongside us. Each one disturbs Bodie a little more. He's up on his feet, glaring and growling, body stiffening for action, obviously not fully understanding the communal activity of movie-going. When one couple reverse their truck into position and then climb in the back with their blankets, it's all over. Every rustle and position shift in the darkness causes him to bark hysterically. I've run out of hot dogs to distract him with and now my nerves are frayed. For the second night running.

There's nothing else for it – we're going to have to head back to the hotel and watch TV.

As we merge back on to the freeway, I realise with a heavy heart that I neither know how to calm my dog nor train my dragon. Darn it.

Not a peep. All night. And this time we both slept. I think it was a combination of all the fresh air and exercise in Santa Barbara, plus the fact that the Cottage Inn feels so safe and clean and cosy. I do love a fireplace and, better yet, the option of being lullabied to sleep by the sound of the waves stroking the shore.

Having conked out by 9.30 p.m., we're up unusually early. I think this is the first time in my life I've arrived for a hotel breakfast to find every offering still intact. The pastries are piled high, there's no line of people waiting to use the toaster or trying to figure out the waffle machine and the coffee flows freely, as opposed to a little sputter from a dispenser and a promise there will be a fresh brew available in ten minutes.

Although Bodie has already eaten, I nip to reception and grab him a few of the complimentary milk bones from the dog-shaped welcome jar (nice touch!), and then we sit on the terrace in the early morning sunshine and consider the day ahead.

Today is a big day. A Big Sur day. We're going to be driving one of the most infamously scenic roads on the West Coast, following in the tyre tread of Jack Kerouac, before spending two nights in Carmel, considered one of the most dog-friendly towns in America.

I have assorted stops planned en route but as it's mostly a car day I want to give Bodie a decent walk, so we head down to the beach. And down and down and down. I hadn't realised just how many steps there would be from our cliff perch – 100 at least – or how steep or how awkward that would be with a dog barrelling down head first. I try to get him to walk behind me so I can act as a breaker but he insists on leading the way. Several times he bashes his head as the staircase switches angles and I fear I'm going to tumble straight over the fencing and take a more direct route to the shore.

Yet somehow we arrive on the wet sand in one piece.

The only people up at this hour are the dog walkers, which gives a very different vibe to yesterday's bucket and spade brigade.

'Morning!'

'And isn't it a beautiful one?'

'Glorious,' I smile. 'Your dog looks like she's enjoying every minute.'

'We come here every morning and she's never short of ecstatic.'

Making small talk with the passers-by, I feel like I could talk about nothing but dogs for the rest of my life – there's just so much to say: everyone has a story about how their dog came into their life or its quirky little foibles. Perhaps it's the American equivalent of how Brits love to talk about the weather – the comfort of a neutral, non-personal subject that everyone has an opinion about. Mind you, people talking about their dogs is actually incredibly personal and revealing once you get past the 'How old is yours?' and 'What breed is he?' You can quickly tell if someone is relaxed or needy or controlling. Whether they are sociable or solitary. Not that there's quite so much interaction today, as all dogs must be kept on a leash here, so you tend to move on after everyone's had a good sniff.

When we reach the baby-blue lifeguard tower, I can't resist getting Bodie to do his best *Baywatch* pose. I shared an apartment with a cast member when I first moved to Los

Angeles – tattooed Tasmanian Jaason Simmons – and I have to say I think he'd approve of the level of vigilant intensity Bodie summons as he studies the waterline.

Next, we go snooping beneath the pier. It's actually a little eerie under here – dark and cool, the water laps black around our ankles as we inspect the spiky barnacles clinging to the sea-slapped struts. Bodie seems happy enough but I can't shake the feeling that some slimy tentacled thing is preparing to ensnare us so we take our paddling feet out into the sunshine.

We're about halfway back to the cliff steps when I notice Bodie is psyching himself up for his first swim – zig-zagging in and out of the water, going deeper each time. I watch with trepidation as a big wave approaches. And we have lift-off! His feet are off the ground, his chin is jutting upward, legs paddling busily. Then he gets a look of mild panic and comes scuttling back to shore.

'Well done you!' I cheer, rather amused to see him trying to shake himself dry while the water is still halfway up his belly. And then he attempts to break into a run.

'Sorry, I can't let you off here!' I tug him back.

Still he pulls and pulls, raring to go. There's only one thing for it. I break into a jog. And then a run. I can feel the soles of my feet pounding at the ridges of sand. I don't know the last time I moved like this – I feel like a child again, totally carefree, running for the pure joy of it. All the while Bodie thrums alongside me, at least until I have to stop and catch my breath. Wow. The things a dog can get you to do.

Chapter 10
Dog Beer at Moonstone Beach

We're all loaded up and on the road again, passing the exit for the Sunset Drive-In and the infamous Madonna Inn with its *Flintstones*-style boulders, pink leather booths and giant cakes – so frou-frou you could wear them to Ascot.

It's a shame they no longer allow dogs in their gorgeously kitschy suites – I loved staying in Carin with its gold Cupid chandeliers, and cowboy-themed Yahoo with the big ole wagon wheels on the side of the bed. For Bodie I would have picked Caveman with its rock walls and waterfall shower, and watched him get in touch with his primal instincts over one of the John Wayne steaks. But for today it's just a drive-by wave and random thoughts of opening a dog lovers' hotel, each room themed according to a different breed: tartan for the Scotties, wall-to-wall white fluff for the Samoyed, mini Buckingham Palace for the Corgis…

The classic road to Cambria would be Highway 1 past Morro Bay with its Gibraltar-esque rock and trio of industrial chimney stacks, but I've been recommended a 12-mile detour that apparently has the dramatic edge…

First we climb through the Cuesta Grade mountain cut-through – I feel oddly excited as the car strains to make the elevation. Then, just beyond Atascadero, we switch to the 46 and that's where the magic begins…

I absolutely adore the gold and green of the Central Coast. The hills look so strokeable here, like they're swathed in suede. On closer inspection I see they're actually a mix of long tickly blonde grasses and mown-short prickles, interspersed with robust vegetation. Bodie and I have pulled into one of the lookout points, parking tantalisingly close to the edge, but something about the Midas touch of the sunlight and the dune-like slopings surrounding us creates a soothing environment. I let my gaze tumble down the valleys and gamble up the other side, roaming widely. Then, as my vision extends to the sea, I realise I can see all the way to Morro Rock.

People often talk about how insignificant they feel in the face of nature on a grand scale but here you feel magnificent. As if you are beholding your gilded kingdom. I feel my chest lift and my lungs expand. I find awe can do that sometimes – instead of feeling 'I am nothing, you are everything', it lets you feel like you are a part of the wonder.

I wish I could release Bodie and let him run wild and free but his coat is an almost identical match for the landscape and I'd probably never see him again. He settles instead for a roll in the crumbly earth, thickening his coat with dust in the same way women might use dry shampoo.

I shake my head at his bulked-up form but I'm smiling as we drive on. Really smiling. 'This is it!' my heart seems to be saying. 'This is the high!'

There's not another car on the road and as we gently swoop and weave on our way, I feel as if I am flying a plane on low-glide. I have the soundtrack to *Out of Africa* somewhere in my CD wallet but even without playing it, I can hear the signature strings intertwining with the horns, sending a ribbon dance across my soul.

We're descending now, heading back down to sea level, but the vistas greeting us at every turn are just as lovely and unspoilt. Nothing ragged or jarring here – it's all soft, caressing lines.

And then I see the crossroads ahead. I'm almost reluctant to bump back down to earth and rejoin the other vehicles streaming along Highway 1. But that's life – these moments are transient. All you can do is fully embrace them and then try to carry them onward with you.

'They're just cows,' I assure Bodie as he sends anxious gurgling noises out of the car window over to the shiny black oblongs in the field beside us.

A minute later it's me doing the squinting and frowning. Are those horse-shaped cut-outs cresting the mound to our left? As we get closer I realise they are real – they just aren't moving, possibly because they belong to the artsy community of Cambria and realise they have struck upon the ultimate Western pose. Someone will be along with a camera or a paintbrush any minute...

The town is snug with galleries and studios and craft shops (and a decent-size dog park). I'm sure it would be lovely to spend the afternoon meandering amid the wind chimes and sitting a while on that nasturtium-entwined bench, but we have two foodie missions to accomplish. The first is to sample the famous Olallieberry Pie.

Linn's Easy As Pie Café has a retro charm with tables covered in floral prints from the 1950s and a selection of those humorous housewife magnets that say things like, 'I understand the concept of cooking and cleaning, just not as it applies to me.' (This one I own and live my life by.)

Bodie and I wait for our order in the pretty garden at the back, perching on the edge of a red-painted picnic bench. We watch a grey-and-blue bird settle on a nearby branch – from the bulge of his tummy I'm guessing he's a regular here at the Crumb Buffet.

Bodie has no issue with our feathered friends so I'm bemused when his body stiffens and he starts barking agitatedly.

'You're surely not barking at the butterfly?' I frown as a Cabbage White dances around his nose.

I catch the elderly couple next to us rolling their eyes at the disturbance of the peace but then, as I look beyond them, I spy a mother deer and two baby Bambis nibbling grass beneath a tree.

'Deer!' I gasp, pleased that we can now claim to have enhanced the old folks' experience.

Bodie falls silent now and we all hold our breath as we observe their sleek lines, exquisite poise and dark, liquid eyes that stare so pointedly back at us.

I always thought Bodie had a deer-like quality but these are something else. It's like seeing Audrey Hepburn wearing a showgirl headdress yet carrying it with regal aplomb.

'Just beautiful,' I sigh.

'Slice of Olallieberry?'

'Here!'

The pie is served warm, on a sheet of red-and-white check wax paper atop a tin plate. The pastry is golden and flakes apart at the touch of my fork, releasing the dark purple sticky-oozy juiciness within – the perfect contrast to my milky coffee. Once I'm done, I find myself sitting very still, wanting to preserve this state of deep satisfaction. But Bodie is eager for his treat.

Down the high street we go, passing the Sow's Ear and the Black Cat and the Bluebird Inn, and then proceed to the more 'modern' end of town where Maddie Mae's Pet Pantry resides.

Quite the contrast to the typical strip mall pet stores, this one resembles a rough-hewn timber cabin accented with a set of giant paw prints climbing roof-ward. The sign hanging from a wrought-iron scroll features an Old English Sheepdog in a chef's hat holding out a tray of canine cookies. These are made by the owners, in memory of Maddie Mae who is now in heaven. Bodie sits expectantly beside the display and then chomps down a bacon bite shaped like a star. I then reach for a six-pack of dog beer. (Apparently, there are lots of B vitamins in malt barley and glucosamine is good for joint health but really I just like the idea of Bodie swigging from a bottle of ale.)

I'm also seriously tempted by the dog horoscope ID tags. Bodie became my charge on 17 March – St Patrick's Day – which would make him a Pisces but the descriptor of 'shy and sensitive' is not a good match. I'm wondering if I could nudge him along to Aries when I see that the savvy people at DogOscopes have created a thirteenth option for Rescue Dogs, seeing as we rarely know when they were actually born.

Now this is more like it: brave, loyal, loving, optimistic and – bringing a little tear to my eye – *survivor!*

Although right now he's mostly displaying the 'inquisitive' trait.

'Come on!' I extract Bodie's nose from the bag of Chicken Soup for the Soul dog food and lead him back to the car. 'Let's go have a quick beer at the beach.'

We get a great parking spot overlooking the sea, opposite a Beagle mailbox. I set out Bodie's foldable bowl and start pouring the cloudy brown liquid, expecting him to start lapping it up mid-flow but instead one sniff causes him to jerk his head away.

What?

'Here you go!' I try again.

He's having none of it and people are starting to give me funny looks.

'Did you see that girl today, trying to get her dog drunk?'

Perhaps he needs to work up a thirst. I'll take him for a little trot along the boardwalk.

Moonstone Beach is an absolute gem, pardon the pun. There's a special sophistication here and everyone we pass seems very genteel and respectful of their surroundings. In fact, the reason for the mile-long boardwalk is to protect the natural habitat, and judging by Bodie's ultra-alert body language, the wildlife is thriving.

'Bodie!' I squeal as he unbalances me with a lunge at a baby bunny.

He even gets all lurchy in the direction of the surfers. There's certainly a nice rearing froth and tumble to those waves. It must be so exhilarating to catch a big one. I'm definitely coming back in my next life as a surfer but perhaps in this one I could live vicariously through Bodie – every year they have a dog surfing competition at Del Mar dog beach about half an hour from San Diego. Perhaps on our next trip we'll go South...

When we get back to the car, I try the beer again. Same reaction. I sigh, pop Bodie in the back and then double-check I have all the info I need for driving Big Sur, as we'll be without a phone signal for several hours.

I'm just taking one last admiring look at the vista when I notice a man approaching the car, motioning me to wind down my window. He has a mop of white hair and kindly gnome-like features so I do as he requests.

'Do you have a dog in the back of the car?'

Before I can assure him that Bodie is being properly cared for, he explains that he bought some chicken jerky for his dogs and they won't touch it.

'Do they drink dog beer?' I ask.

He looks confused.

'Only I just bought a six-pack and my dog wouldn't take a drop – perhaps we could do a trade?'

I hop out and we both produce our respective booty, though I appear to be getting the better end of the deal, since his bag is the size of a pillowcase.

'Fifteen dollars. I spent fifteen dollars on this!'

'Twenty for mine!' I roll my eyes at my purchase.

'I spend a fortune on my dogs.'

'Oh, me too!'

I wonder why he doesn't have his dogs with him, only to realise that he does: they are just so small I didn't notice them wedged into the crease of the back seat of his car – two little fluffy scraps that could easily be mistaken for lint.

'Oh!' I peer at them. 'They don't look old enough to drink!'

'Oh they're fine – eleven and seven.'

He introduces me to Okie – 'Where do you think he's from?' he asks.

'Oakland?' I guess, seeing as we are about 200 miles from there.

He looks at me like I'm crazy. 'No! Oklahoma!'

Then I meet his favourite, Bridget.

'That wasn't her original name – I changed it.'

'From what?'

'Girlie Girl.'

'I think she probably thanks you for that.'

He tells me about how he nursed Okie from when he was four weeks old, and that he has a 'cherry eye' (a disorder that gives the poor pup a bulge of pink in his eye). Bridget, on the other hand, is clearly the apple of his eye.

'I had this big ice-cream sundae yesterday and guess who ate most of it?' He gazes fondly at her before leaning in, 'Do you know what they really love to eat?'

'Tell me!'

'Hot dogs!'

I tell him that we had a double dose of those yesterday.

He asks how much I paid for Bodie and then says he doesn't think shelters should charge you for taking a dog – for the shots, yes, but not for adopting. He volunteered at one place but quit when he saw that their idea of cleaning the cages of a morning was turning the hose on the whole area, without removing the dogs. He watched them whimpering and cowering and hating the blast, so he asked why on earth they didn't take the dogs out first. The guy said it would take too much time and, besides, he was afraid they'd bite him.

'Probably not the best person to work with animals then,' I note.

'I said I'd do it,' he continues. 'Take the dogs out one by one – and when they said no, I quit.'

'It's just horrible to think of these kind of people being in charge.'

'I know. It's supposed to be a *shelter*, somewhere the animals feel safe.'

As he chats on, he mentions his dead wife and says he comes here whenever he's feeling lonely. I have the feeling it's going to be tricky to extract myself from the conversation but then a pretty woman with an even prettier Spaniel pulls up on the other side of his car and he quickly turns his attention to her.

'But we got the treats!' I give Bodie a wink as we pull away.

Chapter 11

The Big Sur Bakery

Each year 750,000 visitors take a tour of Hearst Castle – the historic megabucks mansion belonging to newspaper magnate William Randolph Hearst. His lavish tastes are well-documented and his heyday parties still prompt gossip – understandably when the guest list featured the likes of Cary Grant, Errol Flynn, Joan Crawford and Jean Harlow. (Can you imagine being invited to join their champagne-chinking?) Even long after his death, his publishing empire conveys elite glamour with magazines like *Harper's Bazaar*, *Esquire* and *Elle*. What many people don't know is that he used to breed Dachshunds there on the 'Enchanted Hill', and one Dachshund in particular, Helen, stole his heart.

When she passed away (in his arms), he published a eulogy in his newspaper describing how his 'devoted friend' would always sleep on a big chair in his room, and that her gaze would follow him to bed and be the first thing to greet him when he woke.

'So as your dog loves you, you come to love your dog...' he wrote, 'because love creates love, devotion inspires devotion, unselfishness begets unselfishness.'

Fine words indeed.

Dogs are not allowed to tour the property but I flip on the indicator and pull off the road so Bodie and I can take a moment to admire the Hearst zebras, grazing casually on the sun-blanched grasses, not so very unlike the African plains. They are one of the few species from Hearst's exotic animal collection that have endured. At one time they were mingling with camels and kangaroos, even a few giraffes, and that was just the free-roamers. Caged exhibits further up the hill featured orangutans, leopards and bears, but these started making their way to public zoos in the 1930s.

'What do you think of the zebras, Bodie?'

His body is tense and he appears to be considering a barking spasm. 'Are these horses? Because they look different to the one we saw in Santa Barbara...'

I lower the window. Zebras really are one of the most fascinating beasts to view in person – those dark brown and cream stripes so stark and stylish, the distinct colour bands extending to the tufty crew cut of their manes. To me they are the closest thing to seeing a unicorn – a good match for Hearst's fairy-tale castle, alluringly a-swirl with mist.

And this scene pretty much sets the other-worldly tone from here on in...

Just ten minutes up the road at Piedras Blancas we get to see elephant seals basking on the beach. We're out of the car this time, down by the fenced pathway. Bodie stares intently between the slats of wood but doesn't bark or even growl. I think it could be because they don't make any sudden movements. In fact, most of them don't move at all and with the ones that do, it's a rather laboured, lumbering process. We watch one heave himself out of the sea and then pause for five minutes to catch his breath before his next blubbery undulation. There is a moment of panic when I think he's going to steamroller over the one baby but fortunately the little 'un manages to wriggle out of the way before the 2-ton flattening occurs. And I'm not exaggerating the weight. The adult males can weigh up to 5,000 pounds (that's over 350 stone)! I learn this from one of the elephant seal experts lining the walkway. They answer any and every question. For example:

Q: What do they eat?

A: Females mostly live off squid, whereas the males eat 'bottom-dwelling' species like rays, skates and even small sharks.

(Who knew seafood could be so fattening?)

Q: Why do they flip sand on themselves?

A: It acts as a sunscreen and helps them to keep cool.

Q: Why do only the males have those weird trunk-like noses?

A: The large nose is a secondary sexual characteristic indicating physical and sexual maturity.

I give a little shudder – it's not a pretty sight: all floppy and lumpy and misshapen. I look back at Bodie. He's never looked so handsome.

Ragged Point is upon us before we have time to slow – next time we'll stop for a gawp at its Million Dollar View. Despite being branded as the southern gateway to Big Sur, I'm surprised by the abruptness with which the soft rolling hills rear into steep, rugged banks. Equally, what was a gentle curve of road is now swerving and writhing like a live snake.

'Hold tight, Bodie!'

Sensing a marked increase in elevation, I get a touch of, if not nerves, adrenalin. There's something about driving Big Sur that seems *significant*. It makes me feel all bold and adventurous when really all I'm doing is sitting in the car as normal, albeit making rather more precise life-or-death turns with the steering wheel. I lose count of the times I cry, 'Woah!' – it's all too easy to be distracted by the drama of the scenery and find yourself drifting out of your lane. And there's really no room to do that since, understandably, those driving on the cliff-edge side want to snug in a little. Every sign is a squiggle letting you know that the road is getting ever more winding. An eagle soars above us. I hear myself emit a little squeal of excitement.

As the speed limit grinds down to 20 mph, I start wishing our tyres came fitted with mountaineering crampons. I take a sneaky peek at the coast – the seaweed is a burnished brown, the surf a frothy, zingy white and, oh, you should see the blue! Woah! Again.

I thought about having Bodie up front with me so we could 'share' the experience but considered the potential distraction too risky. Wise move. As we continue on, I realise my nerves have me hunched over the wheel like an old lady and my back hasn't touched the seat in miles. It doesn't help that I now see a sign warning us that this is a rockslide area. What exactly are you supposed to do with that information? I understand they are trying to prepare you for the worst-case scenario but I don't know where you would swerve *to* if rocks did start clattering down on the roof.

I can't help but gawp a little as we pass a lone cyclist. He's shirtless and doesn't appear to have a single thing with him, not even a bottle of water. He must have fantastic lungs – up the hill he goes, powering ever onward. He doesn't even stop for a breather or a snack at the Gorda General Store, though I pull in to let a few cars pass – what a sense of relief! It's so stressful having them on your tail.

Of course no sooner are we back on the road than it happens again. This time we have a little gold bullet of a James Bond car gaining on us. I don't fancy our chances in a car chase and pull over at the first opportunity. He gives us a little toot-toot of thanks, which pleases me enormously. 'Do you see that, Bodie? We just got toot-tooted by a gold Porsche!' What's even better is that it sounded like a little clown horn. Adorable!

As we continue onward I see multiple convertibles with the passenger rearing up out of their seat to take pictures, and one Mustang with a camcorder attached to the top of the windscreen, which is a great idea. I'd definitely watch our trip back, eager to see all the things I missed as I was staring fixedly at the tarmac ahead. It's a shame this route doesn't come with a set number of freeze-frame moments where you could just press pause and take it all in without the risk of crashing. Of course there are lookout points but they are all on the opposite side of the road and I don't fancy our chances of getting back on the right side after – before we knew it we'd be back at Hearst Castle.

'You all right, kid?' I ask Bodie, hoping he's not getting carsick from all the twisty turns. I wonder if this view is impressive to him? Probably not without the accompanying smells. I lower the windows and let the salty air buffet us. Gosh that feels good. I take a giant breath of Big Sur air. And then I snort at the sign requesting, 'Please drive carefully.' Of all the places I might drive recklessly, this isn't one.

'How do you fancy that ride?' I tease Bodie as we catch up with a herd of Harleys. I picture myself on the back with him driving, my hands clasped tight around his furry tummy. Or better yet, his little chops flapping as he's tucked into a sidecar.

'I'm sure you'd rather be out exploring, wouldn't you? We'll be stopping soon.'

A few miles on, we pull into an expansive woodland car park.

Julia Pfeiffer Burns State Park is known as the crown jewel of all the California State Parks – a big, flashing aquamarine jewel. I presumed the pictures I'd seen of the magical cove had been colour-saturated but it really is that vivid, like a splurge of Tahiti turquoise seeping into the Pacific blue. We're standing amid the yellow wild flowers, peering through ragged branches, looking down on it now and I feel on a high. Literally and figuratively. Bodie and I are eager to scamper down Waterfall Trail but then I see the 'No Dogs Allowed' sign.

Here we are, deep in nature, and the humans have decided to ban the animals? I roll my eyes. Who do we think we are?

Everywhere we turn there's another sign blocking our path.

'Sorry, chum,' I sigh as we head back to the car. 'They're trying to preserve the natural beauty so only people with big clompy hiking boots and the potential to litter and start wildfires are allowed.'

When we stop 20 minutes down the road at the Big Sur Bakery (all wood-fired bread and savoury tomato jam), I don't check with anyone to see if Bodie is allowed on the patio, just in case the answer is no. Besides, the table is sufficiently hefty to obscure him from view. As we sit there, glad of an iced beverage and a snack, I register three or four different languages around me, none of which I can identify. It really rams home what a classic pilgrimage this is. I wonder if any of them are quoting Kerouac? My favourite line is: 'Nothing behind me, everything ahead of me, as is ever so on the road.'

He does have a way with words that man. But then the Big Sur Bakery has a pretty profound catchphrase too: *slow down and come to your senses*.

In response, Bodie and I take a moment to wander around the stylishly higgledy-piggledy property, admiring everything from the bright orange blooms nestling beside a large prickly pear to the darling two-pump gas station and the world's dinkiest toilet – a little free-standing wooden hut clad in ivy.

'We're so lucky to be here!' I say, as I smoosh Bodie's face and tickle under his chin.

'Yeah, it's not bad,' he seems to agree.

As we continue on we pass some workmen taking their break, sitting on crates on the roadside, and I feel extremely grateful for all those who toiled to make this dream route a reality. I wonder how long it took? And how did they do it? Was it just a case of forging ahead day after day, paving another foot ahead, and then another? That's what they tell people going through a crisis, isn't it? Just take one day at a time. Which reminds me – I remember reading that if you're not sure whether a relationship is right for you, you should spend less time questioning everything and just keep moving towards what you love. If the person is a match, things will naturally fall into place and if they're not, well, I guess they just fall by the wayside. But you have to keep focused. And keep moving towards what you love. I feel I am doing that right now. I've been so stuck, so frustrated, but this… This is great.

I make a decision that I want to be the kind of person who notices all the beauty in the world, not someone who is so introspective that they miss it. Because if you're human, there's always something niggling at you, be it physical discomfort, a debt, a deadline or a heartache. Everyone has something trying to snatch their attention away from all the wonder. Well, from now on I'm going to resist the naval-gazing woes – I'd rather be a wonder-seeker!

And then I spy a big lay-by on our side of the road and, before I know it, Bodie and I are making a heart-stopping dash across two lanes to the lookout point. The wind blusters us. I have Bodie's leash wound tight to my side, afraid he might lose his footing on these loose rocks as he noses in the crevices. Still, closer to the edge we go.

Kerouac said, 'The greater the fear, the greater the happiness.' And perhaps he's right. I look at the vibrant blue of the sky and sea. And then I look at Bodie – his fur iridescent in the sunlight, his eyes gleaming amber.

My chest expands, barely able to contain my surge of optimism. Suddenly, life's possibilities seem infinite. I feel all energised and 'in the flow'. And then I smile – here we are, on the curviest, most unpredictable road and, for once, I feel right on course.

Chapter 12

Cocktails Chez Doris Day

Gradually, the wild foliage becomes more cultivated and I spy a number of residences peeking through the trees – we must be approaching Carmel. Or Carmel-by-the-Sea to give it its full sing-song name, like something out of a 1920s musical, demanding blazers and cravats and white kick-pleat skirts.

Within minutes I can see why this town has been repeatedly voted the most dog-friendly in America. Dogs are everywhere. The majority of them seem to come in luxe shades of copper and gold with a 'just stepped out of the salon' gleam to their coats. Then there are dogs of a more decorative variety displayed in every other shop – antique china dogs, brass doorstop dogs, chess sets with dogs versus cats and dog logos on T-shirts, the best of which says: *My Dog Makes Me Happy.*

Never was a simpler or truer observation made.

Continuing with the day's fairy-tale motif, the streets of Carmel have a Once Upon a Time quality to them: prettily painted cottages with beamed walls and sloping tiled roofs that I half-expect Snow White to peep out of. The names of the hotels – or rather inns – help set the scene: Candlelight Inn, Carriage House Inn, Cobblestone Inn. So quaint-sounding but take a peek at the shops and restaurants tucked in between and you understand this is a rather grown-up fairy tale, filled with diamond-studded Rolex watches, fine art and sommeliers.

Speaking of imbibing, Yappy Hour is just beginning at the Cypress Inn – Carmel's original dog-friendly hotel, famously co-owned by Doris Day. Much as I'd love to say the décor resembles the interiors of her iconic movies of the 1960s, it's actually far more understated with soft silver-green neutrals, and a Moroccan flair to the wrought-iron lanterns and woven rug hung on the wall behind the reception desk.

We're still at the peering-in stage because I want to get a snap of Bodie set against the whitewashed exterior with its striking black-and-gold accents. I've just got him in the perfect position on the front steps when a man pulls up in a Jag, opens the car door and out burst two untethered pups making a break for it, bounding up Lincoln Street like it's the road to freedom. There seems little chance of the owner's yelling and arm-flailing recalling them, and every chance of them getting run over, but a kindly local with superior dog-herding skills returns them intact. I take some comfort that I'm not the only one this happens to. The doorman looks like he's seen it a million times before – and perhaps he has – because once I step inside I feel like we're entering the world's classiest dog boarding establishment. There are dogs at reception, dogs in the lounge, dogs in the bar, dogs in the courtyard and dogs entering and emerging from the rooms. I wouldn't be surprised to see a dog reading a newspaper or telling some shaggy dog story over a dirty martini. There's even a pair of Dachshunds wearing pearls.

'We got them at the local thrift store!' the elderly owner giggles as she adjusts their baubles.

She goes on to tell me that this is Carmel's best-kept secret in terms of dining with your dogs on a rainy day. Whereas every other restaurant falls foul of health codes forbidding dogs to be present inside, they get around it at Terry's Bar on account of it being partly in the lobby. I think that's the reason. Either way, if I were a health inspector and I was going to give a pass to anyone, it would be Doris Day. For over 30 years she has done incredible animal advocate work with the Doris Day Animal Foundation, although her passion for animal welfare started much earlier. Back in 1956 she was filming Alfred Hitchcock's *The Man Who Knew Too Much* in Morocco and was so appalled by the condition and treatment of the animals on the set that she refused to work until the emaciated creatures – including goats, horses, cats and dogs – were tended to and provided with a feeding and water station. I love it when people use their powers for good!

Today one of the foundation's big initiatives is World Spay Day – I'd never even heard of the word 'spay' until I joined the foundation. It's basically the female version of neutering. Back in 1995, when the campaign launched, there were over 15 million dogs and cats euthanised each year in the US. Now it's down to 2.7 million. But that's still 2.7 million too many. Finally it dawned on me how vital both of these processes are – if every owner (other than those planning to breed their cat or dog) arranged this little op, there would be way fewer homeless animals on the planet. It really is that simple. Plus, spaying/neutering can improve pet health and reduce unruly behaviour. (Which is why only neutered animals are allowed in the dog park!) I can't believe I've spent most of my life not knowing this.

As well as admiring all the work Doris Day has done (including her movies, which I can watch ad infinitum), I also admire how she lives – on an 11-acre estate entirely surrounded by four-legged friends.

'Their affection and care is a release from tensions and anxiety,' she says, seeming perfectly content.

It's certainly an appealing lifestyle option... I once visited a dude ranch in Colorado and the owners had a rescue dog that had spent his whole life restricted on a chain and now he had acres and acres to call his own. He'd go out with the horses every day, running alongside them with a look on his face like he couldn't believe his luck. I remember thinking at the time how fabulous it would be to have a Dog Ranch – some vast expanse of pine-sprigged land populated with all the pups that had ever been confined or cooped up. They'd play wild and free all day then at night they'd trot into the main cabin for dinner and a snoozy sprawl in front of a crackling fire. And I'd sleep right there in the middle of them all.

Now that's a notion worth drinking to.

Mostly I've been avoiding alcohol for fear of getting teary or woeful but I'm fairly certain no harm can befall anyone in Carmel.

The cocktail menu makes for interesting reading: each spirit is assigned a classic Hollywood leading man, including two of Doris's co-stars – Cary Grant (*That Touch of Mink*) and James Cagney (*Love Me Or Leave Me*). Grant has the brandy and Cagney, who I learn used to tend bar on New York's Lower East Side, has the whiskey.

I flip on to the mixed drinks and make the rather bold move of ordering Plenty O'Toole, named for a Bond Girl in

Diamonds Are Forever. Wow. The combination of Baileys and Frangelico is enough to make any woman feel like a Bond Girl. Or, in my case, a Bodie Girl.

My dear dog has settled in front of the large stone fireplace and is offering his tummy up to every passing guest, all of whom oblige him with a rub and tickle. One chap even asks to take a picture and then says, with a slightly creepy air, 'Now I have you forever, my darling!'

I take a few snaps myself back in the bar area where they display vintage movie posters. I loved James Garner in *The Thrill of It All* but my heart belongs to *Pillow Talk*'s Rock Hudson. I have a framed photograph of him at home and some of my favourite images of all time are of Rock and Doris laughing together. Just thinking about them I get a fond pang for my former flatmate James, though really we were more Will and Grace – him the dapper businessman, me the creative ditz. I must say that for every awful relationship I've had with a heterosexual man, I've had an absolutely fantastic one with a homosexual. I mean, I feel truly blessed in that area. Perhaps it's time to let go of conventional ideas of coupledom and start to get really grateful for the way one's life has shaped up naturally. As Cesar Millan says: 'You don't get the dog you want, you get the dog you need.'

Perhaps it's the same with life: you don't get the life you want, you get the life you need.

After our hotel check-in we head up the hill to dine beside a toasty courtyard fire at Forge in the Forest. As well as being a former drinking haunt of Henry Miller and John Steinbeck, this place is known for greeting your dog like a superstar. Bodie is cuddled and complimented and then presented with a special Canine Cuisine menu featuring kosher beef hot dogs, chicken strips and a 'Quarter Hounder' hamburger. There's even an 8-ounce steak option, for special occasions.

I could order every item on the list for Bodie and he would still be finished before I've loaded my fork with my first bite. I certainly find that I eat faster with a dog beside me – less conversation and an extra mouth eager to help you out with an unwieldy portion. (Ironically, I haven't needed a doggie bag since I got him.) I have been surprised at the broadness of Bodie's palate – he loves edamame, the crunch of a carrot, even the creamy coolness of tzatziki. Tonight he has chicken strips and stares with laser-like focus at the bowl, shrugging off any nice people who want to say hello, because all he can think about is the food.

Once he's done with his portion, he angles for any spare flakes of my salmon. And then dessert. I watch as a little droplet of saliva splashes on the floor but I have to draw the line at sugary items and thus, regretfully, I am obliged to keep the mocha mud pie all to myself.

It's still light when we leave so we head back down Ocean Avenue, all the way to the sea.

If there's a more beautiful beach in all the land, I can't imagine it. It's as if nature united with some soulful sculptor to work on the twisting curves of the tree branches to frame the artful sweep of the bay, lining it with darkest green cypresses and blanching the sand to a crystalline white. This sand is so clean it actually squeaks as we walk on it. Add a peachy blush sunset and I am simply in awe.

I have no qualms about releasing Bodie here and watch him trot into the golden path of the setting sun as it reflects on the wet sand. He dances playfully with the waves, allowing them to lift him off his feet and then set him gently back down. Then he starts exploring the rest of the beach, zig-zagging according to the whimsy of his nose, until he notices the sandbanks and charges over to try to scale them. As fast as he climbs up, the loose sand drags him back down, giving the effect of him being on a Stairmaster, pretty much holding steady about halfway up, panting madly.

Someone's going to sleep well tonight.

The darker the sky, the more zingingly bright the stars. This is so magical. Sitting on the now cool sand looking out across the bay I feel a little overwhelmed by the beauty and, before I know it, the tears start to stream down my face. Which I can't understand because I am happy. I'm not feeling hurt in this moment; I just seem to have this incredible sense of longing...

Still Bodie is going like the clappers on the Stairmaster.

Campfires are springing up around us, adding flickering yellow accents to the satin black night. I snug my chin down into the angora of my sweater, craving a little cosiness myself. And then I recall we have the dinkiest, cosiest room in all of Carmel awaiting us at the Monte Verde Inn.

The room is barely bigger than the bed itself but comes with a set of stable doors, French country print bed linens and a cut-glass decanter of sherry.

I wave to the innkeeper as we pass reception and when he responds with a cheery enquiry about our evening, Bodie decides he wants the love of one more stranger before bed and pulls me over to him. An hour later I'm still in reception, sitting in the low-lit nook listening to Randy tell me about his multi-decade love affair with his partner. He's such a delightful man, making me believe in happy endings all over again and, when it's time to head for bed, I leave with a warm glow.

Chapter 13

Beach Encounter

This morning will be forever etched on my memory as Bodie's First Sunday Lie-In.

Normally he's raring to go before my first blink of the day, limbering up with a top-to-toenail stretch, tail wagging in anticipation of his walk.

Today is different. As I begin to stir, he nestles closer, resting his head on my shoulder and placing his paw across my chest. My heart swells with affection – he wants to share his sleep with me! I lie there, revelling in the sensation of his breath upon my collarbone, bewitched by every twitch and vibration of his dreaming. My eyes eventually close but my smile lingers.

An hour later he's still sleeping, now with his top lip splayed out on the pillow. I watch him fondly, just like I used to watch Nathan.

What a beautiful sleeper he was, exquisitely positioned with one arm flung back on the pillow, the other resting over his toned stomach, head angled to the side. So still and silent, I would often place my ear over his heart, just to be certain he was still breathing. If I had sprayed him with satin-finish paint he could've been mistaken for some flawless sculpture. Such contours...

'But he didn't have fur,' I think as I bury my face in Bodie's rucked neck.

He turns and looks at me, and slowly I see him come to this realisation: *'We're still by the beach!'*

And he's up!

I stick my head outside the top of the stable door – the air is filled with an Evian-like spray of mist. No point in properly sprucing myself up until we get back. I pull on a bobble hat then hook the hood of my pale lime waterproof over the top, giving me an extended alien-shaped skull. I'm almost getting a kick out of this outdoorsy dressing now – I love how anything goes!

That said, one man on the beach seems to be taking the notion too far: voluminous misshapen tracksuit bottoms, saggy damp Ugg boots and a pale khaki sweatshirt appliquéd with a trio of dogs.

I don't know if it's because I'm staring, trying to reconcile his George Clooney looks with the crazy dog person clothing, or whether Bodie twists leashes with one of his pack of three, but I find myself talking to him. And then walking and talking. And then, before I know it, two hours have passed. If we were in a bar, sipping cocktails, a vodka-infused kiss might have transpired but we're not – we're on a beach whipped by the wind, blinking sea rain and trying to keep track of all four of our four-legged friends. When I mention that this is my first time with the Chuckit! (the plastic arm for propelling tennis balls), he takes it from me and proceeds to run Bodie ragged with it. Anyone would think we were together. Or at least old pals.

I couldn't be happier – I've longed for someone to skip the formalities and get to that over-familiar stage with me.

I honestly can't quite believe it is happening. This has to be the easiest, longest, most keep-you-on-your-toes conversation I've had in months.

He's playful, sardonic and has the quality that my friend Emily rates above all else: the ability to banter.

The more we talk, the more we establish 'whatever you throw at me, I can knock back, possibly with even more of a spin on it'.

And I don't mean the Chuckit!.

But then I learn he is ex-military and I find myself wailing, '*But why? Why-why-why would you choose that?*'

He looks at me like I'm the oddball. His brother was in the military too. They couldn't wait to sign up. Surely it's the most natural choice for any guy – to want to serve his country?

That's when I see the manliness in him. In the same moment my heart sinks a little.

Then he says, 'My ex bought me a cat, thinking it would help me get more in touch with my feelings.'

Translation: *I can't express my emotions.*

I raise a brow. 'How'd that work out?'

He pulls a 'not-so-good' face.

And then I feel as if the banter takes a turn as he makes a comment about the absurdness of my bobble hat.

'Do you like it?' I grin defiantly.

'Oh I wasn't complimenting you,' he sneers.

'Good thing I don't need you to.'

I'm experiencing mild irritation now – a little glimpse of how he might be in an argument. Snarky. Superior. Needling at your Achilles heel. These are the things I need to pay attention to, to log as a red flag, but there's definitely some giddy lure to speaking to someone of the opposite sex when there is some form of attraction at play. I know what I look like right now so I doubt it's physical on his part but on the inside I feel bright and shiny and energised. Or at least I did until he made the comment about my hat. Still, it's good to get stirred up after such a period of stagnation. Good to be challenged. Good to engage with the human race.

We're heading back to the car park now. He shares his dogs' water with Bodie and then starts to load up the jeep. And so it comes to that awkward parting moment. Awkward for me at least, since I am expecting some exchange of contact information or an offer to meet again on my return trip – surely this encounter must have been equally energising and unusual for him? Yet I sense he's mentally already on the highway home.

I try to stall his departure a moment longer by taking a few snaps of him with Bodie and then ask for his email address so I can send them to him.

He does not ask for mine.

I sit on the wall for a while after he's gone, wondering why I now feel so deflated, other than the fact that I just got a big dose of 'he's just not that into you'. Perhaps he even has a girlfriend and was just passing the time, me mistaking a naturally flirtatious demeanour for something more personal. How quickly the electric thrill of interaction switches to self-conscious reflection.

It's not like I really thought I'd just met the man of my dreams. Other than the fact that he was older, funny, great with dogs and happens to reside within a short drive of paradise.

I suppose, more than anything, I wanted him to be The Buffer Guy. The man who could break the Nathan continuum. I am still in that state where he was the last man in my life and thus, by default, he remains *current*. I need someone to nudge him down a spot and break the hold...

I get to my feet and try to shake off the angst in a bid to revive the pep I was feeling just minutes prior. Look on the bright side – *I've still got it!* In some capacity at least. Maybe that was just a 'getting back in the game' warm-up. Who knows what will happen in Napa or Portland? And, more pressingly, where is Bodie's leash?

I feel around my waist where I had last tied it. Nothing. It must have slipped off amid the rain spritz. I look back at the expanse of beach and all the churned up sand. I don't fancy my chances of finding it again. For now I make do with threading my own belt through Bodie's collar and then, after a shower and spruce-up, we head to Diggidy Dog – Carmel's cavernous dog emporium.

This is the biggest pet accessory/treat shop I've visited to date – it has everything from doggie bow ties to boar bristle brushes and squeaky 'iBones'. While Bodie is sniffing at the deodorising sprays, my eyes light up at the case of artfully decorated cookies. Considering the swishness of our environment, a dog biscuit in the shape of a cocktail glass seems appropriate and I also opt for the squirrel-shaped one, prompting Bodie to sit back on his haunches and do a convincing impression as he reaches up to snatch it from me.

The dog bed section is stacked to the ceiling – I just want to throw myself on to the fleecy, bouncy piles and roll around but decide to get back to the business in hand: a new leash.

I stand and contemplate the row upon row of options. Much as Bodie loves the high life, I don't think the Swarovski crystal studding of the LuxePet range is a good match for his personality, although I do like the bright beading on the 'Kenyan Collection'. The Italian calfskin is soft and pretty but too slim for a dog of Bodie's robustness. I'm running my fingertips along some too-stiff leather when my hand touches foam. Having known only dig-in canvas leashes that slice at my palms, I can't quite believe the sensation of this grip – the main leash is a smooth, strong cord but the triangular handle has a width of rubbery tubing that feels so comfortable and secure, I actually swoon a little. There's even a little toggle for you to attach a spare key, should you head out pocketless, as I often do.

Timberwolf – I nod at the brand name. That's more like it.

'What do you think?' I ask Bodie, checking he approves of the browny-aubergine colourway I'm favouring.

Poop happens! Just pick it up and move on.

He has turned away and appears to be reading one of the humorous, and frankly philosophical, signs. Here's another: *Who rescued who?*

He gives me a knowing look and then delights the cashier by placing his paws up on the counter as if intending to pay. Wouldn't that be nice? It's shocking how much I spend on him without blinking an eye. I'm not alone, of course. The pet industry is currently worth $58 billion and is one of the few sectors to remain untouched by the recession. I just wish dog treats were as resilient. The worst is when you splurge on something that looks like it could keep your pal occupied for a solid half-hour – all tough and knotted and twisted – and then he gives it a cursory sniff and walks away. I dip it in peanut butter, he licks it off and then walks away. I try wedging a malleable treat into its folds, and he hooks it out and walks away... My most expensive splurge was a $25 antler, guaranteed to last a lifetime – he was all over it in the pet store and then the second we got it home he looked at me as if to say, 'Would you chance your teeth on that?' Ah well, that's life. You win some, you lose some.

We're just about to head on our way when a bohemian-chic sixty-something asks if Bodie has some Shiba Inu in him. I tell her that's a new one on me but anything is possible – he's a very elaborate mix. As she leans forward to groove her plum-glossed nails down his chest, I notice the most exquisite pendant swinging from her neck – a miniature glass bottle encased in delicate gold filigree.

'It's from Ajne, just around the corner – you have to go!' she insists. 'It's this beautiful perfume boutique where they custom-blend scents for you. They even do furfumes!'

'Furfumes?'

'Perfume for dogs!'

'Really?'

'You'll find it in the Court of the Fountains by the Mole Hole.'

Which is about as irresistible a set of directions as you are ever likely to receive. Clearly we have to go.

Chapter 14

Kennel No. 5

What a setting. Ajne overlooks a bright blue fountain pool lined with troughs of pink and purple flowers. The shop itself feels like a mini Versailles with its glittering chandeliers and white-and-gold panelled walls, and there's an Alice in Wonderland quality to the ornate scent bottles set on gilded tables. I can't quite believe they allow dogs to pad inside but the first thing I see is a display dedicated to their fragrant wellbeing.

There are four scents available in the Furfume range: Breed, Tro DaBone, Sea K-9 (the dog version of CK1), and the classic Kennel No. 5.

Each has been created to address particular concerns or conditions from generating puppy love to combatting overeating. I think Kennel No.5 is the one for Bodie – a calming floral blend of rose, lavender and geranium.

I am most fortunate that the creator herself, Jane Hendler, is on hand to anoint him. (She and her husband Rex came up with the concept for the entire range over cocktails at the Cypress Inn.)

Although she's a self-confessed cat person, Bodie keels over and lies submissively by her feet from the moment she addresses him.

'First we let him have a little sniff,' she says, holding the bottle to his nose.

He clearly approves.

'Then we apply a dab or two to his fur.'

Instant bliss. It's almost comical how relaxed Bodie is now, ready for a snooze and thus giving me the opportunity to try the human version of the experience.

Jane explains that all Ajne's perfumes are organic, no synthetics, and designed to balance and strengthen your body's chakras. The customisation process is intriguing. It begins with a questionnaire. I am expecting to have to decide between lily and jasmine, musky and clean, but it goes much deeper than that.

'What do you hope this fragrance will do for you?'

This question takes me the longest to ponder because it feels like a genie is offering to grant a wish. I mean, which of these would you pick?

- *Refresh, energise and uplift you.*
- *Give you wisdom and mental stimulation.*
- *Elevate you to new heights.*
- *Provide grounding and security.*
- *Fill you with love and peace.*

Ultimately, I choose 'Elevate you to new heights'. Possibly because I've been feeling so down the only way is up.

Next.

'Which of the following places do you feel most drawn to in this moment?'

Oddly, I don't tick 'Metropolitan cities of Northern America', even though I'm headed to San Francisco tomorrow and then on to Portland. 'Rainforests and jungles' sound a bit sweltering and requiring of a machete so I go for the 'Mountainous regions', such as the Himalayas and the Rockies. I think it's the idea that the purity of the air would somehow bring a sense of clarity... once you'd adjusted to the altitude.

Here's another interesting one: 'Which of the following characteristics do you feel you need more of in yourself and your life right now?'

'Honesty, forthrightness, speaking your truth' is one selection. 'Abundance, creativity, pleasure' is another. I choose 'Courage and confidence' because I feel they are the most key in terms of fulfilling a quest. And that's what we're on, after all.

As the questions get more personal, I start to get a little churny inside. This feels like a soul-searching therapy session. Instead of 'How do I want to smell?' it's more about 'Who do I want to be?' Every choice seems overly significant.

'Should I be responding with my overall thoughts and feelings, or specifically how I'm feeling right now?' I ask.

'Just go with now,' Jane encourages.

I take a deep breath and finally it's complete. I transfer from the private desk to the main counter. It's time to use my nose.

One by one I sniff the samples and assign them to one of three piles – yes, no or maybe. Now this is fun! I can tell that I'm favouring woodsy over floral or citrus and interestingly many of my top choices are unisex. Perhaps it's because I want to be smelling something more manly to compensate for the lack of that presence in my life? Or perhaps I just like cedar.

We whittle the favourites down to four. Then two, then one. I have made my selection. But I'm curious: what would the computer have chosen for me from my answers? Jane slides the printout over to me – the match is exact! Out of hundreds of possible options both my nose and my heart are as one. There's something very gratifying about that. The icing on the cake is picking out the pendant bottle and chain. Jane began her career as a jewellery designer and they really are something to treasure. I forgo the box and decide to wear mine out – I like the idea of having this amulet with special healing powers dangling from me at all times.

'This really has been a lovely experience,' I thank Jane. 'Rare and precious,' I quote their logo. 'Right, Bodie?'

No response. 'Bodie!'

He looks up at me with an easy contentment.

'Time to go…'

We're just crossing the road when a smart businesswoman stops to admire Bodie.

'Is he friendly?' she checks.

'Very!'

'And so soft!' she gurgles as she runs her hand along his side. 'He even smells good!'

Now that is a first. Not that Bodie's ever been called *unfragrant* but certainly no one has ever commented in this way before.

'Well, it's funny you should say that…' I begin.

Time for lunch.

PortaBella has been repeatedly recommended as a great dog-friendly eatery but the weather has really hotted up and I'm concerned that there is no shade available on the front patio seats. One of the waiters notices me hovering at the entrance and says, 'Would you prefer a table on the enclosed patio?' My eyes brighten. 'Follow me!' He turns and walks into the rather posh, carpeted restaurant.

'Really? I should follow?'

He nods.

As the flooring transitions to stone flagging, a gent in a classic beige linen suit offset with a cobalt blue shirt steps aside, bowing his head graciously at our approach. 'Thank you for being nice to your dog!'

I all but splutter, 'It is I who should be thanking you!'

No sooner am I seated than another waiter brings Bodie a bowl of water, served on a linen cloth and china plate.

What a place. I feel like I am in Capri or St Tropez.

The menu is aptly Mediterranean. As I surreptitiously share a piece of lemon chicken with Bodie, I notice a fellow diner watching me. For one awful moment I think she feels I'm disrespecting the quality of the food but when I pass her on the way out she gurgles with delight at Bodie, as if she's been dying to get her hands on him the whole time.

Is there something in the water here?

Perhaps they all drink from the Fountain of Woof in Carmel Plaza. Bodie laps enthusiastically at the water spouting from the mouth of a bronze Labrador while on our afternoon mooch around the shops. It's amazing how dog-friendly every establishment is. Even Tiffany has a dog bowl outside.

One highlight is our tour of the George Rodrigue Studio – the Louisiana artist famous for his Blue Dog paintings. I've seen prints of these eye-popping pop art pictures before but I never knew they were inspired by the legend of the Cajun werewolf dog, said to prowl the swamplands. The Blue Dog of the paintings looks rather less threatening, posing beside a vintage Coke machine or vase of flowers. All the while, the expression on his face is a Mona Lisa mystery. As Rodrigue once said: 'That dog is asking, who am I, who are you, what are we doing here, what is life about?'

Today is definitely a Big Question Day.

I can tell you one thing – Carmel is where I would like to retire. And quite possibly live out the time leading up to that juncture too.

If you had told me that I would be spending the evening conversing with three happily married couples I would probably have stayed in with the sherry decanter. But this is Carmel. There's a dog-twist. And that changes everything.

Of course, I suppose I was asking for it by dining at Casanova – Carmel's Most Romantic Restaurant. I did hesitate on account of that billing but the menu was so alluring I couldn't resist.

Again the staff look thrilled to see that my dining companion is a dog.

'Thank you for bringing him,' the waiter says earnestly.

Again I look back in wonder. You'd honestly think they meant these things.

The couple I am seated next to on the patio have two scrappy little Yorkshire Terriers and tell me that they are trying to train them to give a signal when they want to use the bathroom. Several times the husband jumps up, thinking the little girl dog is tipping him the wink, but each time he returns to the table saying it was a false alarm.

'We'll get there in the end,' he says stoically.

When they move on, a couple with a brand-new, hyperactive rescue dog take their seats. Bodie is still in zen mode and barely looks their way but it doesn't take long to discover they are oracles of all things medical. While she recommends treatments for cuts and hot spots, he locates an image on his phone so I know exactly what product to look for next time I'm at PetSmart. (Sulfodene is their top tip, a classic that has been going strong for 60 years.) In return I recommend Kennel No.5 for their dog – he is proving so restless they are forced to cut their meal short, vacating the table for the third couple, my favourites, both in terms of the people (Ron and Denise from Northern Ireland) and their two magnificent Golden Retrievers (Paddy and Murphy).

I can barely believe two dogs with a combined weight of 230 pounds can fit under the small wooden table but they are brothers and thus prefer to be lying entwined.

'They always touch when they are sleeping,' Denise smiles fondly. 'If one is out of sight of the other there is a moment of panic until they see each other again and then it's, "Oh god where have you been?" and they're all over each other!'

The family currently live in Reno, Nevada (they take the dogs swimming in Lake Tahoe), but Ron's work has taken them all over the US, from Georgia to Texas to North Carolina (where they got 'the boys') and Wisconsin, where the dogs foiled their initiation into frozen chicken bowling.

'It's a tradition when you go ice fishing on Lake Winnebago but the dogs being Retrievers played fetch and that was that – end of chicken-ball, end of game.'

With all their experience road-tripping with dogs, I ask if they have any tips for novices.

'Plenty of exercise before they get in the car, lots of potty breaks en route and I know our dogs love the TV on in the hotel rooms. Reminds them of home and that comforts them.'

They show me some of their snaps from their travels, from reclining on sunloungers to romping in the snow, and it's clear that Paddy and Murphy live the life of Riley.

One photo has the pair of them frolicking at the beach, ears flying high, and it makes me feel bad that Bodie doesn't have a playmate, other than me. Then again, when I do stop to pay attention to another dog, he always gets huffy and either tries to pull me on my way or goes straight up to the other owner and demands attention from them. Perhaps he's happy being an only child.

While he has his phone out, Ron decides to add his review of the Casanova fare to TripAdvisor. Quite the foodie, he tells me about the time he was at a 'gourmet' business dinner in Chicago and they asked if he had any food allergies, to which he replied: 'Yes, I'm allergic to small portions.'

One course was a single tortellini. So he excused himself, saying, 'I'm sorry but I know where these come in packs.'

I must say I could probably manage a third helping of my ricotta ravioli with carrot, coriander and brown butter, but this does mean I have all the more room for dessert…

Over Apple Charlotte pudding with star anise ice cream we chat about living in America and the niggling tug of being so far from family members.

'But of course we do give them a great place to come on holiday.'

'So true!' I concur.

There's something very satisfying about talking with people from 'the homeland' – we've had a good chuckle and I am brimming with bonhomie as Bodie and I feel our way back to the hotel in the darkness.

But then, doing a final email check before sleep, I am greeted by a fourth happy couple…

Sam and Marcus sitting in splendour at the Villa d'Este, Lake Como. It's a lovely picture – both of them dressed to the nines, matching onyx-green eyes shining bright. This time my heart plumps with fondness and delight.

I don't know if it's the Ajne magic potion balancing me up or the fact that I've had a thoroughly sociable night but, as I align myself with an already sleeping Bodie, it feels like everything in the world is exactly as it should be.

Chapter 15
The Dog Mayor

It's a beautiful morning at the beach. Bodie splashes into the marine blue, bounding at full stretch. The only spanner in the works is the woman constantly calling to her new puppy, Bodie, which is confusing my fella, so we decide to explore the new territory at the other end of the bay. At the crest of the low cliff ahead I see a couple of golf buggies trundling along and realise we are now within a short upward putt of the legendary Pebble Beach course. I remember my dad telling me this has one of the highest green fees in the world: around the $500 mark. I'm just pondering the likelihood of a golf ball bopping us on the head when I realise Bodie has scampered way ahead. A couple of jogging guys try to shoo him back in my direction but he ignores them and begins hiking up the rubbly slope with feverish determination. Oh no. I begin chasing after him, scrambling over the algae-slicked rocks, struggling to find secure footing, yet onward and upward he goes, the devil in him now. I'm experiencing the same cold dread as the Santa Barbara road dash – the more urgently I call him, the faster he claws away from me.

He's up and over the edge now, I can't see or hear him. My eyes close in a grimace – I can barely bring myself to peep over the rim – it's one thing seeing a dog tearing across the links but a pre-shower me? Let's just say I'm not exactly meeting the official golf club dress code.

As I do my impression of a gopher, I see two men a few feet away from me – they could well be Jack Nicklaus and Tiger Woods, I am just too mortified to bring myself to look them in the eye.

'Sorry!' I bleat in their general direction as I make a lunge for Bodie, now tormenting me with a ludicrous grin. 'He just got away from me!'

At which point I lose my footing and nearly plummet backwards on to the rocky beach.

'Need any help?' a concerned caddy calls in my direction.

'No, no, I'm fine!' I lie, face burning with shame as I make another ungainly lunge at Bodie.

This time I get him, clamp the leash hook back on his collar and yank him back down to sea level, where we belong.

I later learn that we were just 19 days shy of the US Open. Can you imagine: right in the middle of some tense, televised moment Bodie comes skidding by like one of the streakers that used to liven up British cricket matches in the 1970s.

I shudder at the thought that I would have been following close behind.

As soon as we're cleaned up and checked out, I secure Bodie in the car so we can explore the 17-Mile Drive without any further drama.

Halfway round I wish we'd allotted a day to do it justice. The name had me fooled – I thought it was just a scenic loop, interspersed with golf clubs, to be viewed at a leisurely 17 mph. But certain stop-off points warrant way more than a foot on the brake and a quick camera click: take Spanish Bay, with its expansive powder-white sands and minty-fresh waters, or the picnic area at Seal Rock – perfect if you like your sandwiches with a side of 'arnf-arnf-arnf'!

Bodie is bemused by their honky-barking but my eyes are on the sea – is that a shark fin I see? Or a seal flipper? It's hard to tell with these suddenly choppy waters – one minute you think you see something black and mammal-esque, the next you can't discern it from the shifting seaweed and semi-submerged rocks.

Either way, it's hard to imagine this coastline doubling for Sussex, England, though it did just that in 1944, for Elizabeth Taylor's breakout movie, *National Velvet*, when she was just 12 years old. Now there was a dog lover. Aside from starring in two *Lassie* movies, she actually owned a Collie that was a descendant of her canine co-star – a gift on her sixtieth birthday. When it came time to divorce, her then-husband Larry Fortensky took her to court to battle over the custody. Needless to say, she won.

My other favourite Liz–dog story is this: she was due to film a movie in England with Richard Burton and wanted to bring her Pekingese to the set but the strict quarantine laws of that time would have held them for six months, so she got around it by hiring a yacht and living on the Thames for the duration of filming – that way the dogs never had to touch English soil! Now that's devotion.

She even went as far as saying, 'Some of my best leading men have been dogs!'

Which of course can be taken multiple ways.

I sneak a glance at Bodie. 'You're my leading man now,' I tell him.

He looks back at me unfazed and then perks up at the sight of two enormously shaggy Bernese Mountain Dogs. I wonder if their owner has been waiting all day for it to cloud over. They certainly seem highly appreciative of the fur-ruffling ocean breeze. I sigh – those coats are so luxurious, I think you could survive in the Arctic if you had a Bernese lying on top of you. Definitely one of my favourite-looking breeds, probably because they are the closest thing to having a bear as a pet.

As we drive on, I see a woman cycling by with her little doggy in a basket. I can't imagine Bodie sitting so sedately. As for the Bernese, you'd need a small forklift truck. And then I notice two other women out jogging, waving their arms at the car racing up behind me, urging him to slow down. I decide I can help with that. There is no overtaking on these curves so I ease to a crawl, delighting in the fact that the car behind must now go at my snail's pace. I release them at Crocker Grove and of course they floor it, the second they can. They obviously prefer their scenery at a blur, yet for my money this route rivals the Big Sur in terms of scenic drama. Yes, the plunge-to-your-death aspect is toned down but there is more topographical variety and I do love a road where the tree branches reach towards each other, creating a canopy of lovely dappled light. Unfortunately, the sky has taken on an air of menace by the time we arrive at the Lone Cypress.

For 250 years this infamous landmark has been clinging wilfully to a rocky outcrop, withstanding everything that the elements have thrown at it. I think everyone at some point has felt on the edge and rather blustered by life. It puts me in mind of the quote from Aristotle Onassis: 'We must free ourselves of the hope that the sea will ever rest. We must learn to sail in high winds.'

We'll be finding out whether Bodie is a sea dog later today but we have one more stop prior to our bay cruise in San Francisco...

Talk about going from the sublime to the ridiculous. We are leaving Carmel, where Clint Eastwood was once mayor, and heading an hour and a half north to Sunol, where a dog was once elected mayor. Blink and the words remain. *A dog mayor.*

It started as a joke but the beloved black Lab/Rottweiler mix named Bosco Ramos went on to beat the two human candidates. His term ran from 1981 to 1994 – 13 years. And it only ended because he died. Apparently he was that good.

The first thing we spy as we arrive in this dusty little railroad town is a bronze statue of Bosco. Bodie hurries over to nuzzle into the statue's groin and then feverishly sniff his butt.

'You know that's not a real dog, right?'

I'm amazed that, with all his supposed heightened sensory perceptions, Bodie is still going through the traditional meet-and-greet procedure.

'I do wonder about you sometimes,' I tut as I hoist him up on to the wooden platform so I can see them side-by-side. They look quite the pair in their matching neckties, though Bosco is at least double Bodie's size.

I toy with the idea of leaving the two of them to hang out while I head across the street to Bosco's Bones and Brew but then I notice that the two-storey saloon, with its white slatted balcony and picture windows, has wooden posts ideal for tying up your horse/dog. With Bodie securely in position, I adjust my jeans like a gunslinger and prepare to face the patrons, fully expecting them to fall to silent gawping the minute I enter the room. But they don't. They're actually a rather jovial lot. And they know immediately why I am here…

The real doggie draw in town is not the street statue but the animatronic replica of Bosco set behind the bar amid the clinking bottles of Jack Daniels and Chambord. He's black and furry with a red bandana pinned with a sheriff's badge. And here's the best bit: when the barmaid lifts his back leg, he pees beer.

She sets the glass before me.

'It's a blonde beer,' she explains, perhaps to clarify the striking resemblance to urine.

I hesitate before taking a sip.

'We don't serve it warm here like they do in the UK.'

'No, no,' I shake my head. 'That's a good thing.'

And then I take a gulp. It's actually rather nice. Refreshing even. I make some small talk with the guys propped at the bar and then take a look around, finding a room filled with yellowing newspaper clippings about their star attraction. Seeing Bodie waiting on the other side of the window, I tap on the glass. He grins back at me. I would really rather be somewhere where we can be together.

We stroll beside the picket-fenced cottages then pause to read the postings at the bus shelter, including one from the

Chapter 16

San Francisc-no

I always felt that the person who left their heart in San Francisco must have done so because they had their most vital organ snatched from their body by one of the lurching, bandage-straggled zombies who crowd the city streets.

I've honestly never seen so many eyeball-askew loiterers in one place yet everyone I know loves it there. I certainly loved the *idea* of the place before I arrived – the quirky upsy-downsy terrain, the colourful characters – so much so that I was actually planning on relocating here with my then flatmate James.

We had become so entranced by the 1990s TV adaptation of Armistead Maupin's *Tales of the City* that, with the final credits barely rolling, we jumped on a flight, eager to find our very own Barbary Lane.

Unfortunately James followed a hotel recommendation from a work colleague who, it transpired, liked his accommodations to resemble his office space. I watched James visibly blanch as he scooched up the aluminium blinds to be confronted by a brick wall. Taking in the MDF desk and dormitory-style beds, he railed, *'Get me somewhere expensive!'* It wasn't until he was sipping a Brandy Alexander in low-lit swankiness at the Top of the Mark that the colour returned to his cheeks.

We changed hotels the next morning only to spend the next ten days reliving Mark Twain's famous quote: 'The coldest winter I ever spent was summer in San Francisco.'

Obliged to bolster my flimsy wardrobe, I purchased a heavy Navy-issued peacoat (ironically enough) from a Haight-Ashbury thrift store and braced myself against the biting chill, which was annoyingly interspersed with bursts of sun that would only stay long enough for you to start sweating and shed your coat. Of course a moment later a vicious gust would frisk you until you squealed – I'd had quite enough of that kind of weather in England, thank you very much. In a nutshell, we had the most god-awful time, culminating in petty bickering and a vow never to return.

So why even consider subjecting Bodie to my least favourite city?

Well, first came this statistic: there are more dogs in San Francisco than children – 120,000 canines to about 110,000 kids, according to US Census figures. In fact, the wording of city council code has changed so that you are no longer classified as the dog's owner, but rather his 'guardian'. Which is lovely.

Secondly, there are two iconic and location-specific experiences I wanted to share with Bodie – riding on a tram and taking the bay tour of Alcatraz – neither of which rate as an obvious dog activity but I was surprised to learn that both are possible, so why not give him an ear-flapping thrill?

Rather conveniently there is a cable car route – the Powell-Mason line – right beside our hotel that will take us all the way down to Pier 39 at the Embarcadero. Perhaps this time round I'll have a new view of the city – through a dog's eyes…

Bodie and I are perched on one of the most vertiginous streets in San Francisco, eyes bright with anticipation as we watch the cable car approach. I feel an internal leap of excitement as we hear the metal tracks rattle, the bell ring and the breaks squeak to a halt.

'Ready?'

Bodie looks suitably primed.

We step forward to board but a burly conductor roars at us, *'The dog ain't ridin'!'*

'What?' I bleat.

'THE DOG AIN'T RIDIN'!' he turns up the volume.

'But—'

Before I can show him printouts of the dozens of websites confirming that Bodie is a perfectly legitimate paying customer (same price as a human passenger), the tram trundles off. I am left feeling profoundly affronted on Bodie's behalf. Even he seems a little taken aback.

'Was it necessary for him to be quite so abrasive?'

I shake my head. I hate San Francisco, I really do.

'Well, I guess we're walking. If no one objects to that…'

According to my map it's about half an hour's straight shot down Stockton Street. The only snag is that, within a few blocks, we find ourselves deep in Chinatown. This is not a good scenario. All the shops have their wares displayed out front in low boxes, exactly at dog snuffling level. I shorten

Bodie's leash to get a firmer grip but this only makes him strain and tug more. I've never felt so intimidating – pedestrians part as if Bodie were gnashing and frothing at the mouth when he's really just eagerly taking in the assortment of shrivelled items.

I glance up, attracted by the cheongsam satin, but then find myself wincing at the row of roasted duck carcasses in the next window. Bodie trots on oblivious, entirely unselfconscious about his meaty thighs.

And then it starts to rain. (Bring in the paper lanterns!)

Clearly we're not going to be invited to huddle in a doorway and sip chrysanthemum tea so we have to push through and keep going. The rain is coming at us now from every angle and driving us into a makeshift tourist market to buy what is essentially a disposable umbrella, inasmuch as you'll be lucky if you get one use out of it before it blows inside out and the flimsy fabric whips loose. Bodie is so sodden he has given up shaking himself. Finally, the dock is in sight. Like we need more water.

Bang goes my vision of Bodie with his paws up at the bow of the boat, eyes squinting in the sunshine, nostrils flaring joyfully as he sniffs the sea air. I can barely see out from my water-sluiced eyes to consult with the ticket kiosk lady but apparently we're just in time to board our bay cruise.

'If you hurry!'

We spatter through the decking puddles, rattle down the gangway and are about to propel ourselves head first on to the ferry when some surly deckhand yells down at us: 'No dogs allowed!'

'Oh for pity's sake,' I mutter under my breath. 'Actually, he is allowed,' I yell back, spitting through the rain. 'I checked with the owner.'

'Well, it's not up to him – it's up to the captain.'

'Well, then why don't you check with him before you turn us away?'

He looks a little thrown.

'We'll wait right here.'

He humphs off and then returns rather more sheepishly. 'He says it's okay.'

I give a 'told you so' smirk.

'But you have to keep him away from all the other passengers.'

'Fine,' I grunt.

The second we're on board, I wish I'd let him reject us. The area 'away from the passengers' has no seating and barely any shelter. Bodie is instantly perturbed by the grinding engines and overwhelming stench of diesel fuel. Worse yet, as we begin to surge into the grey waters, the floor starts tilting and sending juddering vibrations up through his paws. I watch him cower, unable to get his footing. This is the first time I've seen him afraid. And I have trapped him in this state for a full hour. What was I thinking? What if I am inflicting permanent trauma? Not that I'm planning on doing a round-the-world yacht race with him any time soon but even so…

I just hope his anxiety doesn't escalate. If he tried to scrabble overboard I'm not sure my slippery hands could restrain him. Surveying the slick metal that surrounds us, one leash no longer seems enough – I attach the spare I have in my bag and now it's the nearby passengers who are looking nervous.

'Look! That dog needs two leashes to restrain him!'

I try tying one to the railing of the nearby metal staircase but we're constantly in the way of crew clattering up and down. I can't believe we paid money to be this wretched. We can't hear the muffled commentary, we can't see anything through the misty haze and the damp is penetrating our bones. God, I hate San Francisco. I should never have come here. Never again – I mean it this time. This is the final nail in the coffin. And a sea burial no less.

The only thing I can think of to distract Bodie from his discomfort is to teach him a new trick with the handful of treats I have in my pocket. Whereas he typically waits diligently for a titbit to be lowered to his lips and takes it softly, I am now encouraging him to jump up and snatch it from my fingers. This he likes. I break the treats into smaller and smaller fragments and then barely-there flecks to prolong the exercise, until he has perfected this new bad habit.

Then, as we pass beneath the Golden Gate Bridge, a shift occurs: we begin to attract the dog lovers among the passengers. Having given up all hope of seeing Alcatraz or trying to guess at the linking words between phrases like 'primitive communications system' and 'sewage pipe', they come over for some doggie small talk and a pat of Bodie's wet fur. In doing so they give me a warming sensation – it's as if we outcasts are being welcomed into the community by a few brave, liberal-minded citizens.

'You know a dog once swam from Alcatraz to the San Francisco shore?' one local chap tells us.

'To escape?'

'No,' he chuckles. 'He was part of an annual race they have. Golden Retriever. Came in seventy-second amongst five hundred humans.'

'That's amazing!' I find myself grinning. 'How long did that take?'

''Bout forty-two minutes.'

'Wow.' I look at Bodie, who gives me a firm, 'Don't get any ideas' look back.

Finally, praise be, it's all over. We can't get back on to the dock quick enough. Even touristy Fisherman's Wharf looks good to us right now. We find a fish and chips restaurant where Bodie is allowed to be tethered in the covered patio area and then, every time the waiter turns his back, I grab another napkin and continue towelling him dry. I always thought dogs looked absurd in those yellow hooded sou'westers but now it seems an essential purchase. There is one pet store at the wharf but it's for dogs so petite that their 'Yap Wraps' would be no more than a pocket square to Bodie. Instead we take the 15-minute walk to North Beach Pet Supply in Little Italy, which, I grudgingly admit, does look rather an appealing neighbourhood even on such a sullen day. Amidst the aging yet characterful cafés Cavalli, Capriccio and Puccini, there's a delightfully bright mural featuring a number of dogs hanging off a streetcar. Just to taunt us a little more.

Now that the rain has abated, my attention switches from a sou'wester to a grey hand-knitted dog sweater with an American flag design – so Ralph Lauren. Bodie looks unspeakably handsome in it, like the dog version of a square-jawed blonde youth from Maine. I buy it but just two minutes up the road he is itching and fidgeting, desperate to get it off his back – the sun has come out and he's now roasting.

'Tell me about it!' I say, wriggling loose of my outer garments.

And so it goes, that familiar routine of hot/cold/humid/damp, flick-flacking between 'oh this isn't so bad' to 'godammit!' all the way back to Bush Street.

Bodie stalls beneath a sign advertising Nob Hill's *World Famous Nude Male Revue*. 'Really? This is where we're spending the night?'

'We're a bit further up,' I urge him past the theatre.

'Hooker Alley?'

'Hooker Alley Community Garden,' I clarify, though I don't find much consolation myself. At least not until I set eyes on the narrow Edwardian building that is the Golden Gate Hotel.

This may sound counter-intuitive but I chose this place because they have a cat in their logo. And because their website uses words like vintage, European and cookies.

The elegant Danish owner, Renate Kenaston, greets us at the reception desk, along with her French Bulldog Patsy.

'Look at those amazing ears,' I marvel. Like two perfect leaves from a Little Gem lettuce or a pair of perky oyster shells.

Though the little dog's eyes are bulging with curiosity, Bodie is far more interested in Pip the ginger cat and is straining towards its position on the stairs.

'Would you like to take the lift up?' Renate offers, motioning to the 1920s birdcage design.

Bodie looks uneasy as she clanks the concertina gating – I suspect he may have had enough of unsteady floors for one day. But it's too late – we're already lurching into motion. Instead of yelping, he looks happily intrigued as he watches the floor disappear beneath us. I have a similar look on my face as I notice the paintings sliding by on the inner walls of the lift shaft – in particular a shimmering, softly tarnished portrait of a dog.

As we emerge, Pip darts ahead along the corridor deliberately tantalising Bodie. But by the time we turn the corner to our room she has vanished in a Cheshire Cat-style vapour, leaving us to inspect our primrose yellow and Wedgwood blue nest with its charming bay windows, white wicker bedheads and ye olde bathroom porcelain.

We both love it – it's so 'tea and comfort' cosy. San Francisco can be as dirty and crazy as it likes; I know we'll be safe here.

Maybe a little too safe.

It occurs to me that this is my fourth snug and chintzy accommodation on the trot: San Ysidro Ranch, Cottage Inn, Monte Verde Inn and now here. I can't deny the homely appeal but wonder if, for tomorrow at least, I should consider something more jet set than twinset. I take out my laptop and begin reviewing sleek, modern options but when I find myself repeatedly clicking on the dining information, I realise that my stomach requires more than cyber sustenance.

'Time for your evening stroll!' I swing my feet off the bed.

For once, Bodie looks less than enthused.

I'd rather stay here too but this being a B&B, there is no dinner to be had and besides, I have a specific venue in mind.

The rain is holding off but the cowing wind remains. This time our route takes us through the deserted Financial District, peering up at eerie statues that look ready to topple and swoop down, like something out of a Batman movie. Or perhaps I should say Dracula, since we are dining at Francis Ford Coppola's bistro: Cafe Zoetrope.

Housed in the Sentinel Building (San Francisco's version of New York's Flatiron), the restaurant is wonderfully reminiscent of Paris – ornate oxidised copper façade, red cloth awnings and an enticing candle glow within. The walls are accented with photos and mementos from the maestro's movies (most famously *The Godfather*) but of course we are not allowed inside. Instead, the waiter kindly assesses the sharpness of the wind at the pavement tables and determines that Kearny Street is less lacerating than Columbus Avenue. Bodie finds shelter in a nook beside my chair and I unravel my scarf and layer it around his neck. He actually doesn't seem too worried about the cold whereas I find myself sitting on my hands with my shoulders hunched up by my ears.

A salad may not be the obvious choice under these circumstances but I can't resist the ingredients of the Insalata Finocchio – fennel, celery, orange, fresh lemon juice and shaved pecorino. It's just as zesty and crunchy and zingy as you might imagine. I then order a little heat with a fiery Penne all'Arrabbiata and pair that with a glass of Merlot from Coppola's vineyard. This is actually the reason I chose this place – it seemed an apt link between today's San Francisco and tomorrow's destination of Napa and California's Wine Country. Coppola's Rubicon Estate permits dogs in the grounds but not the tasting rooms, which is a shame because I was rather hoping to take the Sensory Exploration tour to see how Bodie's nose fared when comparing vintage bouquets.

'Another glass of wine?'

As I glance back at the menu, I notice that, between the Reds and Whites, there is a category named 'Sofia' for his daughter, writer and director of the sublime *Lost in Translation*.

Never had I seen a film capture so precisely the feeling of being a stranger in a strange land. All that wandering and wondering, trying to process the bombardment of a different culture through the woozy distortions of jet lag. Observing other people's lives and holding up your own in comparison. Pondering whether you will ever truly belong to any place or anyone.

The question always seems to bite deepest when I'm dining alone. Of course, if I really were in Paris, say in the 1920s, every café would be overrun with lone writers and no one would bat an eye.

Except perhaps for the fact that I am sitting in the dark on the kind of whistling-wind night that has all the kerbside rubbish riled up and catching on chair legs and lamp posts.

I hand back the wine list and ask for the bill.

Enough is enough. My cocoon is calling. Not even the prospect of Bill Murray and an overhead heater could hold me now.

Chapter 17

The Snoopy Museum

Today we're on our way to see a 60-year-old dog that generates more than $2 billion in annual sales, thanks to its licensing deals with the likes of Hallmark and our friend Ty Warner of Beanie Baby.

Snoopy!

Specifically we're visiting the Charles M. Schulz Museum in Santa Rosa. When I say *we*... Bodie gets to play in the maze shaped like Snoopy's head and sit on a bench with a fiberglass statue but he's not allowed in the museum itself. Handily, there's a doggie daycare just minutes away so he can roughhouse with the boys while I tiptoe around the exhibits.

This really is a splendid museum – spacious, airy and both immaculately and thoughtfully put together. With nearly 18,000 *Peanuts* strips to choose from, the theme of the main room is always changing. Today the focus is heartbreak.

The opening panel talks about 'the disappointment Charlie Brown feels each Valentine's Day' and Lucy's 'unrelenting pursuit of Schroeder'.

We learn that Schulz drew upon his own life experiences to create several recurring plots focused on lost love. Charlie Brown's Little Red-Haired Girl was inspired by memories of a former sweetheart, Donna Mae Johnson, who was proposed to by two men on the same day and did not choose Schulz.

He said: 'I can think of no more emotionally damaging loss than to be turned down by someone whom you love very much.'

And to see your beloved marry another so soon after? That's not something you get over in a finger-snap.

Even Snoopy isn't immune to heartache – one of the cutest sequences shows him snuffling into his heaped dog bowl lamenting having ever fallen in love: 'You try for a little happiness and what do you get?' Cut to him lying on top of his doghouse, his classic profile altered by a huge round belly. 'A few memories and a fat stomach.'

My hand instinctively moves to my own tummy. It's so true and of course the irony is that, in life, the good memories can cause you more pain than the bad. Like now, I can think of Nathan and I side by side in the kitchen, sipping wine, swaying to the music, smiling as we chopped and stirred dinner. It makes my head feel swimmy and my eyes prickle. I blink vigorously. This won't do! I can't have my vision blurring – I won't be able to read the next display.

The more I read, the more I realise how little I knew about the depth of these cartoons – their subtle political and social commentary across the decades with strips touching on everything from the Vietnam war to racial integration in school, equal pay for women in sports and even the grunge movement! And then, of course, there are the exquisitely precise angst and vulnerabilities of the characters... Take Snoopy when he tells Charlie Brown that he's getting married to the most wonderful girl in the world.

'All my life I've felt unsettled... sort of up in the air... not any more. The beagle has landed!'

Of course, come the wedding day, the bride runs off with Snoopy's brother Spike.

Romantic love is such a minefield. No wonder people value the love of their pets so much. One of the few sure things in life.

Upstairs I take a look at Sparky's Studio. (That's what friends and family called Schulz.) He's quite the opposite of me, believing that a change of scenery makes work more difficult – for him coming to the same room every day was 'the only guarantee of keeping going'. I may not relate to that but I do like hearing how he'd often slide back the patio doors and join his children playing by the pool. So he did find love and marriage, first with Joyce and then with Jean, who he was with for 27 years until his death in 2000.

He really seems a lovely man with a gentle, grey-haired, V-neck sweater handsomeness that puts me in mind of Andy Williams. I'm surprised to hear him described as melancholy. It makes me sad to think of him sad but as one of his close friends said, 'We've all got some melancholy in us, Sparky used his to make us laugh.'

I'm sitting in the screening room now, watching a documentary on his life.

Apparently the family dog that inspired Snoopy was quite the wayward character, given to ingesting tacks and even, on one occasion, a double-edged razor blade. He'd often disappear for hours and the only way the family could get him to come home was for Schulz's dad to drive around the neighbourhood honking his horn. The dog would come running from wherever he'd been plotting his next mischief and jump aboard, never happier than when he was riding alongside his master.

Just like Bodie!

Schulz talks about the comfort and security of being in the back seat with your parents up front, taking all responsibility for the direction and the driving. But part of being an adult is 'being reconciled with the fact that you can't go back, you cannot sleep in the back seat any longer, you have to sit in the front, *you have to drive your own way*'.

Wow.

This whole experience has been way more moving than I was expecting and I wander back outside in something of a daze. It's a little too soon to pick up Bodie so I head over to the Warm Puppy Café, which I'm rather surprised to see is housed in what looks like a large Austrian chalet. Even more unexpected is the full-size ice rink within. Cue lots of teenage girls with buns and mums with bedazzled hoodies. Turns out Schulz had a long association with ice sports and I have to say the flagstone fireplace is most welcoming. I snug up with my hot chocolate and try to reconcile what I have learned about Snoopy's creator: the man fulfilled his childhood dreams, led a successfully creative life, made millions, had a loving wife and children and a world class sense of humour, and he still got the blues? Is there no cure for the human condition? I remember Shirley MacLaine talking about the reasons she got into spirituality – since she had already acquired and achieved all the things that most people spend their lives in pursuit of, she knew for a fact that money and fame were not the answer. There had to be more. I've certainly read my share of spiritual and self-help books and they do put you on a better path. But I have to say, in terms of actual, tangible, instant-gratification happiness, a dog is far more effective.

In gratitude to Bodie, I visit the vast gift emporium across the way and purchase a cuddly Snoopy for him to chew on. Well, it's a dog-eat-dog world out there.

Chapter 18

Yappy Hour in Napa

You have to drive your own way...

In the half-hour drive to our next stop I feel my spirits lifting again – it's a beautiful leafy route and, though I never thought I'd be the kind of girl to even notice such things, the road surface is a dream. This is what happens when you have a dog that freaks out when there are bumps or ridges or anything that makes the car judder.

So what on earth will he make of the Petrified Forest?

As we head into the attraction I'm picturing Bodie bundled in my arms, gibbering with fright, and thus gasp when a passerby declares, 'He looks just like Scooby-Doo!'

In actuality the Petrified Forest offers Bodie a blissful sniff-a-thon: millions of years of smells condensed into select tree trunks. One is named for Robert Louis Stevenson as he had such a fascination for this place he wrote a booklet about his visit called *The Silverado Squatters*.

I expected the whole area to be a devastated, ashy wasteland but instead it provides a delightful woodland amble, with some unusual extras: what looks like grey concrete splurged across the pathway is ancient volcanic lava. That old grey trunk that you might have casually stepped over in any other scenario is as hard as stone. Over an eternity of time the molecules of silica have replaced the molecules of wood, turning these trunks and stumps to solid quartz. Bodie rises up on his back legs to put his paws on top, as if to connect to the history.

Most of these fallen trees are fenced off – one is particularly intriguing, as it leads all the way down what looks like a mineshaft. I can't help but marvel at people's dedication to excavate and preserve these trees. It was a farmer who first discovered them back in 1870 and a woman named Ollie Bockée who determined to turn the forest into a public attraction around 1914, to ensure the trees would always remain protected.

Bodie and I take advantage of every seat en route, pausing to cool off in the shade and enjoy the leafy peace. One bench has assorted lovers' engravings and heart-shaped cut-outs. I muse that my heart definitely feels more whole than hole here. There is something about being away from the general population that makes you less inclined to compare yourself and find yourself lacking. Perhaps it's that simple: everything is relative. Sitting with Bodie amid the beautiful trees, I feel extraordinarily fortunate and at peace. If we switched to a room full of canoodling couples I might feel all self-conscious and at odds. Of course, you don't want to avoid every situation that can conjure feelings of inadequacy or left-out-ness but you can certainly balance out those experiences with something more life-affirming.

I get to my feet but for once Bodie doesn't follow suit. He wants to sit a while longer. And so we do, fully immersing ourselves in this feeling.

We have an option a few miles down the road to visit the Old Faithful geyser but I think we can both do without the startlement of 175°C water shooting out of the ground. I'd rather watch a barista whooshing that into my coffee. Besides, it's time we headed for our hotel.

As we take the St Helena Highway, we pass countless sprawling vineyards offering tastings. The names I recognise – Robert Mondavi, Beringer, Rubicon Estates – are all dog-friendly, but we have something special planned for tomorrow so we ignore the temptations, even those of the exquisite Domaine Chandon (of Moët & Chandon fame), which has a red rose entwined at the end of every row of vines. So romantic.

Much of the Napa Valley has a historic olde worlde charm and so I find Yountville, where we're spending the next two nights, ultra-neat and new-looking by comparison, even though it has an old train caboose turned hotel and a vast red-brick building clad in age-old ivy.

Aside from their weekly Yappy Hour, I chose the Bardessono resort because it is the latest addition to the wine-based accommodation scene and by far the greenest, on a mission to prove that eco and luxe can go hand in hand. The vibe is very angular-zen, with boxy modernist apartment-style suites using weathered wood milled from salvaged trees. In fact, every material used in its construction is non-toxic and non-allergenic. Naturally they have their own organic vegetable garden. Which Bodie will not be peeing in. Got that?

I spend a bit of time getting Bodie to do the MGM lion roar beside one of their rough-hewn stone archways and then we head up to our vast room – so many sleek lines and sharp edges, I feel I should go round childproofing the place.

Of course, Bodie is more interested in the complimentary dog biscuits presented in one of those metal-hinged jars with a rubber suction ring that makes a satisfying pop when it opens.

I slide back the balcony door and Bodie immediately takes the opportunity to splay out and sun himself. I too have come to a standstill. I have enjoyed the cosiness and chintziness of our lodgings to date but now I'm loving the minimalism. The crisp, white linens on the bed feel like a fresh start, a cleansed palate. The bathroom is like your own personal spa. Even looking at the simple artwork on the walls feels like a meditation.

We order room service and all but adopt yoga poses while we watch the day draw to a yawn-filled close.

Chapter 19
Fou Fou Le Blanc

The next morning I'm in up and at 'em mode but Bodie wants to play. He's doing his little prancy dance with his squeaky toy in his mouth and how am I going to resist that? The room is plenty big enough to throw the toy and he skids delightedly around the tile floor, ricocheting off the bed and then rising off the ground as we engage in a tug of war – and before I know it we're breathlessly behind schedule.

It actually feels good. Even though I've been freelancing for years, I've always been breathing down my own neck, enforcing deadlines and feeling guilty when I'm not at the peak of productiveness. To do something purely for fun feels liberating.

Besides, our first appointment is only five minutes' walk away.

Bouchon Bakery is famous for its foie gras dog treats (and all manner of Parisian pastries). Bodie waits patiently, tied to one of the courtyard tables as I line up to add an almond croissant and latte to his order. He practically loses his mind as I give him a scent-waft while concealing the biscuit in my hand. The treat is gone in seconds and then he looks expectantly at me for more. But by then I've Googled foie gras – which I only knew as a delicacy up until this point – and learn that it's made from the forcibly fattened liver of a duck or goose. So he has to settle for croissant crumbs after that.

'What a lovely dog!'

A middle-aged couple are watching him from an adjacent bench.

'We couldn't bring our two and we're missing them terribly.'

'Where are you from?' I ask.

'Virginia Beach,' they reply.

Nathan's base. It feels like a punch to the stomach. Fortunately they're a jolly pair and chat on regardless. It's ridiculous, really, my reaction. I wonder if the shock feels so great because I've been so happily absorbed in the present moment and thus spared my usual forlornness? Suddenly I can't help but think that I might, in another life, have said: 'Oh, what a coincidence! I'm moving to Virginia Beach just as soon as my fiancé returns from his deployment!'

'Really?' They would have laughed and we'd have planned to take our dogs on a play date.

In my dreams.

Instead I say, 'I need a drink.' Not out loud, of course. But it seems apt that our next appointment is for a wine tasting…

The Mutt Lynch Winery goes beyond dog-friendly to being dog-themed. Each of their wine bottles features a dog on the label, so for example you have Fou Fou Le Blanc featuring a pointy-toed poodle, Unleashed Chardonnay showing a dog leaping for joy and Merlot Over and Play Dead with its chompy-jawed English Bulldog.

Mutt Lynch also actively supports local animal rescue organisations as diverse as Hounds for Haiti and the Dirty Dog Squad. The year of my visit they donate $10,000 to Adopt-a-Pet.com, which is a brilliant nationwide online search system for finding the next animal love of your life – you can be as specific as breed, sex, size, even colour!

Oh and the Mutt Lynch motto is: 'Bark Less, Wag More.'

What can I say – you had me at Merlot!

It gets even better when we meet the dog behind the brand. Patch is an ex-champion greyhound racer, quite the celebrity in his native New Zealand, now curled slim-limbed on his bed.

Owner Chris Lynch tells us how Patch would sprint in ovals around the local park, though everywhere else he loves to sleep.

'Each year we think about updating Patch's photos on our web page and each year we take a new round of pictures… and each year they look the same!'

Just being in the presence of his quiet, slender beauty is touching and Bodie takes a leaf out of his book and settles dutifully at my feet as I taste the wine. Which is really good – award-winning good – all without the poncey bow-tied bouquet-sniffing I had rather feared. At the time of my visit the bar is a plank of wood in a charming little barn-like structure off the beaten track. These days Chris and his lovely wife Brenda have a smart tasting room in Windsor (just 10 miles from the Snoopy museum), sharing a space with Deux Amis Winery, famous for its Zinfandels. There's also a new range of wines featuring black-and-white dog portraits on the labels and a stack of the *Winery Dogs* books I've been seeing in every pet store in the area – big, gorgeously lit photos of dogs grinning: *viva la vineyard!*

It's funny, before I came to the Napa Valley I thought dogs would be a bit thin on the ground on account of grapes being so very poisonous to their system but, *au contraire*, they're everywhere. I'm surprised, therefore, to find myself having a little pang for human companionship, since I can't actually chink glasses with Bodie. I think it would be a delightful way to spend the evening, stumbling from one tasting room to the next with your beloved, discovering a new favourite wine together and then heading back to your hotel room or perhaps even going for one of the famous mud baths in Calistoga. That bit Bodie would probably enjoy. The only thing he likes better than being clean is being clean and then rolling in mud. Loves that.

I get my wish for some wonderful company when we spend the afternoon at the Chappellet Winery in St Helena.

I contacted Blakesley Chappellet when I discovered her range of gourmet-themed dog accessories, including a dog bowl stand made from a wooden wine box, branded with a charmingly snooty 'Domaine du Chien' logo.

When I mentioned Bodie and I were going to be in the area, she invited us to take a stroll around the family vineyards.

Blakesley is instantly likeable, reminding me of Debra Winger but with a voice that is melodic rather than husky. She radiates positive energy throughout our tour, though there is a palpable sense of loss when she speaks of the recent passing of her beloved Anatolian Shepherd, Omar. She misses seeing him running amid the wild flowers and encourages Bodie to roam off leash, and he responds with vigour.

As we progress up the hill, Blakesley tells me the story of how her business got started, which is essentially when her husband Cyril came home with a gallon of concentrated dog shampoo that he had traded for wine.

'It was the best dog shampoo we'd ever used. Even though we already had enough to last Omar's lifetime, he traded some more and suggested we give it to our friends for Christmas. So then I thought, "Let's have some fun with this!"'

She sourced some squeezy wine bottles, created special Chien Cuvee labels, put a note from Omar on the back and everyone loved the present so much they demanded more. Initially she told them that they had to wait until next Christmas but one of her friends, who was in the pet accessory business, insisted she start selling her design. Before too long she launched an entire collection under the Dogs Uncorked brand.

'My bowls ended up in Target, the Bowluga treats were in *InStyle* and my dog treat jar was featured in *Oprah* magazine,' she marvels. 'That sent me to the moon! Oprah! You couldn't ask for more!'

But, she says, all winemakers are farmers at heart.

We're standing atop Pritchard Hill now, looking across mile upon mile of undulating hillside and, far below, a shimmering lake. The Chappellets were the first winery to plant vineyards at high elevations and this gives their wine a uniqueness, not to mention a great spot for summer picnics and tastings.

'That's the Sutter Home Winery down there...' Blakesley points to a well-known rival.

I ask if there's much competition between the grape growers but she makes this good point: 'Most people don't just drink one kind of wine,' adding, 'so we all support each other.'

As we continue traversing the vine-accented acres, Blakesley notices that Bodie is about to disappear from view. She whistles to him and he immediately stops in his tracks.

She looks impressed. 'He listens when you whistle!'

'He listens when *you* whistle!' I clarify.

And then he starts bounding towards us, running dead centre down the rows of young vines. I lift my camera and manage to capture him with all four paws off the ground – the doggie version of a wine flight. I've never seen such a spring in his step. Perhaps the reason Nathan and I didn't work out is that I'm supposed to be with a vintner – I can just see Bodie roaming the land whooping, 'It's mine, all vine!'

As Blakesley leads us back down the hill, she asks a little more about our trip and then laments the fact that she could never take Omar to a restaurant.

'The Anatolian Shepherd breed is traditionally a livestock guardian so he would have to check out every person at every table to see if they were okay, and of course he was so big – 160 pounds – and essentially designed to intimidate and make any foreign presence go away…'

I can see how that might be an issue.

'People would be scared to even look at him!'

On the plus side, these traits are currently being put to excellent use by the Cheetah Conservation Fund in Namibia. Ranchers have permission to shoot and kill any big cats that come after their cows or goats but the presence of an Anatolian Shepherd changes the whole dynamic because they will face down the cheetah. Unused to this, the cheetah has a mental shift: 'Whatever this is, coming at me, I'm getting out of here!' And everyone gets to live!

So cool.

I could listen to Blakesley until the Namibian cows come home but it's time to say goodbye. Even this she turns into a happy moment by presenting Bodie with a gift basket of her best-selling items, including the much-coveted wine box dog bowl stand, a pewter dog tag with a sommelier logo and a laminated mat with a doggie-diner theme.

I chuckle as I read the food options from pâté de paw gras to paw-shaped pancakes. There are even multiple water options – puddle, lake, toilet... Or you can upgrade to a cocktail such as a Muttini or a Cosmuttolitan.

Love it!

I give Blakesley a heartfelt hug. I've enjoyed every minute of our time together and I know Bodie has too.

It's our last night in California. Tomorrow we'll be on the road all day, making the 300-mile trek to a $49 motel in Oregon. But tonight we plan to dine in style in Calistoga, a pleasingly sleepy winery town with a main street topped and tailed by soaring mountains.

We're just crossing a seemingly empty car park when a tannoy blares out the words: '*THAT'S A CUTE LITTLE FELLA – I LIKE HIM!*'

We jump and turn to see a chap waving from the cab of his big black truck. I wave back. It's so nice to be travelling with a furry goodwill ambassador, eliciting compliments wherever we go. Imagine if we were as appreciative human to human! Actually, that's one of the things that first struck me about America – how complimentary strangers were to one another. Back in London I was used to keeping myself to myself, so I was quite taken aback the first time a passer-by said, 'I like your dress!' They weren't trying to strike up a conversation or even ask where the dress was from – it was just a thought bubble come to life. My favourite compliment came when I stepped into a tiny elevator in an office block and was greeted by an enthusiastic, 'You smell yummy!' just as the doors hemmed us in. This would typically be a moment of excruciating self-consciousness on my part but the breeziness of the American delivery put a spring in my step for the entire day.

I'm barely a few paces on in Calistoga when it happens again.

'Well, who's this chap? I don't think we've seen him around before?' A navy-blazered gent stops to greet us.

'This is Bodie.' I find myself giving a little bow. 'We're just passing through.'

'What is he?' His rather more brassy wife enquires as she leans in to give his face some love.

I toy with the idea of coming up with a new breed name – perhaps a 'Chingo' for the Chow–Dingo combo. Or a 'Sharpit' for the Shar Pei–Pit types. But that last one sounds a bit too much like carpet so instead I simply tell them, 'He's just a mix!'

'Oh here we say a blend,' the man corrects me, sounding even more like Roger Moore.

'So much more refined,' I concur.

'You got kids?' the wife wants to know.

I'm momentarily thrown by the non sequitur but quickly reply, 'No, no, this is it.'

'Me too. My choice. We have Spaniels.'

As they drift on their way, I feel she leaves behind a trace of sadness. As if that's something she must tell herself daily – *my choice…*

But though I feel for her, I don't feel the same. Not any more. I crouch beside Bodie and look into his amber-glow eyes. What if he were my child – how proud would I be? He's brave and funny and goofy and instantly likeable, at turns gentle and energetic, he rarely complains or tantrums, he's teddy-bear soft and he makes people smile and fills up my heart with all things good.

What more could I want? If he's all the child I ever have then he's more than enough.

One of the reasons Solbar pipped so many of the local dog-friendly restaurants to the post is that I heard a Great Dane regularly holds court beside the firepits, extending almost the entire length of the outdoor sofa. He's not here tonight sadly, but that leaves all the more room for Bodie.

Unlike a child who gets increasingly tetchy and irritable when tired, Bodie just conks out. Even with so many fragrant plates glancing by, he's already jaw to the floor.

'Your menu,' the waiter presents me with a swoon-inducing list of options including such fanciful terms as 'blistered' beans and pea 'tendrils'.

I tend to lean towards the vegetarian option but since Bodie came into my life I often find myself choosing my dinner with his under-the-table titbits in mind.

The lemongrass-poached sole sounds good but I think he'd prefer the pan-roasted chicken or seared loin of lamb. Either way, I have to try the starter with the lavender-honey vinaigrette. And roll on the dessert of chocolate marquise with its 'cocoa nib dentelle'. Whatever that is.

My dad says I should have been a food writer as talk of my travels so often revolves around what I ate. While I'll certainly never be a connoisseur, I do find that the older I get the more I relish a beautiful meal. And that extends beyond the actual taste of the food. I get misty-eyed as I look around me: the lights strung in the trees, the chatter of elegant conversation, the near-perfect temperature as the day eases into evening.

As I sip my glass of chilled rosé, I reflect on our Californian adventure, from the deluxe doggie massage in Montecito to running wild and free through the Chappellet vineyards... It feels satisfying to my soul to know that Bodie is having such a good time. As am I. It hardly seems possible that a week ago I was a sobbing heap, so depleted and weighed down by heartache. I know I'm still a work in progress but there's an excitement in the air now, a sense of hope...

'I'm so glad we came away,' I say as I reach for Bodie's velvety head. 'Hasn't it been wonderful so far?'

He looks back at me as if to say: 'Let's always live like this.'

I blink back the tears. He's the best thing to have happened to me. The very best companion.

I lean back in a dreamy haze, hold up my glass to the evening sunlight, enjoying the dewy sparkles and the rose glow within.

'A toast,' I sigh, 'to Bodie and to California.'

Part Three
Into Oregon

Chapter 20
I Heart Weed

I squint at the clock – 3.54 a.m. I wanted us to make an early start but this is ridiculous.

I spend an hour trying to find my way back to sleep but the 'new state' excitement of venturing into Oregon has me all a-fidget so I decide to make like we're doing a runner and creep out under cover of darkness.

Initially it feels all daring and ahead-of-the-game – the lone headlights on an empty road, stealing onward while others sleep – but then fatigue begins to droop my eyelids and a mere half an hour down the road we're back in Calistoga, pulling up to Yo el Rey's organic coffee shop. While the server is frothing the milk for my latte, a local comes in and is horrified, no exaggeration, to learn that she missed haiku night.

'Noooo!' she wails repeatedly. 'Haiku? *I can't believe it!*'

This strikes me as oddly appealing – a world revolving around fair trade beans and petite Japanese poetry.

I glance over at the quiet guy in the corner with his artfully shaped beard and marvel at all the options we have for how we live our lives. Of course, in the scramble to survive the day it rarely feels like it comes down to a simple choice – there are just too many obligations and distractions. We feel bound to live out the consequences of our earlier choices, so many of which are hopelessly out of date and out of sync with who we are and what we want *now*. We get so used to living amid the chaos and the noise that we become a part of it.

Is there really an option to unhook from all the mind-mangling media, to snug yourself between a couple of signal-blocking mountain ranges and enjoy the more sensory pleasures in life?

Bodie and I ponder this question as we take in Calistoga's rustic charm – from a quiet park with an elegant gazebo to a high street reminiscent of the Old West. We stray as far as the Indian Springs resort where all pampering needs can be met, including immersion in volcanic ash mud followed by a Chardonnay bubble bath.

One of my favourite things about Calistoga is how it got its name – California's first millionaire Samuel Brannon purchased 2,000 acres of land and said he was going to make it the Saratoga of California. At least that's what he meant to say but in his excitement he proclaimed it the 'Calistoga of Sarafornia.' And it stuck. The Calistoga part, anyway.

Speaking of quirky names, our next stop is Weed. It's 250 miles away so I suppose we should get a move on.

Despite the traffic-free roads, this isn't quite as easy-breezy as I had imagined. The road is suddenly so steep and twisty it feels as if I'm fighting a dastardly centrifugal force. I wrench the steering wheel from left to right, leaning and tilting as I do so, pressing my elbows and knees to the side of the car as if this will somehow help to keep me on track. On and on this goes, mile after mile. It's scenic and mystically misty but it's also annoying. Must we keep going up and up? I wonder if

I picked the best route? I'm straining muscles that have been left un-flexed for years.

After about an hour of this amusement arcade driving, we approach Clearlake and I find myself flashing back to 12 years ago when my friend Emily and I went on a quest to find a 'nice' man in the nearby town of Nice. Turns out there's a fundamental flaw in picking a place purely based on its name – Nice was a world away from its Côte d'Azur counterpart and known locally as the 'Methadone Amphetamine Home-Brewing Capital of California'. I remember our innkeeper tutting at the futility of our mission, informing us that the men there had 'more tattoos than teeth'. His wit was bewitching to Emily and it didn't hurt that he was a ringer for Leslie Nielsen (so her type) but sadly he wasn't single so we hit the road again. I smile as I recall our shenanigans and then glance at Bodie, wondering how I've gone from Thelma & Louise to Turner & Hooch.

Switching to the 5 Freeway, I watch the clouds cast dark shadows across the pines and marvel at the utter vastness that surrounds us. Bodie is less impressed. He can't seem to settle, just keeps making complaining, pawing noises.

'Sorry, buddy, there's nowhere for me to stop here – we have to keep on trucking.'

I wonder if he's sick of being in the car or actually carsick? As soon as I find a rest area, I release him.

'Praise be!' His bound speaks volumes.

He explores the gravelly pet area, and then we edge over to where the land drops into a valley and gawp at the folds of spriggy green, layering deep into the distance. This is the Pacific Crest Trail, running for 2,650 miles from Mexico to Canada. If I were a bolder individual, I would take Bodie on a hike, just for a taster mile or two. Perhaps the pair of us could roll in the dirt and look like we've been trekking for days. Then again, considering we got lost in the woodland at the back of the San Ysidro Ranch, the likelier scenario is that we'd set off and never be seen again. So it's back in the car. All the way to Weed.

I decided Weed was a must-stop because dogs love to pee but there's no ignoring the marijuana connotations and, true to form, the first people I see are three long-haired stoner dudes. They are in fact the *only* people I see on Main Street. Despite the town's catchy motto of '*Weed like to welcome you!*', the population has dwindled since its lumber heyday. I look up at the buildings painted in hippy hues of purple and wonder what it was like back when ladies would get a fancy updo at the Best Little Hair House and the doors of the Black Bear Saloon were a-swinging.

'Are you coming in?' a voice calls as we peer into the local gift shop.

'Well, I want to,' I call back. 'Do you allow dogs?'

'Is he nice?'

'He's lovely.'

'Well, come on in.'

Every possible souvenir is branded with an 'I Heart Weed' logo and, against my better judgement, I purchase a dog T-shirt for Bodie. As I pay, the cheery chap asks me if I'm a teacher. I'm not quite sure what prompts this or how to take it – except that I do look especially exhausted today – but I explain that I'm a writer on a dog mission. In return he tells me how he came to work here after a long period of unemployment, culminating with him moving back in with his 82-year-old mother.

'Oh, I'm sorry,' I say. Though I'm sure she's glad.

'It's not all bad, look...' He leads me to the doorway and points off into the distance.

Bodie and I stare open-mouthed at the extraordinary snow-dusted volcano rising up 14,000 feet ahead of us.

'Mount Shasta,' he tells us. 'Last eruption 1786.'

'Wow.' How had I not noticed this on the way here?

'When I first caught sight of it, I was fifty miles away and afoot, alone and weary. Yet all my blood turned to wine, and I have not been weary since.'

Now I'm staring at him open-mouthed. 'Perhaps you should be writing too?'

'Oh that's not me,' he chuckles. 'John Muir. Circa 1874.'

'Ah.' I nod, thanking him for teaching me a thing or two.

Later I learn that Scottish-American naturalist Muir wrote a dog-centric memoir called *Stickeen*, first published as a magazine article titled 'An Adventure With A Dog And A Glacier'. The glacier in question was in Alaska and the dog is described as a 'little, black, short-legged, bunchy-bodied toy dog'. During their stormy ordeal, Muir discovered that our 'horizontal brothers' are not so dissimilar to us, and this in turn led to insights about unity and kinship that he considered the most useful message he had to bring back from all his wild walks.

Unity – and the notion that there is no 'other' – seems to be a common theme with the spiritually enlightened. (And at total odds with less scrupulous politicians.)

'Oregon welcomes you!' I point to the hand-sculpted metal sign marking our transition into the Beaver State.

'See that, Bodie!' I catch his tired brown eyes in the rear-view mirror. 'Another twenty minutes' drive and we'll have the utter luxury of two nights in the same place!'

Well, perhaps luxury isn't quite the right word when you're staying at a $49 motel…

Chapter 21
The Dog Show

Dubbed 'Oregon's City of Sunshine' on account of its 300 days of sunshine a year, Klamath Falls sounds idyllic. I picture log cabins nestled around the base of a waterfall that doubles as your shower facilities. But it's not like that at all. For a start there are no falls, just mislabelled river rapids. The land is flat and sparse and instead of butterflies and woodland creatures we find McDonald's and Burger King and shops you have to drive between, at least in this newer part of town. We're basing ourselves here to be near tomorrow's American Kennel Club dog show and we are not alone. Looking out across the car park, the Cimarron Inn appears to have more canine guests than humans but I'll happily take the odd bark-spasm and yelp over the sound of an amorous couple in the room next door.

At under $50 a night including breakfast, this may be the cheapest accommodation of our trip but I have to say the reception staff are models of efficiency and hospitality. While I sip on complimentary Stash tea, Bodie is presented with a foldable water bowl and invited to check out the trail directly behind the motel. It's always a welcome bonus to have an adjacent dog-walking area and this one just happens to be Oregon's longest linear park – 109 miles of rail-to-trail conversion, utilising the former tracks of the OC&E (Oregon, California and Eastern) Railroad.

The tracks where timber and cattle used to rattle along have been paved over, but set off to the right there's a bright yellow and ivy-green caboose. Bodie Jones hops aboard the back ledge and does a fine impression of railroad engineer turned American folk hero Casey Jones, gazing off into the horizon. This may not be the most picturesque place in the world (a tad too much broken glass at large) but the grass is dotted with dandelions and the blue sky is blurry with sun-flares, giving me a 1970s summer feeling.

Continuing on, our evening stroll takes us past some stray farm equipment, a Kung Fu Panda Chinese restaurant and the Chevron gas station where I stopped earlier and was told that it was illegal for me to pump my own gas. Apparently Oregon is one of the last states to hold on to this law. I even had to hand over my credit card for the guy to insert in the machine. It's a bit like being carjacked, only they clean your windscreen and fill your tank.

'I'm not being racist but Hispanics are the best tippers,' the guy told me as he pocketed my paltry dollar.

On the way back to the motel we cross paths with some purebreds (perhaps making them cross-breeds for a few seconds?). They seem eager to play, just like a normal dog, but I respect the fact that Bodie is a little too rough and tumble and their owners need to keep their pristine forms away from the dust baths he so enjoys.

And so we settle in for a night of take-away pizza and catching up on emails.

'One from Sam!' I go to read it out to Bodie but find my voice trailing off mid-sentence.

Marcus has asked her to move in with him.

There it is again. That sinking feeling that we're pulling in very different directions – Sam into the snug of a shared home, me and Bodie into the wild, blue yonder. Well, when I put it like that, it doesn't sound so bad. But then I think of them sizzling up dinner and sipping wine together and I look down at my makeshift pizza box tabletop and Bodie chomping at a discarded crust. Why do I feel I'm moving further away from the chance of finding my person? When I set off I felt that anything was possible but right now I feel as detached as that lone train caboose.

I sigh. At times like these, how do you stop feeling sorry for yourself? I know the most instant cure is to count your blessings. But I'm too busy counting Sam's to see my own.

I attempt to give myself a Cher-like 'Snap out of it!' slap.

Everyone's life is paced differently. Some will peak while others trough. Sam and I experienced that when I was initially so happy with Nathan and she was lovelorn. Is this payback?

Stay in your own lane! I chide myself. Comparing your life to others is the quickest way to feel bad. Unless you compare yourself to those less fortunate… And there are plenty of people worse off. It's really so silly – it's only heartbreak I'm experiencing. Why does it feel so wretched and ruinous? Perhaps it's because it jabs at the universal core fear: *I am not lovable.*

Bodie is. Unquestionably. And yet he wound up in a dog pound. He's been abandoned. He's been homeless. He's been hungry. He doesn't complain one bit, even though someone who once loved him let him go and numerous people peered into his cage and kept walking.

None of that made him a bad dog. It ultimately just made him *my* dog.

I pull him closer, soothed by his presence and the distant whistling toot of a train.

In the morning Bodie and I go our separate ways: him to doggie daycare, me to the American Kennel Club dog show.

As doggy an attraction as that is, Bodie is not permitted to join me – only registered show dogs may attend and all show dogs must have a pure pedigree. I have mixed feelings about endorsing an ethos that places zero value on mixed breeds but coming from the land of Crufts, my curiosity has got the better of me. I mean, there are 'dog people' and there are 'show dog people' and I can't resist the opportunity of seeing this particular breed of person up close. Ironically Bodie would be the better infiltrator since, despite being *canine non grata*, he gives great show-dog stance. It seems to be his default pose when assessing a scene or inhaling a breeze – he stands proudly, hind legs set back at an angle, chin up, tail erect, perfectly still and statuesque, until I tug him onward. I shake my head. There are 22,000 American Kennel Club events taking place each year – would it hurt to have one rogue category? They could call it the Under Dogs.

The show is being held in a big airport hangar of a venue with all manner of RVs and dog crate camps clustered around the entrances. As I enter the fray, I see one woman pushing a shopping trolley full of dogs instead of groceries and another pulling a hefty flatbed trolley, puffing like a beast of burden as her giant dog maintains a regal air, wondering where the raffia fan-wafters have got to. But what surprises me the most is the dress code. I was expecting a muddy-boot country vibe so I'd worn my jeans and a faux tweed jacket but the look is far more 1980s power dressing, with flats instead of stilettos on account of the running involved. I watch a bevy of teenage Alexis Colbys trot around the ring with their canine charges. Based on beauty, there's an outright winner in the combination of an immaculate Akita and a girl who looks like Elizabeth Taylor circa *National Velvet*. I'm therefore stunned to see her receive a low ranking from the judges.

As she bursts into tears and falls into her mother's comforting arms, I ask around for an explanation. Apparently this was a Junior Handler section and it was the girl, not the dog (who goes by the wondrous name of Reign), being judged.

'That's probably the toughest experience she'll have in her career,' a fellow teen tells me. 'She was supposed to be walking with her own dog but she's on heat so not allowed.'

I nod understanding – I know this to be true based on the episode of *Sex and the City* when Charlotte competed with her Cavalier King Charles Spaniel, coincidentally named Elizabeth Taylor.

I feel bad that the girl is so upset. And that she missed her chance to truly shine. Still, she has plenty of opportunities ahead of her – case in point a glamorous 70-something posing for photographs with her award. I'm impressed that she's perfectly matched her two-piece with the ice-blue eyes of her Siberian Husky. As I lift my camera she bends to adjust her dog's back leg and, when I look back at the image, it appears as if she's taken on the dog's habit of sniffing a rear end.

'Oh!'

I turn away and find myself beholding *my* perfect dog outfit. It's akin to something you might wear at the hairdresser's – voluminous black nylon with a front zipper – but printed with cute dog images. I suppose it's meant for professional dog groomers but I always get drenched when I give Bodie a bath so I feel this could be a great wardrobe addition, especially if worn with bubblegum-pink lipstick and big hoop earrings. Now if they only did a matching shower cap...

'Can we help you find something?'

Vendors Bill and Mike gleefully point out some of the more absurd grooming products they have on display, including pet colognes ranging in every scent from baby powder to designer imitations such as Timmy Holedigger and White Dalmations. Then come the deodorising, conditioning and finishing sprays, again in an array of fragrances. I wonder if Bodie could carry off Pina Colada? I think perhaps he's more of a Lemon Vanilla...

'We have an aloe vera and witch hazel aftershave spray,' Bill notes, though Bodie doesn't have that morning ritual. Or, luckily, the need for a breath-freshening dental spray.

Judging by the extent of stock dedicated to white dogs, they must be the highest maintenance. Understandably – they must have similar upkeep to white clothing. I inspect a pack of Angel Eyes tear stain remover and discover it is made with marshmallow root, and then attempt to read the label on a 2.5-gallon glugger of whitening shampoo, but it's too heavy for me to raise to eye level. I'm just wondering whether the Red on Red shampoo might succeed where a gazillion human hair dyes have failed, when I notice the café area. Time for a reviving beverage.

I'm hoping the drinks will be offered in dog-themed sizes – perhaps Miniature (Pinscher), Standard (Poodle) and Great (Dane) – but it's just regular-event catering. As I sip my tea and gaze out across the cavernous arena, it occurs to me that there's barely a bark to be heard – quite some feat considering how many hundreds of dogs there are at large. And while I anticipated a stressful, fussy environment for the competing canines, I'm beginning to think they're revelling in the attention. One rosette-studded dog swaggers by, all but nodding 'Crème de la crème, baby!' I suppose it is a beauty contest of sorts but each contestant also has to be in peak health so you know they are well-exercised as well as groomed, which is no bad thing when you think of all the dogs that barely get further than a backyard pee.

And then there's the cliché of the show-dog owner being a neurotic, pushy stage parent… Instead I'm seeing a lot of doting, dedicated men and women who will admit that being part of the circuit is 'a lot of driving and a lot of waiting' but do it for the love of dog. We all need to have a sense of purpose and passion in our lives and they certainly have that. They also have admirable skills when it comes to manoeuvring their obedient, focused dogs. I should really have better control when it comes to Bodie, especially since I come from the Barbara Woodhouse school of dog training – almost literally, in that we went to the same school (Headington School, Oxford) a mere 50 years apart.

(Barbara Woodhouse was the brisk, tweedy, sensible-shoed precursor of Cesar Millan. At the age of 70 she had her own TV show and her '*Walkies!*' catchphrase was on everyone's lips.)

I remember the day she returned to the school for a visit: the whole building was abuzz and when a classmate caught a glimpse of her in the driveway we all flocked to the window, much to the irritation of our starchy, elderly history teacher. She shooed us away and had us return to our books. History books. Not a thing in them that couldn't wait until our next lesson. I think I might have objected, which just further enraged her. I bristle now at the fact that she blocked our opportunity for a fleeting thrill and moment of pride. Was she jealous? Did she feel the rush of attention was undeserved or simply uncouth? This was nearly ten years prior to *Dead Poets Society* or I might have stood up on my desk and rallied, 'Oh Barbara! My Barbara!'

Soon enough my day of swooning over Salukis and beaming at Beagles comes to an end, and I head back to the doggie daycare.

'I'm here to pick up Bodie!'

'Oh!' the woman on reception starts. 'He's strong!'

I'm just wondering what he's done to prove this when he appears around the corner.

'Bodie!' I can't help but exclaim in delight when I see him. I've observed some exquisite specimens today but, for me, none can hold a candle to Bodie, for he is a true one-off.

Chapter 22

Bobbie the Wonder Dog

After a low-key evening dining on supermarket snacks, we arise ready for our 250-mile drive from Klamath Falls to Silverton, home to a Collie who got the whole world talking in the 1920s. Silverton is just an hour and a half shy of our destination city of Portland but it's a little too far for us to push through in one go. One thing I've learned in recent years is that Google Maps timings rarely match my own. You pull off the road 'for five minutes' to fill up the tank, have a wee and grab a drink, and before you know it an hour has passed and you're behind schedule. No clock-watching today – we're just going to ease on down the road...

Some scenery really takes you out of yourself, frees you up, lets your thoughts and dreams fly. The California coast did that for me, peaking as we drove along Big Sur. Here, as we leave Klamath Falls and head deeper into Oregon on Route 97, I'm having the opposite experience. Burrowing through the flat uniformity of the Winema National Forest, I feel like I'm on some never-ending pine-lined treadmill, and for some reason my life seems to be reflecting back to me, requiring scrutiny.

It's making me a little uncomfortable. Part of the pleasure of this trip so far has been the escapism, the distractions, the break from having to consider how I live back home.

Of course I have to go back and face it all in a week or two so perhaps now is a good time to take stock – when I know there are still good things ahead.

Let's start with what's working: I like where I live – I like the people that live around me. I wish I could take my favourite people from the UK and have them as my neighbours too but I understand that is not possible, though I do one day hope to have an apartment with a welcoming guest bedroom. (Or, better yet, one of those guest houses you see in the grounds of Hollywood mansions – a girl can dream!) I like writing and, most of all, I like my dog.

So what's not working? Relationships. That appears to be an ongoing, lifelong torment. And as a result I can feel a little disconnected from the world, as if I have yet to find my place in it. I feel that now as I look around me and there's not another car on the road. I wonder sometimes whether I have the capacity to sustain happiness. I seem to have glorious, giddy highs but then come back to earth with such a bump. It's like the day after you get back from holiday – your carefree, beachy persona disappears as soon as you're back in the office and suddenly it's as if all that magical sunshine and romance never happened. Everything goes back to being ordinary again and that's when I panic that I'm letting life pass me by. I don't want that to happen. I want to feel like I am engaging, not observing.

I glance back at Bodie. Perhaps I could take a leaf out of his book – always fully embracing all excitement and adventure but happy to chillax through the more humdrum aspects of the day.

'Wake me up when it gets good again!' he seems to say.

He's quiet today, perhaps a little sleepy from yesterday's play day. I leave him to his snoozing for another hour or so but his stirring coincides with a prettier, woodsier area so I pull over by a stream to let him have a little break.

He forages in the mossy, fern-fanned undergrowth then catches sight of the water and turns back to me and smiles his bright-eyed approval directly into my heart and I feel good again.

Stepping over fallen branches together, I marvel at the entertainment factor of moving through the world with an animal by my side – I love Bodie's sniffing technique and the way he seems in danger of tipping over like a wheelbarrow whenever he lifts his leg. Basically I'm interested in everything he does, never quite knowing how he's going to react or behave. I'm also grateful that the mum-like instinct to put his needs above my own offers wonderful relief from my navel-gazing.

We stay a little longer than planned, which is a good thing, since the promise of a sunny patio lunch and afternoon amble around the university town of Eugene is cancelled by an almighty downpour.

They say Oregonians don't age, they rust. As we emerge from the car my flip-flopped feet skid every which way. Bodie tries to shake himself dry every other minute and the best we can do is run for shelter under the jutting ledge of a sandwich shop.

'Sorry about this, bud.'

I tie Bodie to an insubstantial twig and duck inside. I'm trying to be swift, repeatedly turning back to check that Bodie hasn't been washed downstream, but the sandwich-maker chap is struggling to come to terms with my Englishness.

(Not least because he first pegged me as Australian and then South African.)

'But what are you doing here?' he asks, confounded.

'Just driving through.'

'From where?'

'Klamath Falls,' I tell him.

'Well, I know you're not from there. I'm from twenty minutes south of there and really there's nothing—'

'I'm on my way to Portland,' I cut in. 'My dog has an urgent appointment with an English Mastiff named Winnie.'

That seems to do the trick – now he thinks I'm nuts.

Which reminds me: Ken Kesey, author of *One Flew Over the Cuckoo's Nest*, went to university and then later died here in Eugene. I was planning on getting a snap of Bodie beside the life-size bronze sculpture of him reading in Broadway Plaza, but there's really no option other than to return to the car.

I tuck myself under the back hatch and huddle beside my bedraggled dog, sharing the filling of the sandwich and trying not to think about the unpleasantness of the wet denim clinging to my skin.

There's really nothing else for it – we've got to hit the road again.

As we reconnect with the freeway, I turn on the heat and direct it to dry off my feet. I have no idea what I'm driving through or by – all I can see is the white spray thrown up by the other cars. An hour passes before my grimace becomes a smile – passing through Oregon's capital city of Salem we cross a street named Wolverine. (Thoughts of Hugh Jackman are never unwelcome.) Then suddenly the sun begins to emerge and now, as we reach our destination, there's a rainbow!

It seems an apt symbol for the quirkily colourful town of Silverton – a mix of historic murals, one-off cafés and rummage-inducing knickknack shops. I'm particularly drawn to the Books-N-Time store which sells 'new and used books and old and new clocks'. How well they seem to go together. I like the idea of dressing a table with an old mantel clock, a potted aspidistra and a stack of worn leather spines but Bodie is tugging me on to Main Street where I'm tickled to find signs announcing 'Entering China Town' and 'Leaving China Town' on either side of Chan's Restaurant.

But best of all is the pair of vintage gas stations – one repurposed into a cool little coffee shop and the other into a dog-grooming salon called Le Pooch. It's not quite a drive-through dog wash but it's the next best thing. (I picture Bodie getting lathered up in the passenger seat while I read a newspaper.)

Of course, the real doggie attraction, famed the world over, is the 70-foot-long mural honouring local hero, Bobbie the Wonder Dog. His is an amazing story: in 1923 a two-year-old Collie mix was travelling through Indiana with his family when somehow they became separated and he was lost. The family hunted high and low but were forced to head back to Oregon (around a 2,500-mile drive) without him. They never expected to see their dear dog again.

Cut to six months later, Bobbie stumbles into town, paws shredded from endless padding – day after day, month in, month out. It is estimated that he averaged 14 miles a day across all manner of terrain – plains, desert, mountains – all in the bone-chill of winter.

The story of his incredible loyalty and determination went the 1920s version of viral: letters of admiration flooded in from around the world, as well as reports from people who had housed and fed him along the way. Some tended to his wounds and tried to get him to rest a while but they said he was always up and on his way again before breakfast.

He earned the title Bobbie the Wonder Dog, went on to become a featured attraction at Ripley's Believe It or Not!, played himself in a silent film called *Call of the West* and, when he died in 1927, the German Shepherd movie star Rin Tin Tin laid a wreath on his grave.

All these years on, he is still honoured every year at the Silverton Children's Pet Parade. (Sadly we're missing this by just a day, as it overlaps with our main event – the Oregon Humane Society's Doggie Dash in Portland.)

Around the corner from Bobbie's mural there's a life-size replica of the courageous canine beside a wooden doghouse. So he always has somewhere to come home to.

I experience a little heart pang. Every now and again I wonder if there's someone waiting for Bodie to come home. Perhaps they were separated through no fault of the owner. Perhaps Bodie was on his way home when he got picked up by animal services? If I let go of his leash, would he start making his way back?

'Don't get any ideas,' I tell Bodie as I step back to take a picture of him beside the wording, 'Dog travels 3,000 miles.'

'It's a bit late for that,' he seems to roll his eyes back at me.

At least our base for the night is just strolling distance from here – a mile down the road at the Oregon Garden Resort.

Chapter 23

The Oregon Garden

Talk about a warm welcome: we're greeted by a toasty hearth at reception and then our very own flickering fireplace in the corner of our gentrified/countrified room. Better yet, our unit is called Dogwood.

This really is a great place to stay with a pup. Set amid 80 acres of the botanical wonderland that is the Oregon Garden, every guest has unlimited access to the gardens so even though it's getting close to closing time, we can stay on after hours and have the entire place to ourselves.

It's beautifully done, with just the right blend of clever design and nature going its own sweet way. Bodie and I weave through the 20 speciality gardens, from the lavender and oregano of the Medicinal Garden to the Ponderosa pines and Salmonberry bushes of the Lewis and Clark Garden. This is a living museum to the botanical finds documented on the duo's expedition, charting new territories in America in the early 1800s, complete with streamside campsite.

I decide that Bodie and I would make excellent explorers – Lewis and Bark if you will. Bodie sniffing out the treasures with me documenting them.

As we track our way to the Rose Garden, I find myself doing a double take. 'Wait! This fella looks familiar!' I step towards a blackened bust of a Collie, raised to eye level on a plinth. 'Look Bodie – it's Bobbie!'

But my pal is more interested in the life-size bronze Lab down at ground level, introducing us to the Pet Friendly Garden – a mossy, rocky nook trimmed with whiskery palms designed to educate visitors on how to 'construct a landscape that both you and your pet can enjoy'.

Plaques advise working with your animal's habits rather than against them, like paving the perimeter of your garden in stone for a dog to patrol, rather than complaining that the shrubs bordering your fence get crushed under-paw. If you do want to keep your pup away from flower beds they suggest using 'decorative pickets' or stakes made from bamboo or wood to prevent your dog lying down and thus crushing delicate blooms.

And instead of having to worry about toxic plants they suggest planting edibles such as apples and blueberries for dogs, and catnip and wheatgrass for cats.

The biggest no-no in terms of toxicity appears to be the yew tree, with the foliage even more poisonous than the berries. If a 50-pound dog (i.e. Bodie's size) consumed just 0.08 ounces (one-tenth of 1 per cent of its body weight), it could die.

I'm busily taking notes, though I don't know quite when – or if – I'll ever have my own garden. It's one of those things you expect will come to you with age, along with the house and husband and kids, and yet… I can't quite see how any of that will come my way at the moment. But that's okay. At least there are plenty of public gardens for us to roam. I look back at my guide. There's a lot more to see but I think we'll save the rest until morning – dinner is calling...

Too chilly to eat on the Garden View Restaurant patio, we bring a portion of vegetable linguini (with added chicken for Bodie) back to the room and, even though I'm eating from a cardboard box with a plastic fork, I have to say this is the best pasta I've had outside of Italy. Bodie licks the last of the juices then snuggles up with the box like it's his new best friend. I feel happy again. So I'm clear on two things at least: I am deeply affected by a) my environment and b) the yumminess of the food I am eating.

As I recline on the bed and gaze at the faux flames, I ponder why I'm so drawn to cosy of late... I guess we all need to feel cushioned from the outside world at times. When I was with Nathan he was my comfort and my centre. Without him I've been reminded how transient my lifestyle is. I only ever seem to stay about a year or two in whatever apartment I'm renting (I've moved 27 times in my life to date) so I never really get settled in. I've always been a fan of chasing down the new. But when you are experiencing an emotional wobble, staying somewhere with cream-and-sage décor and a hand-painted writing desk is very soothing. Plus *Castle* is on TV, which, despite assorted homicides, I always find reassuring.

With Bodie already asleep, I soon follow suit. It's one of those ideal slumbers where you remember nothing and wake with a full starfish stretch. I count my lucky sunbeams that we can linger a while before all the action of the day begins. In just a few hours we'll be in downtown Portland.

I love a hearty breakfast buffet. I like the return trips, the multiple courses and the obligatory stash of pastries in your purse – even though these rarely appeal later with serviette stuck to the jammy bits. Bodie likes the fact that he gets his own serving of sausage instead of having to share with me.

We also get a kick out of being able to take the residents' route down to the gardens, feeling as if we have one up on the day trippers, in the nicest possible way. It's like we belong here. At least for a few more hours.

'Oh look!' I quicken my pace. 'There's the tram – fancy taking the tour?'

Bodie hesitates, perhaps recalling the reception we got in San Francisco.

'Are you joining us?' The cheery driver encourages us on board.

It's good to feel welcome and Bodie shows his appreciation by making a surprisingly attentive passenger.

'And if you look to your left, you'll see the Bosque Garden with its reflecting ponds and Pacific Sunset Maple...' Bodie dutifully pads over to that side of the tram. 'And on your right...' He crosses over, peering intently at the cascading waterfall and wild lilies as we are introduced to the Amazing Water Garden. We hop off here so we can explore the Sensory Garden and then, on the way back to the Pavilion, discover a hyacinth-blue butterfly bench. Bodie sits dead centre looking as if he has sprouted magnificent wings.

Even though this is the perfect end to our stay, I'm reluctant to leave. Back at the car Bodie settles quickly but I hesitate over starting the engine. What I wouldn't do for another night of linguine and *Castle*. But then I remind myself that the whole point of this trip is to get to Portland – to reunite Bodie with Winnie and join in Oregon Humane Society's Doggie Dash. And so we hit the road.

Chapter 24
Keep Portland Weird

After so much flora and fauna – from dense, stoic forests to whimsical botanical gardens – I feel like I'm entering some kind of futuristic city as I approach the skyscrapers and Meccano-style bridges of Portland.

The volume of people overwhelms me: students traversing the university campus, locals weaving down Morrison Street, shoppers bustling in and out of Macy's, blue-haired youths asking passers-by for change. And now, as we pull up outside The Nines, three valet guys clamouring to get their hands on Bodie.

Our hotel is smack dab in the centre of town, opposite historic Pioneer Courthouse Square and its attendant posse of characters determinedly upholding the city's motto: *'Keep Portland Weird'*.

It feels disconcerting not to be pulling into a parking space opposite our room for the night. 'Just give me a second!' I apologise to the valet guys. 'I need to rearrange a few things.'

I may be a frequent traveller but I'm a horribly disorganised one. It suits me to make multiple trips to the car, pulling out what I need from cases, bags and seat pockets, but that's just not feasible with so many eyes upon me. I end up getting virtually everything loaded on to the cart and tut to myself for not keeping a cleaner ship.

'One more shoe!' I add a stray trainer to the pile. 'Oh and the snack bag. Just in case.'

The elevator ride to the eighth-floor reception is swift but long enough for me to notice just how ragged and dirty my nails are. I have paid so little attention to my appearance over the last few days (dogs and nature care not a jot for mani-pedis, just where you put your hands and feet) it hadn't occurred to me to smarten myself up for city life. It hadn't even fully registered that we were headed to a five-star hotel because I got it for such a steal on Priceline. And yet the clue was in the name – The Nines. I tut myself again – barely dressed to a three.

'Oh wow!'

As the lift doors open we take a moment to gawp at the cityscape before us and then reel back as we are confronted by the modernity of the vast glass-ceilinged atrium. It's all angles and squared-off areas with metal-framed cubes set with lime moulded chairs and orchid-purple rugs.

While I'm assessing the headless mannequins, Bodie tugs ahead to the black lacquered reception desk, rears up and sets his paws on the countertop.

'Reservation for Bodie Jones, could be under Belinda...'

I catch up with him, ready to apologise and seek assurance that they really mean to allow dogs in such a fashionista setting, but before I can speak Bodie is presented with a pouch of dog biscuits and superstar adulation, both suiting him well.

'Your key!'

'Th-thank you!' This still feels a little too good to be true.

Back in the lift. Up and up.

I gasp as I open the door to our room – Bodie may not be having breakfast at Tiffany's any time soon but this is the next best thing: crystal drop chandeliers, an iridescent Tiffany blue chaise, silver-and-mink embossed wallpaper, draped voile curtains last seen on Grace Kelly in *To Catch A Thief*...

As Bodie performs his sniffer-dog routine, I stand for a moment taking it all in. This 'Hollywood Regency' décor is the style I most aspire to in my own home – they have a white tufted leather headboard, I have a white tufted leather sofa. The one time I had an office I painted the walls this very aqua. Even the carpet has the same blend of colours as my own rug at home.

So why, pray tell, am I feeling slightly at odds with our surroundings? Surely I can't have changed so much in ten days?

I step into the bathroom and admire the marble-topped corner unit, teal boudoir stool and glass vase of delicate flowers. And then I startle at the sight of my reflection in the three-panel mirror. The surroundings conjure an expectation of upswept Elnett hair and diamond drop earrings and here I am: a vision in fawn-coloured fleece. All that's missing is some campfire soot on my nose. I step back into the room and eye my suitcase. No cocktail dress in there. Even if there were, I fear that I'm too far gone. At least I can switch from dog-walking fashion to, well, something clean.

Bodie, meanwhile, has opted to forgo soul-searching in favour of couch-surfing, reclining on the velvet chaise like Marie Antoinette. His gold fur looks so beautiful set against the rich, shimmering aqua.

'You've come a long way, baby!' I smile.

And perhaps I have too.

I haven't cried in days. And if I was given the option to share this room with another human I would choose Sam, a diehard Audrey Hepburn fan and luxe-lover. I'm not wishing Nathan were here – why would you want to share a bed with someone who doesn't want you? Although I experience a heart stab at this realisation, I also feel more resigned to the fact than ever before. I am now living in a very different world to the one I inhabited with him. That one was about pairing up and settling down. This world with Bodie is more onward and outward.

'Fancy a sniff around the city?'

He doesn't need asking twice. I'm just taking a photograph of the pair of us reflected in the mirrored lift doors – realising for perhaps the first time just how unflattering my mid-calf denim skirt is – when they open and reveal a silver-haired toff heading to a black-tie ball.

'What is he?' he all but sneers as Bodie pads inside.

I do my usual spiel – bit of this, bit of that...

'Oh we just say Pound Pup.'

I give a little snort. I hardly think Bodie wants to be reminded of that experience. Besides, I don't see him as being defined by his former lodgings. Then again, I suppose we humans do the same to each other, asking, *'Where are you from? Where did you go to school?'* when really these days, like Bodie, we can all be our own unique creation.

The lift doors open again a few floors down.

Now we're joined by an ultra-glamorous couple. He's a jet-haired Bond, she's Oregon's answer to Rosie Huntington-Whiteley. If they were famous they would have their names conjoined. He smiles warmly, she arches her brow. I want to assure her that I know I am from an entirely different gene pool and really have no business sharing a lift with them, but as I go to step further back Bond reaches down to pat Bodie. Bond Girl's disapproval is palpable. Perhaps she's concerned the ensuing waft of dog fur might attach itself to her dress. I try to give her a sympathetic glance but she averts her eyes. I've seen this a few times – easy-going, open-faced men with frosty ice maidens. I wouldn't have thought they would have been attracted to the nose-in-the-air type but Nathan used to say they had little choice: the woman would set her sights and the man in question would be too nice to object. Of course there's no denying her beauty. I wonder what it's like to have such long limbs and lustrous hair. I give my straggles an involuntary pat – more dog's dinner than gala dinner.

'After you...'

Off they go to their swanky do while Bodie and I head to Cupcake Jones, chosen both for its name and the fact that they serve Pupcakes (complete with Fido-friendly frosting). While he wolfs his treat in one bite, I peruse the 'human flavours', including Peach Cobbler and Orange Creamsicle, but ultimately opt for The Pearl (white velvet cake with vanilla bean buttercream) as we are exploring the Pearl District.

This is a hipster haven with music venues, galleries and bars galore. Even Bodie gets a cool source of refreshment in the grassy North Park Blocks – we approach a chequerboard effect of stone slabs and contemplate what appears to be a forgotten tin dog bowl. This is, in fact, the Portland Dog Bowl – an ever-burbling fountain of fresh water designed by William Wegman, the artist known for his amazing photographs of

Weimaraners looking deadpan and dapper in assorted outsize jackets and mock-human poses. I love his work and, if you wanted, you could stroll from here and buy a copy of one of his many books at Powell's City of Books, which also offers a city block's worth of used tomes. It was named one of the ten best independent bookshops in the world by the *Guardian* newspaper alongside Shakespeare and Company in Paris, which offers the opportunity to sleep amid its crammed shelves, and Acqua Alta in Venice, which has books heaped in an old gondola.

There are many tempting eateries in this area but we have decided to dine in true Portland style – in the legendary food cart quarter.

Bodie is in his sniffing element here, nostrils flaring between The Dump Truck's dumplings and Viking Soul Food's flatbreads, tongue busily connecting with spillage from assorted burritos, wraps and tubs. This is pretty much Nathan's idea of hell – too many unidentified ingredients and unfamiliar tastes. In over a year together I never once saw him deviate from his sandwich filling of turkey and cheese with a dab of mustard and emphatically no mayo. The most daring order I ever saw him make was on our first Valentine's Day together in a swish French-Asian restaurant in Chicago. They were offering a special five-course 'his and hers' menu and he told me he wanted to order the 'hers' as the tastes were milder.

'But just think – if we order both we'll have ten dishes to try!' I didn't know at the time just how much horror that must have struck into his heart. But, bless him, he went along with it and, despite looking like he was facing a Bushtucker Trial, he ended up loving every morsel.

Now it's me having dilemmas as I study food truck offerings. 'Hmm, succotash... sounds familiar but is that just as a Daffy Duck swear word?'

Lucille's Balls has to win the best pun title and the sweet potato balls with coconut curry sauce sound enticing. I definitely feel bolder trying new things around Bodie knowing that, provided it's not too spicy, he can easily help me out with finishing it off.

As it is now too cold to eat on the street corner, we once again lower the tone as we enter The Nines, wafting our cardboard cartons up to the room. Well, we need an early night in preparation for tomorrow's main event...

Chapter 25

The Doggie Dash

I awake with a rush of anticipation.

Today is the Oregon Humane Society's Doggie Dash – thousands of dog owners congregating for a sponsored walk aiming to raise $250,000 in a bid to 'End Petlessness'!

After a quick breakfast I set off with Bodie, thinking, 'Great! Two and a half miles – that's a decent morning stroll!' But of course we are heading into the fray with his energy level at full charge.

'Easy…' I struggle to keep up. 'No need to rush!'

Progressing down Morrison in the Sunday morning hush we attract dog after dog streaming in from the side streets, almost as if we are part of a choreographed flash mob. They're everywhere – Danes to the left of me, Boxers to the right – all heading for registration.

Bodie can be a handful when there's just one other dog. Here at the Tom McCall Waterfront Park there are already easily a thousand. And now we have to stand neatly in line to get our kit and number. In theory. Bodie is getting frisky with the dog in front of us, the one with the Cesar Millan wannabe for an owner.

'Hey!' she snaps, jabbing Bodie in the soft spot below his ribs.

My eyes narrow: *Handle your dog, not mine!* I wonder how she'd feel if I jabbed her in the kidneys? I'm tempted to find out but instead I note that she appears to be growing a goatee just like her hero, albeit a blonde one.

The man behind me has a growler. I like him. He can't control his dog either.

For some reason everyone seems to want to cut through the line precisely at our juncture, regardless of how many paces we shuffle forward.

'Have we got a target on us?' he asks.

The man and I try everything: standing with our back to the masses, closing the gap between us, getting our dogs to sit, but still they barge through. It gets to the point where I let Bodie jump all over their dogs just to make a point.

Of course the majority of people are lovely – revelling in the sunshine and the hoopla, just happy to be out with their dogs. The location is great – a vast expanse of riverside greenery decked out with all manner of stands and booths and a stage for the competitions, including doggie kissing and fancy dress. I've seen a few contenders for the latter already – a Dachshund in prison stripes, a Pug dressed as a bumblebee, a Terrier wearing a punky leather jacket with the fur on the top of his head sprayed green – every one of them causing a Mexican Wave of smiles.

But I do meet one more sour face as we join the line-up at the starting position. Her dog is pleading with Bodie to play – literally prodding and stroking him with his left paw. He's only a little fella but couldn't be any cuter, with gorgeous floppy ears that make him look like the puppy version of Dumbo.

'What is he?' I ask, with obvious enchantment.

'He's just from the shelter,' she dismisses my inquiry and pulls him closer.

I get the feeling she's one of those girls that would glass you just for looking at her boyfriend. Don't think I'll be keeping pace with her.

Suddenly the starting announcement is made and we're off!

The flow of dogs and people traversing Hawthorne Bridge is surprisingly un-chaotic. Of course, some dogs are more competitive, vying for position as if they are contenders in a track race, but most appear content to be padding forward. Or, in Bodie's case, zig-zagging hither and thither. He does seem a tad overwhelmed, 'So many bottoms, so little time to sniff!' But he's definitely having fun.

As am I. It feels good to be part of something big. I'm certainly enjoying the 'demonstration march' element – demonstrating just how much people love their dogs and how important it is for the ones in shelters to get the best possible care and chance of adoption. I wonder if Bodie knows he's paying it forward?

It's incredible to think that the money raised on this one day will be able to vaccinate 10,000 pets adopted by the Oregon Humane Society, feed every animal at the shelter for a year, buy medical supplies for 1,250 spay/neuter surgeries and keep two animal cruelty investigators in the field for a full year. Astounding. It just goes to show what well-organised public support can do – and everyone is having fun in the process. Win-win.

We're on the Eastbank Esplanade now, taking in the city skyline and the iconic old neon signage of a leaping stag with the words 'Made in Oregon' in a fabulous 1940s font, reflecting the date of its initial illumination. I consider this to be Portland's version of the Hollywood sign (interesting that both began as advertising) and duly take a snap. Apparently at Christmas the deer's nose glows red!

As Bodie and I gain on a pair of stunning Dalmatians who, in turn, are sidestepping a tiny Chihuahua, I give a little chuckle. I don't think I'll ever get used to the sheer variety in the canine kingdom. There must be at least one of every breed represented here today.

We shuffle along for a relaxed-pace hour, pausing for nuzzles into the surrounding foliage and the occasional sizing up of another dog. It's fascinating watching all their common rituals en masse. I imagine co-ordinating the leg-cocking so that they form a doggie conga line – step, step, step, lift-pee to the left, step, step, step, lift-pee to the right.

There's a slowing of pace as we approach the narrower walkway to the Steel Bridge but, despite the congestion, no one is stressing. There are lots of groups and families so they are happy to chat away or give their dog a slurp of water. I crouch down beside Bodie.

'Can you believe we're actually here?'

He looks back at me with wild eyes, like he's attending his first rock concert.

'I know! It's crazy!' It feels like the dogs have taken over the world and the humans are just along for the ride.

And what a wonderful world that would be.

By the time we reach the opposite riverbank people are opting to splay on the grass, not wanting to miss the chance for a great picnic or snooze spot.

Bodie and I forge on – we've already travelled a thousand miles to get here, we're not going to stop short of the finishing line.

We savour the moment as we reach it, just sorry there's no ribbon to burst through chest first.

'We did it!' I ruffle his face.

It's been a while since I had such a sense of accomplishment. Bodie, meanwhile, is just interested in taking advantage of all the free samples on offer at the assembled stalls.

'It's like trick-or-treating for dogs,' I decide as we go from table to table, gratefully accepting a double allowance from the Greenies dental chew lady. 'Thanks very much!'

We pause and watch the Frisbee action for a while, pick up some literature for Stay Pet Hotel and pose beside a giant inflatable pup with a rolled-up *Oregonian* newspaper in his mouth. But for me, one display is a stand-out: *Run! Day Camp for Dogs*.

Firstly, they have the hippest dog-mobile I've ever seen. I love the retro colour combo of chocolate-brown and sky-blue set against a clean white background. I'm equally enthusiastic about their lively photo board posing the question: '*Why walk when you can run?*'

And why send your dog to some local daycare's concrete yard when they could be running wild and free at Run!'s 200-acre private forest.

'Did you hear that Bodie? A two-hundred-acre private forest!'

I get tingles on his behalf and am eager to find out more but co-owner Dave is giving his gift-of-the-gab spiel to a potential customer. Sensing he could be some time, Bodie ducks under the van to get some respite from the sun while I lean in and eavesdrop, ever-more impressed when I hear that they pick up the dogs directly from your home, office or hotel in the morning and return them clean and exercised in the evening, all for $33 a day. And they work closely with vets and clients regarding the dog's health and wellbeing.

'We consider ourselves fitness trainers for dogs,' he grins.

I'm all but bursting now, so keen to get Bodie signed up.

Finally, he turns to me.

'You're English!' is my ecstatic opening gambit.

'So are you!' he cheers, extending a hand. 'South-east London!'

'Islington!' I reply.

'Yayyy!'

It's strange how having the same motherland engenders instant familiarity. All formality is out the window now – it feels more like we're chatting at a summer picnic having been introduced by mutual friends.

'So where do you live now?'

'Los Angeles.'

He rolls his eyes. 'When are you going to move to the Northwest?'

I frown in bemusement. 'You make it sound like it's only a matter of time!'

'It's the best. The people are real – if they invite you over for a barbecue they mean it.'

'Yes, but how many barbecues can you have with Oregon weather?'

As we chat on, Bodie takes it upon himself to take a pee on the van tyres.

'Oh, I'm so sorry!' I gasp, yanking his cocked leg away.

'Happens all the time,' he shrugs.

'You were saying...'

Before he can continue, Bodie tangles himself in their A-frame sign, sending it crashing into the side of the van.

'Oh my god! There's no dent, is there?' I leap to assess the damage.

'No, no, it's fine.' He smoothes the still perfect paintwork.

'Sorry,' I cringe, adding the disclaimer: 'he's American.'

And then I take a breath. This may not be the best time to be asking a favour, but I do anyway: 'Do you think it would be possible to book a slot for Bodie tomorrow—'

'Of course!'

'And for me to come along as well?' I hold my breath.

He must have comprehensive insurance because he says yes.

Chapter 26

The Pack Run

Our pack run pick-up point is The Dragonfly Coffee House, which is just as lovely as its name would suggest – the kind of café that makes you want to move into the neighbourhood just so you can hang out daily amid the old books, tinkly chandeliers and intriguing patrons. I compliment one guy on his dapper lilac suit and envy the bohemian styling of the women.

And then it's my turn to order.

It's funny how getting ripped off for what is, for the most part, a cup of boiled water can make you so happy. I think the home-baked treats are a big part of the pleasure principle. Yes, it may be true that the word 'muffin' was invented to distract people from the fact that they are having cake for breakfast, but everyone else here is getting a cardamom apple cake or date bar so it can't really be that much of a sin, can it?

I get my chai to go and loiter with Bodie on the street corner. Though cool in the shade, it's glorious in the sunshine and I'm just thinking that we could quite happily spend the day here when up pulls the Run! van.

It's good to see Dave again. He felt like an old friend the first time we met so now we're practically related. We still have a few stop-offs to make, collecting dogs, and when I hear him on the phone to his fiancée/business partner Erica, I like him all the more because he says, 'I love you!' every time they have so much as the briefest exchange about the day's schedule: 'Just picked up Coco and don't worry about Logan – I've already got him! Okay, I love you!'

For a typical English 'bloke' he is remarkably unselfconscious in his affections. The other thing that surprises me is the lack of scrapping amongst the dogs piling into the back of the van. (Bodie is up front with me.)

Amid the mix I see a mischievous Beagle, a wise old Schnauzer, an imposing German Shepherd and a brutish Bulldog – they look like the motley crew assembling for a bank heist.

'Isn't there ever any aggravation?' I ask as Dave adds a Vizsla.

'Why would there be?' Dave frowns.

I look back at the dogs.

'Are you trying to start something?' They squint suspiciously at me.

I shrug and face forward, eager to learn more about Dave's former life as a professional mountain bike racer and then, even more fascinatingly, his disastrous previous relationships.

There's a lot of, 'Noooooo! She didn't! And she never did get arrested?' coming from me.

'If you think that's bad, wait till you hear Erica's stories.' He shakes his head.

Of course I'm curious to meet her. As is always the case, she is not at all what I was expecting.

Erica is basically a beautiful blonde woodland sprite, complete with pixie crop and make-up-free face. Straight away

I get the impression that she has the most genuine, earnest heart and I feel protective, and frankly outraged, at the thought of any man trifling with a thing so pure. Luckily, she has the grit of a long-distance runner (her other great passion beside Dave and the dogs) and used this to extricate herself from the horribly abusive relationship she was in before she met Dave. My main relationship before Nathan was equally dicey and demeaning and the similarities in our experiences are uncanny. It's cathartic to speak with someone who has been through the same mire (as opposed to trying to explain why on earth you put up with such nonsense in the first place). So much so that just talking to her gives me real hope that someone like me can find a good guy, who also happens to be sparky and have a twinkle in his eye.

But, for now, it's time to hike.

The dogs have already transferred from the van to a huge holding pen where they can limber up and stretch before the main event. The only thing holding up proceedings is my outfit: it's started to rain and though my top half is deemed appropriate – hooded mac, fleecy scarf and snug hat – my cropped jeans and flip-flops are cause for concern.

'We'll lend you some waterproofs.'

'Oh, don't worry, I'll be fine.'

They give me a 'bless' look. Apparently I am underestimating the terrain.

'Try these.' Erica offers a pair of synthetic rain trousers.

I give the narrow waistband a dubious look. 'Are they yours?'

'Yes,' she smiles encouragingly.

'Thank you for even thinking I could fit into them but...' I grab at my hefty rump.

'Let me see what I've got,' Dave offers, returning with a man-size (me-size) pair and a range of chunky wellies.

I may now feel like I'm wearing the bottom half of a clown outfit but it adds to the surrealness of the fact that the reigning Miss Slovenly Couch Potato is about to go on a pack run in the wet, wet wilds of Oregon.

'Ready?'

I must confess I am a little nervous about entering an enclosed pen with so many hyped-up dogs – 30 is a lot. Which I suppose sounds silly after the 2,000-strong Doggie Dash but all of those dogs were attached to their owners. These are free to lunge or snap or chomp unchecked. I've never been more keenly aware of my inexperience. I'm still getting a handle on Bodie's foibles. I don't want to inadvertently rub anyone up the wrong way – one false move and I fear there could be a sinew-shredding riot.

'Perhaps I should just wait here?' I offer, explaining that I don't want my nerves to unsettle the pack.

David insists that everything will be fine.

'Really?'

I'm still not sure.

But into the pen I go, muttering Cesar Millan's 'No touch, no talk, no eye contact!' mantra as if my life depended on it.

I even ignore Bodie – well, I don't want to be like the overprotective parent at the school gates, setting up their child for ridicule by coddling and fussing. I'd rather give him the chance to assimilate as if I am not here.

He seems on the same page. So much so that when a few dogs try to make the connection, he swears he's never seen me before in his life.

'Okay, we're going to head out,' Dave alerts me.

As the dogs crowd together in frantic anticipation I begin fretting about whether I'm going to be able to keep up or get trampled face-down in the mud.

Either way, it's too late now: Dave reaches for the gate latch – and they're off!

It feels like Pamplona's running of the bulls as they cut loose. And I mean loose.

I watch in awe as this seething, weaving river of live fur moves through the long wet grass and bright yellow Scotch broom, heading for the forest and hills that give way to endless mountains and sky – not a barrier or a boundary in sight.

'B-but...' I struggle after them. 'What if one of them goes off? Or gets left behind? How can you keep track of them all?'

Dave smiles confidently. 'Dogs are pack animals – they naturally want to travel together.'

'Well, I understand that in theory but—'

'Watch...'

He whistles and holds up his hand to alert them to a new direction. They all follow. All of them. The sprightlies and the slowcoaches may have their own pace but they all get it. He does it again. Total about-turn. Same thing. And yes, some of them are regulars but Bodie, who has completely abandoned me, is in the flow too.

I am in awe.

Down the muddy slope we go and along a woodland path. Some make independent explorations, others romp and tussle. All within 50 feet of each other.

This is probably as close as I'll ever come to being part of a wolf pack. Better yet, I've teamed up with an aging Huskie that seems glad to have someone keeping a similarly leisurely pace.

As we walk through a corridor of pines, I reach down and give his rain-kissed head a pat and he looks at me as if to say, 'I let the youngsters go on ahead – they're all a bit noisy for me. Someone needs to bring up the rear.'

'Quite right,' I assure him, now feeling that I am serving some purpose. No dog left behind and all that.

Besides which, from this vantage point I can see all the action, like Dave getting playful with a cream-and-brown Springer Spaniel with shaggy ears: Dave calls his name and the pup leaps high into his arms, resting on his shoulder with a huge grin on his face.

It really is the coolest thing seeing people who love dogs and know dogs interact with them without all the syrupy baby talk. Erica and Dave are like the cool teachers at school that everyone likes and respects – easy-going but mess around in class and they'll soon set you straight. And today's errant pupil?

Bodie, of course.

Oh jeez, I cringe to myself as Erica is forced to repeatedly disengage him from a dog who clearly wants no part of his horseplay.

'Can't you see he's not having any fun when you bother him that way?' I try to reason with Bodie.

'I'm going to wear him down!' he seems to reply. 'I'm gonna make him like it!'

'Oh no, you're not!' Erica steps in again.

'Sorry,' I say weakly, knowing I'm powerless to contribute any authority. Not least because my waterproofs have sprung a leak and raindrops are a-trickling down the small of my back. Very strange sensation.

'Do you think he walks funny?' I ask as I catch up with Dave. 'As if something is wrong with him physically?'

He studies his wonky gait. 'Well, he does look like John Wayne from the rear.'

'Is that a problem?'

'Not necessarily – shelter dogs rarely get enough exercise so it could be as simple as the fact that he's building up his muscles again.'

'Really?' I like that explanation and it also makes sense – think of how unfit I am and I'm sure I'm no picture from the rear either.

Hmmm, I wonder how many of these sessions it would take to get us *both* into shape?

They really do offer a great service at Run!, especially when you compare these two possible scenarios: owner leaves dog home alone while they go to work, dog paces a while before slumping on the carpet, falls asleep, wakes up, turns on to his side, sleeps some more, yawns and sighs ad infinitum until his owner returns. Or, he has a heroic al fresco adventure and gets to be his best dog self.

By the time we return to the pen, a good couple of hours later, the mass of dogs have become distinct personalities. I've even registered a few names, like Jasper and Cookie and Frankie and (my personal favourite) Cassidy. I'd be hard-pushed to rile them now: they are too blitzed with fresh air – all oxygenated muscles and lolling tongues. Though the rain has ceased, it is now time for the hose down. I don't envy Erica in this moment. No dog likes to— *wait*. What's going on? One by one they dutifully make their approach and get the requisite dousing while standing accommodatingly still. Some even lift a front or back paw. I can't believe my eyes – they're all but donning shower caps and blowing bubbles.

I hold my breath for Bodie's turn, praying he won't act out like he would with me. But up he goes and takes it all on the chin. Amazing.

'You have a magic touch,' I tell Erica.

She shrugs in a 'just doing my job' way.

Now that the ensemble is clean and ready for a snooze, we head back into the house for some lunch.

Dave and Erica's home has a very outdoors/indoors feel, with a window wall showcasing both the far-reaching countryside and the lawn where they are planning to marry a few months from now. As my eyes adjust, I notice a small dog sunk deep into a cushion. The dear chap has been very sick and is on his last legs. Just seeing the look in Erica's eyes as she contemplates him makes me want to cry so I am relieved when we move through to the kitchen. Bodie included.

I can't help but smile as I watch their coupley interactions at the countertop. Dave gets all *Masterchef* creating sublime avocado salsa quesadillas while Erica furiously blends every green vegetable she can lay her hands on.

'My friend Sam calls this Swamp Juice!' I laugh as she hands me a glass.

'You don't have to drink it if you don't want to.' Dave gives me a significant look, gagging slightly as he takes his first sip.

'It's good for you,' Erica insists.

'I just don't understand why it has to taste so bad,' Dave frowns.

It's funny but, with them, I don't feel any queasy pangs of 'It's all right for you!' I just feel pleased. As if a wrong has been righted in the world since two such fine people got to heal their hearts together. They strike me as the real deal. And so hard-working. I bet they sleep well at night.

And so the time comes to return to the city.

As we get into the van, I haul Bodie on to my lap so that I can safely close the door without clipping him and seconds later he has fallen asleep in my arms, jaw resting heavily on my forearm, bottom curving at my knees, all four paws retracted neatly to his centre. I didn't even know that a dog his size could fit on my lap – then again, my thighs do have a sizeable span. And for that, for once, I am grateful.

'Now, that is trust,' Erica smiles as she slots behind the wheel.

I feel oddly proud, as if this simple act is an endorsement of our bond.

And today certainly has been a bonding day. A great day, actually. Challenging and thought-provoking and different. And all the while I got to be in the presence of two people who received a belated but well-deserved happy ending. It's just so gratifying and hope-inducing.

'I wish you lived here,' Erica says when we finally part, all dogs safely returned to their homes.

There is a simplicity and genuineness to her words that touches me. We have only known each other a day but I too feel a sense of kinship. It's such a pleasure to feel noticed and welcomed. I can almost feel myself transitioning from one of life's nose-pressed-against-the-window onlookers to invited guest.

Chapter 27

The Pet Psychic

I have no qualms about bringing our mud-spattered selves back to the Hotel Monaco – we checked in this morning and it may be literally around the corner from the swishness of The Nines but the vibe is quirkier and even more dog friendly. In fact, all hotels in the Kimpton group have zero pet charges and an 'if your pet fits through the door, we'll welcome them in' size policy.

There's a Collie-shaped blackboard in the entrance hallway with the names of the current dog guests in pastel chalks – Bodie is etched beside Riley, Shelby, Willie et al. – all of whom received a welcome by the resident Director of Pet Relations, Timmy: a jolly, enthusiastic yellow Lab and former Guide Dog for the Blind.

There have been canines at Kimpton hotels since the company's inception in 1981 – founder Bill Kimpton used to bring his pup Chianti to work, knowing that dogs have 'an innate ability to lift spirits'. Then along came Jack Russell Terrier Lily – she used to tag along with the Director of Sales and Marketing for Denver's Hotel Monaco and ended up being the most lauded 'staff member' on guest comment cards. And so the role of Director of Pet Relations was born!

I therefore shouldn't have been quite so surprised that, as Bodie and I approached the reception desk, a white Labradoodle reared up and placed his soft front paws on the marble countertop.

'Now, that is what I call dog friendly!' I muttered.

'Oh hello!' The human receptionist stood up from rummaging in a low drawer. 'Sorry about that.'

No apology required – it really was the perfect start to our stay, which just kept getting better as far as Bodie was concerned. Our room featured a big red stripy dog bed laden with treats and coupons for the LexiDog Boutique & Social Club. A postcard from Timmy showed his ten top pet-friendly picks around town and his face even beamed out from the label of a bottle of red wine.

'I think this one is for me,' I said as I propped myself up against an orange plaid pillow and contemplated the flying birds print on the walls – giving new meaning to the term 'flocked' wallpaper.

'Very nice indeed.'

Despite the lingering 'eau de wet dog' from today's pack run, I'm in no hurry to shower and, while Bodie snoozes, I take a moment to flip through the hotel binder. I've seen some cute doggie extras on my trip but this is the first time there's been a pet psychic on the list...

Bridget Pilloud of Pets Are Talking discovered her ability to communicate with animals in 2001 when her rescue dog Beaulah woke in the night with a pressing question. Beaulah had been given up by her male owner of nine years when he chose to marry 'a lady who hated dogs'. So there was Bridget, wide-awake and wondering why she suddenly felt so overwhelmed with grief. She looked over at Beaulah and heard her ask, *'What did I do? What did I do that he made me leave home and come here?'*

And so Bridget explained the heartbreaking situation as best she could, soothing Beaulah and helping her learn to love her new life.

I look at Bodie. I've never got that sad vibe from him. I think he was in survivor mode by the time we met and now he just wants to enjoy himself. But what if I'm wrong? What if he needs reassurance in a voice he can understand?

I scan the case studies section on Bridget's website. One tells of a Terrier's relentless barking in the home. When Bridget asked Ellie why she barked, she replied, 'Because it works.'

Ellie explained that if she barked people kept walking, which meant she'd done her job of keeping the family safe. Bridget reasoned that perhaps some people were simply walking past and not planning to approach the house, so she could wait and see if they came to the door and then trade crazed barking for a low 'grrrr'.

Her owner Patrick reported that he had never heard her make this sound before but she practised it right there while Bridget was on their phone consultation and, a few weeks later, he confirmed that the low 'grrr' had consistently replaced the barking.

Now that's a change a lot of dog owners would welcome.

'It's important that we understand what our dogs get out of their behaviours, and how they think they're helping us by doing what they do,' Bridget says. 'It keeps us from confusing them and hurting their feelings. And then it's easier to find solutions that meet the spirit of their intentions, while meeting our needs too.'

I find myself sufficiently intrigued to make an appointment for tomorrow morning. It would be great to get an insight into Bodie's heritage and who wouldn't love a bit of 'spiritual healing'? Mind you, as far as reading his mind goes I have to say that right now he's sending a clear message: 'Where's my dinner?'

'Coming right up!' I tell him.

I go to close the hotel guide but then experience a heart dip as I catch sight of the page offering guests the option of having a goldfish (in a bowl) brought to their room. That might startle the uninitiated but I've seen this sweet suggestion of companionship before – at the Hotel Monaco in Chicago, with Nathan.

Being responsible for the wellbeing of the shimmering little fellow brought out the parental side in us and we spent the weekend discussing every aspect of our future child's upbringing.

Against my better judgement I find myself reaching for my laptop and locating the pictures of us in the hotel's zebra and tiger print bathrobes, looking so carefree and besotted. That was just a couple of months into our relationship. We were invincible then.

I look up from my computer screen. I was planning on taking Bodie to the hotel's dog-friendly wine reception but suddenly socialising seems on a par with scaling Mount Shasta.

Room service it is.

'You like carrots, Bodie.' I put on a brave face for him. 'How about these ones with a honey and orange glaze?'

I've been to a few psychics in my time. Now I come to think of it, the last one (hired by a friend for an all-girl house party) told me that Nathan wasn't The One. I referenced him early on, gearing up to ask a series of questions, but she dismissed him in an instant, eager to move on to topics she felt were more pertinent.

If only I could shrug him off with such ease.

I check my watch – 10.55 a.m. Bridget should be here shortly.

I've got us a spot in the exotic jewel box of a lounge – the richness of the colours and abundance of tasselled floor cushions put me in mind of a satin-swathed Yul Brynner stepping forward to ask, 'Shall we dance?'

Bodie's had a good walk and by rights should be settling in for a hearthside snooze but the minute we make the Bridget–Belinda–Bodie introductions, his energy goes askew and he becomes unbearably restless. Though Bridget doesn't need to gaze into his eyes or study his paw to make her reading his fidgeting is wildly distracting. I repeatedly apologise and try to settle him but the more Bridget makes claims like 'he became separated from his owner in a maze' and 'his mother was a large blonde dog', the more uncomfortable he becomes.

'Get outta my head lady!' he all but screams.

I really have never seen him react to anyone like this.

'Shall we take a walk?' Bridget suggests when it becomes impossible to get through an exchange without disruption. 'There's a pet store just down the road – we could get him a chew.'

'Yes, yes, great idea.'

It's drizzling but Bodie has us moving at such a clip the raindrops glance off us. Conveniently the pet store has a quiet area with chairs for us as well as the vital chew for him.

Bodie accepts the distraction and channels his distress into feverish gnawing. I feel disloyal asking her to rummage in his head any more so I ask about her pets – two dogs, Olive and Marvin, and cats Bo and Leo – and soon our time is up.

'Just one last question,' I say as she gets to her feet.

'Yes?'

'Is Bodie enjoying this trip?'

Which I suppose really means, 'Is he happy with me?'

She pauses for a moment, as if waiting for the message to come through. 'He says he's having a great time – he's just slightly concerned you may be lost.'

I smile. 'Because we've been away so long?'

'He wonders if you've forgotten the way back home.'

This feels oddly metaphoric but I have to postpone my pondering for now – the time has come to reunite Bodie with Winnie.

Chapter 28
Puppy Love

Back in Los Angeles Bodie and I could walk to Molly's apartment but here we are relying on the satnav to guide us to leafy suburbia. This is new territory for me – the land of grown-ups. The only time I've lived 'out of town' was the nine months I spent in Las Vegas, and even then our cul-de-sac pad was just 20 minutes' drive from the Strip (and ten from Liberace's mansion). It was a surreal existence but I was quite partial to desert living – there's something about those tumble dryer hot summer nights, looking out across the sandy mountain ranges at sunset. Portland couldn't be more different – here the lush greenery spills out over the garden walls of a series of craftsman houses with pretty sit-a-while porches and two-tone paintwork. I admire one in cocoa and lemon, another in smart ivy and white.

'Come and have a nice life,' they seem to say. 'The kettle is whistling, the cat is purring and later this evening local academics will gather for gin-based cocktails.'

'Any minute now...' I slow to a crawl, searching for Molly's house. 'Here!' I pull in, turning to contemplate Bodie. 'Do you have any idea what's in store?'

The Bodie–Winnie reunion exceeds all expectation.

Molly's place is immaculate and spacious, with an open-plan kitchen and dining room leading to a large, multi-tiered garden bordered with pink-and-white azaleas. Not an inch of it goes untrodden as the two dogs launch into a high-speed, high-energy wrestling match – tearing hither and thither, rearing up like fighting bears and then rolling and tumbling like circus acrobats. Bodie tries his classic move of clamping down on Winnie's leather collar but she writhes free, the pair of them now facing off, jaws wide, teeth and tongues clashing in a canine kiss.

'They are in love. You know that, don't you?' Molly notes as she hands me a drink.

I nod contentedly.

'So you realise you'll have to move here now,' she continues. 'To keep them apart would be tantamount to animal cruelty.'

I can't tell if she's joking and even if she is, I feel she has a point. Bodie's happiness is paramount and he simply can't get enough of Winnie.

'Refreshments, guys!'

Molly really is the hostess with the mostest, bringing them water bowls to glug at, biscuits to crunch and toys to tussle with. But her *pièce de résistance* is the Frosty Paws dog ice-cream.

It's just a little cardboard tub, the size you'd enjoy during intervals at the theatre, but somehow these two dogs manage to tilt their chunky heads and alternate licks so that they can share the creamy, cooling vanilla. Right up until the point when Bodie hooks out the last lump, swallows it whole and then reels, *'Brain freeze!'*

They take a moment to pant and rest and then they're at it again. And again.

'Of all the places they can play!' Molly tuts as they repeatedly bring their limb-tangling into our personal space.

Of course, we love it this way.

'Let's do some photos!' Molly suggests.

Up close, I admire the smoky-black velvet of Winnie's face set against the backdrop of her fawn-coloured folds and smile at the way her tongue lolls out to the side of her mouth like she's carrying a pink sock. At one point she nudge-sits on me and it's like being hit by a furry bumper car.

When I try to get a picture of Bodie with Molly he is still in play mode, snapping excitably at her hands. Fortunately she's a pro and gets him to simmer down and pose beside her as she sits crossed-legged in her skinny black jeans. I study the picture – basically Heidi Klum posing with a street kid with overly gelled hair, as styled by Winnie's saliva.

By the time Bodie comes to me he's too exhausted to do anything but recline and we turn to the camera with matching grins. It's the closest I've been to a 'proud mother with child' pose.

I wonder if this is what it's like for mums having play dates with their kids, only with the mute button on – for all the romping and rolling there's barely a peep from our charges. The noisiest part is the water-lapping.

I really like dogs.

'Are you at the Monaco tomorrow night?' Molly asks as I bring her up to speed on our itinerary.

I shake my head. 'Some old-fashioned place with very dark interiors.' I tell her the name.

'No, no,' she winces. 'Come and stay with us.'

'Really?' I brighten.

'I think these two should spend as much time together as possible, don't you?'

I can't disagree with that.

'You can have your own room, brand-new bed linens. I'll cook dinner.'

I all but swoon at this.

'I have a tour of the Oregon Humane Society in the afternoon but we could come after that?'

'Perfect!'

As Bodie staggers like a jelly-legged triathlete to the car, I get a 'job well done' feeling. All the happier for knowing there's more to come tomorrow.

I have cornflakes for breakfast – encrusted on my French toast with a slathering of maple syrup and a side of bacon for Bodie. Mother's Bistro is a popular choice, mixing country chic and chandeliers with an abundance of mama memorabilia and photos. Each month they feature the story of a local M.O.M. (mother of the month), honouring her exceptional ways. I raise a cup of spiced plum tea to my own mother and for the first time it occurs to me that it's actually right that our family line of child-bearing women should stop with her. I used to feel like I'd dropped the baton and brought our genealogy to a grinding halt but now I see we ended on a high with her – you couldn't find a kinder, more nurturing person.

'We can only wish that the rescue animals at the Oregon Humane Society find such a loving home, eh Bodie?'

While I take my tour, he will kick back at Stay Pet Hotel (another find from the Doggie Dash day). Like so many dog-boarding establishments it has a shack-like exterior but this one steps up the hipster vibe with a cool neon sign in the car park and a countertop of kitschy dog porcelains (from pink Poodles to doe-eyed Cavalier King Charles Spaniels) alongside a silver platter of pastel-hued dog treats sprinkled with hundreds and thousands.

Normally I'd want the staff to run Bodie ragged but today I ask, 'Can you make sure he gets some rest?'

They raise a quizzical brow.

I show them a picture of Winnie and lean in, 'He's got a big night ahead of him.'

When you think of visiting an animal shelter you don't necessarily think of whooping and high-fiving everyone you meet but this is how I feel on my tour of the Oregon Humane Society. I cannot imagine a better-run organisation. A quick look at their figures speaks volumes: dog adoptions are at 96 per cent and cats at 98 per cent. To put this in perspective, the national average is 20 per cent for cats and 25 per cent for dogs.

Even more startling is the average number of days it takes from the time an animal enters the shelter to when it goes home with its new owner: nine. That's just over a week! I've never heard of such a swift turnaround.

It certainly helps that the 140 staff are helped by 2,000 volunteers (doubling the overall staff hours) but at the heart of this success lies the OHS slogan: 'There's a furry soulmate for everyone.'

Back in 2008 local marketing company Leopold Ketel donated their services and created what I think is an utterly genius campaign: instead of showing sad dogs with pleading eyes, all too often causing soft hearts to turn away, their series of 'End Petlessness' artworks depicted cosy home and leisure activities enhanced by the presence of a pet. So there's a girl with a guitar howling a tune with her Beagle, an outdoorsy type in a green beanie relaxing beside the campfire with his dog, a gym enthusiast getting a back massage from her cat, an old archaeologist getting some enthusiastic assistance on a dig, and so on.

It's so clever – playing to the modern 'What's in it for me?' mindset in the coolest, sweetest way.

Of course anyone with a pet will vouch for the myriad benefits, always happily confirming what excellent company they are. And to think that just a few weeks back circling the word 'companion' as my reason for adoption felt like an awkward admission, shining a light on my personal deficiencies. Now I see this reason embraced and emblazoned in murals running several stories high in downtown Portland!

And it's not just local rescues that get the benefit of this brilliance. My tour guide – events manager Rebecca Ramach – explains that because Oregonians are such big-hearted adopters, the OHS is able to travel into other states and scoop up their excess of shelter animals. Plus, whereas Bodie's former South Central facility has a four-week maximum stay (before they are put down), there is no time limit on how long an animal will be cared for here.

(On the rare, rare occasion when an animal is slated to be euthanised due to an extreme behaviourial issue, an email is sent out so that if any staff member or volunteer felt strongly enough that they wanted to step in and adopt, they can do that. And they often do.)

Rebecca shows me the remaining four of an original haul of 67 mistreated Akitas rescued from an unscrupulous breeder – a woman in her sixties living just an hour north of here, who kept the dogs in airless, squalid conditions. The beauty of the dogs is untainted but they stand at the very back of the kennels, staring out through wary, troubled eyes. The scene is all the more poignant so soon after seeing the magnificent show dog Reign strutting proudly at the Kennel Club show.

'How long have they been here?' I ask, sensing they have surpassed the nine-day average.

'A year.'

My heart winces. 'But you found homes for sixty-three of them, so there's always hope?'

'Always,' she confirms.

Of course a great deal of that hope comes in the form of funds raised by the annual Doggie Dash. My jaw drops when Rebecca tells me that, when the event was organised and promoted by a local radio station, they would raise about $16,000 but since they've taken over the running, they've upped that by a quarter of a million dollars. (In 2016 they sailed past the half a million mark!)

Not bad for a company that started with one humanitarian and a dozen or so volunteers.

Back in 1868 the mission was to prevent the abuse of draft animals (those drawing heavy loads) but this expanded to include companion animals and even orphaned children, right up until 1933. It must have been an enormous comfort for the children to be surrounded by so much furry love, though I suppose they could never get too attached.

Animals and humans still cohabit today, as a certain number of medical students live on site.

'One time we came back from an event and found that a puppy had wriggled free of its IV, so we just called upstairs and had one of the students reinsert it,' Rebecca smiles, explaining that the programme offers great hands-on experience for them. 'They arrive never having spayed a cat and by the time they leave they will have done thirty.'

She turns my attention to the immaculate surgery room but even glimpsing a cat belly-up on the table has me feeling faint. I certainly won't be tuning into their special channel where medical students can watch the operations remotely. More my speed is the cat playroom with a live internet feed… You take your place in line and then, when your turn comes, you can engage the cats in play by pressing keys that activate springy arms with tantalising feathers on the end. This you can do from anywhere in the world.

'Is there anything you don't have here?' I marvel.

'Oh we're not shy about asking for these things,' Rebecca smiles. 'That system was kindly donated to us.'

Our last stop is a large room used for training and workshops (tonight there's one on how best to photograph cats and dogs). The walls are lined with artwork from local schoolchildren and each one has written a little message beside their drawing, saying what they like most about their pets.

'We find it helps to develop their respect and appreciation,' Rebecca explains. 'If they can understand from a young age that they need to treat animals with kindness, there will be a lot less mistreatment down the line.'

They really have thought through every aspect of animal welfare here, from the soothing, tinkling piano music to the temperature of the building being set to be preferable for animals (not too hot) and requesting the humans dress accordingly.

I feel filled up with admiration and hope as I thank Rebecca for her time and then pause to look back at the building before I return to the car – if I ever did take up Molly and the Run! crew on the idea of moving to Oregon, this is where I would want to work.

Chapter 29

The View from Mount Tabor

Bodie and I arrive at Molly's with a bottle of wine and six Chocolate Labs – of the truffle variety, complete with hand-piped eyes, noses and collars. (Oregon-based Moonstruck Chocolate Company is so acclaimed that their goodies were featured in Oscar gift bags two years in a row!)

'Winnie has been waiting!' Molly shows me the nose prints on the window overlooking the street. 'I can always tell if I've been gone too long by the number of smudges.'

While 'the kids' play, Molly prepares the ingredients for dinner and I take a seat at the breakfast bar, feeling like I'm watching a live cooking show. The sizzling is tantalising and her culinary skills keen, though somewhat wasted on Winnie since she only eats raw food.

I learn that this alternative dog diet of unprocessed meat, edible bones and select fruits and veg is gaining popularity, not least for the amazing results for dogs with allergies.

'It's the healthiest option for all dogs,' Molly affirms, offering Bodie a bite of one of the pink burger patties.

He rolls it around his mouth before letting it plop to the floor.

'Not for me, the steak tartare.'

It's then we hear a crunching in the background and notice that Winnie, the purist, has powered through the bowl of dried food I had set down for Bodie.

'Kinda like popcorn,' she seems to say.

'Ah,' I grimace. 'Sorry about that.'

Molly decides to reach for the peanut butter – a great unifier, holding both dogs in rapt attention as they await their tongue-slapping spoonful.

And now it's our turn.

As she serves up our steak I flash back to Dave's quesadillas and tell Molly I must give her the contact details for Run! – Winnie would have a blast.

'Oh no, she wouldn't like it.'

I blink back at her. 'But she loves to play!'

'I don't like the idea of her picking up bad habits from the other dogs.'

'What kind of bad habits?' I frown, imagining a huddle of dogs trading tips on breaking and entering.

'She's too shy,' she counters.

When I suggest this might be just the thing to help, she shakes her head in a 'no is a complete sentence' way.

I look back at Winnie, in her element with Bodie, but reason that this set-up works because it's a controlled, one-to-one environment. Molly's doing right by her dog and I'm doing right by mine. We're both being the parents we want to be. She wants Winnie to have a secure, regular, balanced regimen with the purest foods, freshest air and most luxurious bedding. And I want Bodie to let his freak flag fly and know fearless, boundless joy.

Maybe it's a good thing I don't have children.

'But, Mum, I don't want to go paragliding – I have a physics test to study for.'

'Nonsense! You'll love it, you'll see!'

The steak is cooked to perfection and the conversation as invigorating as ever, even in this homely setting. Her take on the military challenges my resentments and presumption that it is a miserable way of life for anyone. She speaks of the Navy, and her father who served from the age of 18 to retirement, with great reverence and respect. I feel rather humbled.

Though we are clearly cut from different cloth we are both still looking for love, both quite particular and independent. Mind you, I'll wager she gets rather more offers than me – the aforementioned Heidi Klum to my English Pear. Or Patsy to my Edina if we have any more wine.

When we take the dogs out for the last wee of the day we look up at the stars and then down at the grass and Molly tells me that it's only female dogs that bleach out the green, on account of the increased oestrogen in their urine. I feel like there's a lot she could teach me about dogs and life but, for now, it's time to hit the hay.

'Thank you for your hospitality, both of you.' I give Winnie a gentle pat. 'It means the world.'

Tucked up in the guest bedroom, I feel so safe and taken care of.

'Can you believe this is our last night in Portland?' I reach for Bodie. 'I must confess I feel a little nervous about moving on.'

But he's already snoring, little paws twitching as he plays kiss chase with Winnie in his dreams.

'Bagels for breakfast?'

'Don't mind if I do!'

Before we head off Molly suggests a hike to the local volcanic cinder cone – aka Mount Tabor.

Spanning a magnificent 200 acres, this is the walking-distance park of a dog owner's dreams. Shady and sprawling, the ever-changing pathways weave around reservoirs, picnic spots and neck-crickingly tall trees. There's an amphitheatre for summer concerts and a bronze statue of Harvey W. Scott (former editor of *The Oregonian*) sculpted by one Gutzon Borglum – the very same artist who etched four presidents into Mount Rushmore in South Dakota. He was actually working on both projects simultaneously – because you must have so much time on your hands when you're carving 60-foot granite faces that will blow people's minds for decades to come.

As we reach the brow of the mount, Molly directs my gaze to a stop-and-gawp view of downtown Portland, exquisitely framed with evergreens.

As the four of us shuffle up to a bench, it feels as if we are taking a front row seat to one of the finest collaborations between nature and architecture – the jut of the angular tower blocks softened by the dense greenery and sloping mountains, rather like a Christmas centrepiece with pillar candles nestled among sprigs of pine.

'Now that's a good-looking cityscape,' I acknowledge.

'Just trying to make it that little bit harder for you to leave,' Molly smiles.

She seems almost as proud of Portland as she is of Winnie. I love it when a person finds their perfect-match place. (Later she will find her perfect man here: a doctor with three children, all of whom will fall profoundly in love with Winnie.)

But destiny has other plans for Bodie and me, moving us on from home, hearth and human companionship and placing us firmly back on the road.

Part Four
The Way Home

Chapter 30

Grumpy Dog

Even though we are travelling an entirely different route with lots of new stop-offs, it never seems quite so thrilling on the way home. 'Getting away from' offers so much more energetic promise than 'returning to'.

Of course we have activities planned – a graduation ceremony at the Guide Dogs for the Blind facility, a romp across the Oregon Dunes and a photo op beside a drive-through tree to name but three – but still I feel oddly deflated as we pass through an unpretty stretch of suburbia.

'Come on! Buck up!'

I have to ditch the notion that 'it's all downhill from here'. If anything, these last days are to be treasured all the more, because they now carry all my hopes that something miraculous *could still happen...*

So many people are resistant to change; I seem to have a greater issue with the status quo.

'Here I am, back to square one again!' I lamented when Nathan left.

'No, you're not!' my mother would protest. 'Think of all you've learned, how much you've grown!'

But it didn't feel that way. I didn't feel more evolved – I felt less so. The only thing I felt I'd gained was further evidence that I was unlucky in love or destined to be alone or any of the things we tell ourselves when we just don't have the energy to be optimistic any more. I wanted to throw in the towel and just call it a day but of course bringing your life to a halt isn't a real option. You have to keep going. So, if what I had been doing wasn't working, it could be time for a rethink... This trip has certainly revived my inner nomad – perhaps solo is the way to go? Could I embrace that instead of fearing it? Especially now I have such an amazing sidekick in Bodie. Not all of us can be meant for long-term human relationships. For some, the enduring part always starts to feel like something to endure. Who's to say it would have worked out with Nathan anyway?

But things are working out, even better than expected, with Bodie.

'Isn't that right, pal?' I smile at his ever-lovely face.

Suddenly I feel back on track.

And, before I know it, we're arriving at our first stop on the Oregon Coast: Lincoln City.

Having a penchant for all things retro, I'm particularly pleased with our accommodation for tonight. The owners of the Ester Lee weighed modern upgrades against throwback charm and, though adding motel rooms in the 1970s, chose to preserve the 1940s heritage of their cottage rooms. As we pull into the car park, I imagine myself in Katharine Hepburn slacks and a silk headscarf, with Bodie transformed into a Westie with a red velvet collar.

'Oh the things you'll see from the Ester Lee!'

I read the sign with sing-song pep. Turns out that Esther was misspelled on the original signage and the couple (husband and wife Esther and Lee) were so eager to open their doors that they accepted the flaw and went ahead.

The reception windows have particular wow factor, giving the impression of being aboard a cruise ship with their curved white edges and endless seascape beyond. I step closer, eager to glimpse the beach below – it stretches for 7.5 miles and there's not a soul in sight.

I can't wait to take the cliff path down there but Bodie becomes sullen and scowly the minute his paws meet the sand. I don't know if it's the excessive bluster of the wind (this area offers the best kite-flying on the Oregon Coast) but he doesn't seem to want to run or play or dig or even sniff. I've never seen him like this before and it's a little disconcerting.

'What is it, chum?' I fish for a clue but, like a sulking boyfriend, he refuses to communicate.

Of course dogs are entitled to have their moods and off days just like humans – I just hope it's not something I've done. Like part him from his new pack and most beloved Winnie.

'Come on,' I attempt to gee him up. 'Let's see if we can make it to that big rock!'

As we push through the wind, the wind pushes back at us, whisking my hair upwards, sending it dancing erratically and ruffling Bodie's fur in new, seemingly uncomfortable directions. His ears are pinned back now, possibly to streamline his passage.

Were it not for him, I suspect I would be sitting at the picture window, feet up on the ledge, sipping tea and feeling cosy. But not much else. Sometimes it's good to be blustered. It's like an invigorating exfoliation of your senses, sloughing away the stagnant outer layer brought on from watching too much TV and wasting time wishing your life was some way other than what it is.

But when the sand starts to sting we seek shelter behind a blanched tree trunk. I try to pull Bodie into me to protect him with my hunched body but he shrugs me off, scowling even.

It's moments like these that make me most feel like a parent – your child won't always like you and you have to be okay with that. At least with Bodie I can't pepper him with questions, trying to diagnose the nature and origin of his mood, like I always did with Nathan. All I can do is leave him be and let him come around to me in his own good time. Now if only I could apply that simple strategy to relationships: *stop fussing and let it be.*

Maybe Bodie just needs some space. We have it all around us but little between us, ever linked as we are by his leash. I unravel it to its full extent as we head back and try not to watch him so closely, for once relieving him of my constant scrutiny and fascination.

He does perk up a little when he spies an empty plastic water bottle to chew on, then digs himself a bunker and hunkers down, closing his eyes to limit their streaming. He has no interest in paddling today, which is probably for the best as the white surf is racing, layer upon layer, across the thrashing minty sea.

My brother Gareth was a lifeguard in Devon and still trains the new recruits known as 'Nippers'. I decide to call him, burrowing into my coat as I dial. I want to know if he's ever rescued a dog.

'About once a year and it always goes like this,' he begins. 'Dog is swept off the sea wall or gets in trouble retrieving a ball. Owner goes in to rescue dog and drowns. Meanwhile dog scrambles to safety unscathed.'

'Every time?'

'Every time.'

He then tells me about a 200-pound Newfoundland named Bilbo who worked alongside his lifeguard owner at one of the most dangerous beaches on the Cornish coast. For three years Bilbo assisted in swimmer safety but when the RNLI (Royal National Lifeboat Institution) took over the beach they banned Bilbo, causing a public outcry.

'Please tell me he was reinstated!'

'Well, a petition to bring him back garnered twenty thousand signatures and the RNLI were forced to make a compromise, allowing him to participate in safety education.'

'Interesting.'

'Google it,' he tells me.

I do and I'm rather amazed by what I read. I would never have thought these big, shaggy, bear-like dogs would have been well-suited to the water but they are in fact natural swimmers with large webbed feet, extra-large lungs and a double coat that keeps the layer closest to the skin completely dry.

Bilbo's owner – Steve Jamieson – started taking his dog to the beach when he was 14 weeks old. He trained him to recognise a person in distress and Bilbo would swim out with a float attached to his harness. When he felt the weight of the person grabbing on to the float, he would then swim them back to the beach, saving the day.

I put my phone back in my pocket and pull up my collar. When it comes to romance, being 'saved' is a common motif. But as much as I want to take on the Prince role in the fairy tale by making everything all better for the object of my desire (and thus indebting them to me for all eternity), I wonder how I would feel about being rescued myself. I don't know that I was ever under the illusion that a man could right every wrong in my life. I'd see couples glowing and gazing googly-eyed at each other on their wedding day and think, 'What happens now?' Besides, what would I be rescued *from*? I've always gone to great pains to create a life I love. I suppose the answer is loneliness. That's something you can't really fix by yourself. I remember Nathan used to talk about wanting to 'belong' to someone. He used to say that I was the human representation of the feeling he had craved his whole life. And I too would feel all high and filled up after one of his calls. I noticed that I didn't feel so vulnerable as I moved about the world. I didn't have to be so on guard or wary – I felt loved and protected and there was even a sense of relief that it wasn't all 'on me'. I didn't have to have all the answers because maybe he would chime in and help me to solve a puzzle or two once in a while.

So why, when I asked relatively little of him, was it still too much to give?

Now I'm in a slump.

I can't even ask Bodie to make it all better like he usually does because he's still in a contrary mood.

Time to head back to the Ester Lee.

If I could just find the path we came down on…

On the way here I was too entranced by the frothing surf to register landmarks for our return. All the rickety wooden staircases seem to be leading up to private homes. Did we really walk this far? I squint along the cliff edge but there's no trace of the Ester Lee. At least it doesn't look like the tide is coming in to cut us off. Sooner or later we'll find a way back up the cliff…

Naturally it is later rather than sooner. And colder.

But all it takes is a portion of fish and chips to make everything better (or should that be batter?).

My eyes stream from the vinegar fumes and I can't resist tearing into the paper to snag a few chips as we return to our hotel room. It's been a while since I tasted anything this good and in my distracted state I trip over our doormat and send the whole lot flying across the floor.

Bodie all but rolls his eyes. *I suppose you expect me to clear that up?*

Thanks, you're a pal.

Now darkness has fallen and we can no longer distinguish sea from sky, I turn on the old-fashioned boxy TV and become hypnotised by the live footage of a local council meeting. It's a bit dry but real in a way that reality TV never is any more – no one here is expecting to get 'discovered' or make money from their appearance and there's no dramatic music underscoring their words; they are simply arguing their case regarding the local animal shelter. It's strange how in life, once you find a new passion, you seem to magnetise related items to you. I absently work my way through a bag of chocolate pretzels as I watch.

'No, sorry, you can't have chocolate.' I repeatedly move the bag away from Bodie.

Watching this animal advocate speak with such conviction, it strikes me that people always refer to guard dogs, protecting the home and the family members within, and here she is returning the favour – guarding the health, safety and indeed *lives* of the local dogs.

It seems reasonable reciprocity – you guard me, I guard you.

I go to reassure Bodie that I've always got his back but he's already soundly asleep. And, once the case to make the shelter 'No Kill' is won, I join him.

Chapter 31

Bad to the Bone

The morning light gives the beach an almost mystical quality – as the surf drags back, the sand becomes a gleaming mirror reflecting the pewter and white streaks of the clouds and clean blue of the sky. I falter as I walk, barely able to tell which way is up.

And then I feel my heart pang, as I always seem to do when I behold a breathtaking scene. I wonder why this is? Could it be because the human instinct is to want to share the moment? Or because great beauty touches you in a similar way to desire? Sometimes Nathan would take off his glasses mid-conversation and the loveliness of his eyes would take me by surprise. I remember my Auntie Gill actually gasping via Skype: 'You're so much more handsome without them!'

He really has the prettiest eyes. And the prettiest nose. And don't get me started on his ears. Of course, the same could be said for Bodie. I take his face in my hands, pull him close and plant noisy 'mwah-mwah-mwah' kisses all over his cheeks. Though he tolerates this with the same grace as a teenage boy being fussed over by his mother, I'm relieved to say that we're back being pals again today.

'All right, all right. Let's get some breakfast.'

If I were choosing the food establishment based on the name alone it would be a toss-up between Eleanor's Undertow Café and Pirate Dan's Pastry Shop, insisting 'You'll treasure the taste!'

But the Nelscott Café has a walk-up window 'for our friends with dogs', which makes it the clear winner.

We then spend rather too long at Paws On The Sand, which isn't so much a pet store as a gift shop for animals. The staff are extremely friendly and one lady tries to show me how to use clicker training with Bodie. The basic principle is positive reinforcement – every time you click the clicker (a basic little gadget not much bigger than a pencil sharpener), you give the dog a treat so it comes to associate clicking with food and will then rush eagerly to your side. She says the fact that Bodie is so 'food-motivated' makes him a good candidate. I can't argue with that but we'll see whether I can keep up my side of the training.

After a quick pack and check-out, we're back on the road. There are some wonderful vantage points to watch the waves crashing around Depoe Bay – home to the world's smallest harbour and a collection of equally dinky shops. One offers 85 flavours of salt water taffy but I manage to keep us moving, past Cape Foulweather and on to our first stop at Yaquina Head historic lighthouse.

According to the website this 'Outstanding Natural Area' has offshore islands that attract harbour seals, nesting seabirds and grey whales. And then there's Cobble Beach, which has basalt rocks worn into pebbles – or 'cobbles' as they are locally known – producing a sound like applause as they tumble over each other. At low tide a vibrant ocean floor of orange sea stars, purple sea urchins and giant green anemones is revealed. Sounds wonderful, but I have to take their word for all of this because the first thing that greets us as we step from the car is a sign bearing the words: 'NO PETS'.

I could have sworn they were allowed. I check the website again and see that there are a few areas they can visit but with this proviso: *'Any domestic animal observed by authorities to be molesting or killing wildlife may be destroyed if necessary for public safety or the protection of wildlife.'*

Destroyed? Do they have snipers in lookout towers here? I think we'll just move on.

Rogue's brewery in nearby Newport made our itinerary when I read about Brewer's Memorial Ale Fest – an annual dog-friendly event that raises funds for the Oregon Humane Society and pays tribute to Rogue's founding black Lab named Brewer. We're going to miss the festival by just a few days, which is a great shame as I love the sound of the tail-wagging contest and had my eye on an 'IN DOG BEERS I'VE ONLY HAD ONE' T-shirt.

Our intention is to stop by and raise a glass in their honour but as we roll into town I start to feel uneasy... The area has an industrial feel, populated with warehouse-like buildings, and I'm beginning to doubt whether it will be tourist-friendly. Which usually means my English accent becomes extra hoity-toity and absurd-sounding: 'Why hello good sirs, how does this fine day find you?'

I falter in the bar doorway. Should I or shouldn't I? But then the menu catches my eye and I spy Kobe beef 'haute dogs' for lunch. In that moment I realise I'm just as 'food-motivated' as Bodie and step inside...

Instead of the conversation cutting dead so everyone can gawp at the 'strangers in town', Bodie is welcomed like a long-lost pal. I'm so relieved. Also rather impressed – I've noticed the distinctive Rogue beer brand in liquor stores and admired their bold angular artwork depicting raised fists and men with beards and hairy forearms. They are equally innovative with the flavours – how about Voodoo Doughnut Chocolate or the extra strong Dead Guy ale, which lists a surprising note of 'caramel-drizzled dried apricot' and recommends spiced pork as a food pairing. This is clearly a passion project and I'm all for that.

After a shared lunch, Bodie and I exit via the patio where we discover the most beguilingly fluffy dog – black and amber with a tail like a feather duster. He looks back at us, seemingly unsure of how to react. 'I wasn't expecting company...'

'Hello chum!' I say as I drop down to his eye level and Bodie moves in for a sniff.

Nose-to-nose I can see just how similar they are, both in build – with their short legs and stocky bodies – and with their equally handsome faces. This dog's energy is quite different to Bodie's, however, more tranquil and gentle. Looking into his dark eyes I feel like he's trying to convey something to me. 'What is it?' I ask. And when he doesn't reply, I follow up with, 'Do you have any idea how good-looking you are?'

'Don't go near that dog – he's a mean one.'

I look up and see the snarliest-looking man I have ever laid eyes on. It's all I can do to stop myself from cowering back and preparing myself for a swipe.

'Really?' I falter. 'He looks so sweet…'

The man scoffs and looms closer. He clearly wants me to leave his dog alone. I scramble back to my feet and guide Bodie out of the gate, quickening my pace as we proceed up the street.

But as I go to start up the car, I hesitate. Something tells me that dog needs saving – he just couldn't actually tell me so. Or is that true? Did he just tell me with the expression in his eyes? Now I feel worse. I consider turning back but what would I say?

'Forgive my impertinence but I get the impression that you don't treat your dog with the impeccable kindness he deserves and I think he would be better off coming with me.'

I imagine the man flicking my face with saliva as he spits out his curse-riddled response. He wasn't like the other good-natured folk in the bar. Perhaps he's just passing through?

So what if I just slowed by the patio, opened the passenger door and whistled? Would the dog see his opportunity for a better life and hop in?

Ultimately my uneasiness and I move on. The dog certainly looked healthy enough. Perhaps the man is a softie in the privacy of their own home.

Later I see a T-shirt saying, 'DOG IS FRIENDLY – BEWARE OF OWNER'.

To me that says it all.

Back on the coastal road the drive is soothingly picturesque, until we round a corner and behold such a gasp-inducing vista that I have to pull over.

The sloping hills are a bright St Patrick's Day green, plunging towards sand of the finest beige and sea of a metallic silver-blue. All three stretch for mile upon mile upon mile. Is it just because I'm English that I hadn't heard how stunning the Oregon coast is? You'd think people would always be raving about it. Perhaps the weather doesn't show it in its best light often enough. Then again, right now the sky is a gloomy grey and it still looks stunning. A few more years of global warming and this could be the new Hawaii.

Bodie is too tired to climb out of his cabin at the back of the car, merely leaning out his weary head, looking for all the world like a frail patient about to draw his last breath. I surmise he's had quite enough sea air for one day and will be glad to turn in for the night. Not long now...

The Park Motel in Florence is another accommodation with a retro feel, this time set amid 5 acres of Douglas fir with cabin-like rooms of 'vintage knotty pine'. I suppose a clue to the clientele might have been 'ample parking for those with big rigs'. Not that I see any truckers as I pull in, just a bevy of burly bikers. Apparently of a superstitious persuasion, they have booked a run of rooms either side of number 13, leaving that one for me. The bikers in 12 and 14 are sitting out on the porch, chatting across my doorway, all leather and chains and unruly whiskers. I feel excruciatingly self-conscious as I pull up. Mostly I forget that I'm a woman travelling on her own; here I feel like Little Red Riding Hood. I pretend I'm sorting my bags when really I'm trying to get up the nerve to walk past them. Short of driving around the back and wriggling in through the bathroom window, there's no getting around it. I take a deep breath, count my blessings and head for the door.

'Oh what a cutie!' Their faces light up at the sight of him. 'We just love dogs!'

They seem to be going out of their way to show themselves to be nice, friendly folk and I am supremely grateful. That'll teach me to judge a book by its cover. As we settle in I recall reading about Rescue Ink, the New York state bikers on a mission to fight animal abuse and neglect – now in that context a big bad biker is nothing but thrilling.

'When there is a situation that gets out of control, you can rely on us,' their website assures. 'We are comprised of street guys, military personnel, police officers, private investigators and lawyers. Rescue Ink does whatever necessary within the means of the law – that's what our lawyers tell us to say – to fight abuse and neglect of all kinds.'

On the Team page of their website you can see a profile on Jimmy the Bull, a marine sergeant who has travelled the globe working with bomb dogs and once held a world record for bench-pressing 1,000 pounds. He and his big ole biceps help to 'educate' abusers on how to treat animals with the respect they deserve.

Now I feel safer than ever and settle down to sleep humming George Thorogood's 'Bad to the Bone'.

Chapter 32
The Oregon Dunes

Running for 40 wind-sculpted miles, the ever-shifting Oregon Dunes rise as high as 500 metres above sea level and yet they are nowhere to be seen as we pull into a woodsy parking area.

Bodie and I spent the morning at a classic car show tapping along to Frankie Valli as we admired pink Cadillacs and cherry-red Chevys, but I'm suspecting this natural wonder will have the edge for my canine pal. If we can just find it...

'I can't believe we're playing hide-and-seek with a 300,000-acre attraction!' I tut as we pad down a shady path, piebald with playful sunbeams.

The surrounding forest has an enchanted quality and just a few minutes in we find ourselves gazing across a glinting green pond resplendent with water lilies. Bodie's eyes gleam with appreciation.

So here's the oasis, now where's the sand?

Forging onward we cross a wooden bridge and pass sprinklings of pink-and-yellow wild flowers, until the trees part and reveal a seagrass-tufted bank. We clamber up and then reel back as a full-on *Lawrence of Arabia* scene plays out before us – mile upon mile upon mile of soft-sloping wonder. Far off in the distance we can see the sparkling semaphore of the sea.

This is a truly magnificent sight, far more vast and other-wordly than I imagined. And we have it all to ourselves.

'Ready to run wild and free?' I entice Bodie.

I can feel him revving up, ready to hit the accelerator. The second I unclip his leash, he's off – bounding and pounding ecstatically up and around the dunes. He tears off in one direction then curves back in a wide loop. His muscular body is at full extension, his heart at full expansion. His enthusiasm is contagious. I too start running and whooping, lumbering up a dune then skidding back down at speed, now inviting him to chase me as I make a break for it across the open basin. Unfortunately he's now whipped into such a frenzy that he decides to take me down in the same way he would another dog – i.e. with his teeth. As he sinks his fangs into my leg I hit the ground with a searing zing of pain to my thigh.

He just bit me!

I'm in a state of disbelief as I grab my leg, fingertips meeting punctured denim.

He's still pogoing excitedly around me, no doubt waiting for me to take off again. But I can't.

I raise a hand – 'Calm down, calm down...' I implore and then quickly retract my arm, not wanting to give him any ideas about chomping on that.

I did not see that coming. I lie back on the sand in shock until slowly the pain starts to ease. That was totally my fault – I baited him. It was just innocent play on his part; he didn't break the skin. Even so, I am wary about any more games of tag.

'How about some digging?' I suggest.

He doesn't need asking twice.

I watch as he burrows and burrows, occasionally toppling over, only to right himself and begin again with renewed vigour. Deeper and deeper, but never deep enough. He settles for a second and then he's up, digging again, always managing to spatter me with damp sand. Finally he collapses, resting his jaw on the ledge of his bunker, black nose now encrusted with sand, like the sprinkles on a cupcake.

He puffs out a breath. Finally peace.

The drama is over.

For a while we just lie there. It's almost like being on another planet. I wouldn't be surprised to see a half-buried spaceship over yonder.

Time has no bearing here. And heartache has no hold. I feel happily neutral. None of it matters – all the bad stuff that has gone before is just that: *gone*. It doesn't even seem real any more.

On the way back we pause to take in the distinct line where the sand meets the dark green of the trees. It's such an unusual sight I find myself sinking back down into the sand, wanting to savour the moment. Bodie remains standing, looking so noble and wistful, like the breeze-caressed hero looking into the future, half-focused on the horizon, half-lost in thought. If he had a pen, he would write *The Alchemist*.

If I'd known the dunes were going to be so majestic, I would have allotted an entire day to them. We would have trekked to the shore and had a paddle and a picnic.

As it stands, we're all out of snacks and our scheduled dinner stop is 40 miles away. So on we go.

It's a beautiful drive to Bandon. At one point there's an expanse of glinting blue water either side of our two lanes of tarmac and then the magnificent Coos Bay Bridge raises us so high we can't see any land at all.

At North Bend we draw level with a drive-up window at the Top Dog Espresso Company but, despite having a 'there in your hour of need' Saint Bernard for a logo, it's closed.

That's okay. Within 30 minutes we've traded their bright yellow wooden shack for a baby blue one decorated with a shoal of rainbow-coloured fish.

It's love at first bite for Bodie at Bandon Fish Market.

I'd read that dogs go crazy for their pepperoni-style salmon sticks and Bodie duly turns into a ravening beast in their presence.

'Mind my fingers!'

I buy him a couple more and a portion of chips for me and then lead us out along the wooden boardwalk, set with hand-carved artworks and surrounded by gleaming white sailing boats.

I'm cosy as can be in my peach mohair sweater and as we settle on a bench I tilt my face to the sun and luxuriate in its golden glow. Once again we have the place to ourselves and I realise that a sense of peace and appreciation is becoming the norm. Alone but not lonely. I check my body for twinges of sadness and Nathan-ness, and find none. Weird.

We sit a while longer and then, taking a peek in my guidebook, learn that Bandon used to be known as the Cranberry Capital of Oregon and before that, during the steamboat age, the Playground of the Pacific. Passengers sailing between Seattle and San Francisco would stop off for some fun ashore but a devastating fire in 1936 put paid to that and now the main appeal is a world-class golf course (steering Bodie well clear of that) and a rock formation called Howling Dog, which does indeed bear a striking resemblance to a Spaniel sitting on the sand with his nose to the sky.

From here we have a little mooch around the Old Town with its artsy stores, including The Cobbler's Bench and Washed Ashore, which has a window display inviting: *Give us your ocean debris and we'll make art to save the sea!*

It's starting to drizzle so I chance my arm at WinterRiver Books – 'You don't allow dogs inside, do you?'

'Yes, of course, come on in!'

I couldn't be more delighted. Bodie is thrilled too, eagerly tugging me to the Children's section. Really? Ah. He's after the soft grey tabby cat peering out from the back room.

'That's our stray, Bookish,' owner Grover tells me. 'Our store manager, Gina, first glimpsed him out the back door – he was very timid and would dart up the hill and hide amid the plants if he was spotted, but if the staff had the back door open while they ate their lunch he would return!' he smiles.

Before too long the green-eyed beauty would jump into their laps to be petted and he now has a shelter behind the store – with a bed and a warm blanket – that he calls home.

'If the store is quiet he will come all the way to the front counter but he is still very wary and retreats if a customer comes in.'

Especially if that customer is a nosey dog.

I tell Grover that I love the name Bookish: 'Devoted to reading and studying'.

'My wife Debby chose it. Bookish is never seen wandering around the rest of Old Town – he always stays close to his area behind the bookstore.'

'It's perfect,' I note, thinking how well cats and bookshops go together.

Moving Bodie on to the Animal section, I'm delighted to find multiple shelves stacked with dog books, including a bundle of discounted treasures that make their way into my arms.

On the way to the till there's a sepia greeting card I can't resist – a 1950s woman leaning on the bonnet of her car, frowning at a map with the caption, *'Where the heck is Easy Street?'*

On the way back to our car we pass a toyshop with a window display of almost life-size dog soft toys kitted out in Western attire – there's a Golden Retriever in a straw hat and red bandana chewing on a strand of dried grass, a Beagle with a leather waistcoat and a sheriff's badge, a white fluffy dog in a pink Stetson and a Rottweiler in cowboy chaps.

I'm peering in the doorway, half a toe inside, trying to see the price tags when the shopkeeper calls, 'Is your dog all wet?'

'Yes, sorry!' I go to back away but instead she invites us in and starts blotting Bodie with paper towels, making a lovely fuss of him.

I'm regretting not choosing Bandon as our base for the night. This is my favourite Oregon coast town so far. I purposely planned ahead so as not to miss the best bits but you can't always plan for how a place makes you feel. Or the fact that you catch yourself wondering, 'What would it be like to live here?'

But with fatigue setting in I realise we'd better hit the road – just one more hour and we'll reach our room for the night.

Or so I think...

Chapter 33
The Speeding Ticket

I'm bombing along the Oregon Coast Highway, loving the tree-dappled early evening light, when the 70 mph speed limit plummets to 35. I apply the brakes but, not having been to stunt school, don't quite slow in time and suddenly – *wah-wah* – here come the sirens and the police car and the not-so-casual invitation to pull over.

Bodie raises a brow as if to say, 'You want me to look remorseful or bite?'

I tell him to look remorseful and I'll work the English accent – it hasn't failed me yet.

The traffic cop is having none of it. He actually brags to me about the number of fines he's issued that day.

'I get nearly every car that comes through,' he puffs up. 'The last one was a family of six!'

I frown. Does he get extra points for a full vehicle?

He takes my licence and registration and heads back to his car to make his checks. I don't have a good feeling about this.

'The odds of him turning out to be a Strippagram are dwindling,' I tell Bodie, looking to him for support, but he's ducked out of sight. I'm on my own.

'All set?' I smile as the officer returns.

He's being extra pally now – keen to chat a while, find out where I'm from and hear more of my wacky accent. I would be more than happy to indulge him, if I wasn't now holding a piece of paper demanding $270 of our road-trip funds.

It really does seem a lot. I mean, it's not like there are any pedestrians to take out even if I wanted to. Nothing's open and he's the only human as far as the eye can see. (I suspect the community of 1,000 has used the stash of fine money to relocate to Florida.) Still, he's having a great time embodying what I imagine to be the town slogan: *'Come to Port Orford and get a speeding ticket!'*

After he's gone, I continue up the side street to get a closer look at what promises to be a beautiful sunset. Perhaps I'll have an epiphany here that I wouldn't have had without this diversion and then the $270 fine will be worth every cent. But the one bench is occupied by an elderly couple gazing out to sea, probably enjoying one last look before they too relocate to Palm Beach.

Maybe it's because we arrive after dark but our accommodation, though scenically waterside and considered a resort (at least by the person who named it), gives us the creeps. The room is spacious but that just gives Bodie all the more room to pace. We've had such a good run of sleep since that first unsettling night at the San Ysidro Ranch. Yes, there was a ridiculously early start in the Napa Valley but Bodie has taken all the ensuing accommodation switches in his stride. How can I blame him for having the jitters now when I do too? Every few minutes we look up at each other as if to say, '*What was that? Are you freaked out? I'm freaked out!*' and then spend the night clinging to each other, teeth chattering in anticipation of the axe about to slice through the door. Three times I get up to check that the car is still there, seeking reassurance that we'll have the means for a quick getaway in the morning but, now I come to think of it, repeatedly opening the door to welcome in the bogeyman.

Come sunrise you'd think we'd want to get the hell out of Dodge but we actually backtrack to an attraction we passed last night after closing time.

The Prehistoric Gardens are the passion project of sculptor and dinosaur enthusiast E. V. Nelson. He welcomed the public to his version of Jurassic Park in 1955 and went on to create 23 life-size replicas over the next 30 years. I thought it would liven up Bodie's morning walk – a few stegosaurs and pterodactyls to break up the giant ferns and skunk cabbages of this 300-year-old coastal rainforest.

'What do you think?' I ask.

Bodie eyes the long-necked, tail-trailing beasts with great suspicion, a couple of times turning back to make sure they are not advancing on him.

'Look at this!' I pause to read one of the wooden signs. 'Cynognathus – literally means dog-jawed.' I look between Bodie and the green-and-yellow reptile. 'I can't see it myself.'

It's actually too terrifying to even contemplate being amongst these animals for real – all those spiky crests and earth-quaking feet. I prefer the dopey *Flintstones* version of the time period, complete with dog-substitute Dino and his big, slurpy tongue.

As we come to the end of the loop, passing Mr Nelson's pride and joy – an 86-foot-long brachiosaurus – I watch Bodie's nose for a reaction but none is forthcoming. Sometimes I wonder about his sense of smell as he tiptoes up to a stone carving of a rabbit or indeed the statue of the dog mayor in Sunol, responding first to the shape, which then draws him in for a sniff. Perhaps because the forms here are so outlandish and unrecognisable he doesn't seem fazed. 'Ah, you've seen one T-Rex, you've seen them all.'

Still, a walk in nature is a walk in nature. I realise now that I like doing pretty much anything as long as it's with him. Equally he'll hop out of the car and roam around a quirky roadside attraction with the same enthusiasm as a car park in a strip mall. He's game. He's curious. He doesn't talk much. I like that in a travelling companion. He may be my favourite yet.

Back on the road we cross over the Rogue River Bridge, give a quick shudder as we pass last night's accommodation and then settle in for the easy 30-mile drive to our final port of call in Oregon. But within minutes I'm swerving into a gravelly lookout point, eager to get a closer look at the attention-grabbing diversity of Meyers Creek Beach.

The rock formations jutting from the water are striking – giant raggedy forms, some topped with greenery, others dark and pocked. Then there's the elephant's graveyard of blanched driftwood and the flutters of white birds, luring us across the grassy dunes down on to the flat, brown-grey sands. The beach itself is vast. Bodie may have already had his morning walk but nothing compares to a full-tilt run. I propel the ball with all my might and watch him race after it, occasionally surprising us both as he disappears into a rock pool. I chuckle as I watch him trying to grab the ball from the water's surface, looking like he's bobbing for apples. After a delicate sniff of the barnacles he moves closer to the frothy surf. The waves here don't move in one steady line but lap and overlap from all angles, prompting Bodie to dance at the unpredictability.

Every once in a while he comes to a halt and raises his chin to revel in the salty breeze, the wet sand reflecting a perfect mirror image as he strikes his 'Best in Show' pose.

And then he trots back over to me and starts digging, gleefully kicking up great clomps of damp sand.

This is a world away from the scowly dog at the Ester Lee beach. Here he is youthful, playful and full of vigour, which gives me a sense of immense satisfaction. I'd say that this and Carmel beach have been our two most heart-soaring shorelines.

I'm just gazing heavenward, following the powdery streaks across the expanse of blue, when Bodie emits a low growl – his grumpy old man alert. I scan the horizon for intruders and spy a white horse with a red-jacketed rider. A black dog scurries ahead of them, seemingly recceing the route, his slim legs going double speed as the horse lollops silently, all clip-clopping absorbed by the sand. Bodie is now as mesmerised as me by this movie-like scene and together we watch them traverse the curve of the bay, the rumply, pine-sprigged hills creating the perfect backdrop. I sigh and dig my hands deep into the sand, as if to anchor this memory forever.

I'll say one thing for this trip – it has made me seek out all things naturally beautiful. When arriving in a new town the old me would have homed in on the shops but now the prospect of an Azalea Park seems far more appealing.

I don't know if colour amplifies the joy of sniffing for Bodie but it's certainly an added bonus for me – the silky clusters of peach, coral and hot pink contrast so vibrantly with the bright green foliage and clear blue sky. This is Brookings, our last stop in Oregon, but it feels more like one of those hilly worlds from children's TV – all rainbow palettes and sunshine. Any minute now I'm going to start skipping. I am skipping! Bodie trots along beside me, occasionally diverting to bury his face in low-lying blooms.

As we take a moment to enjoy the gazebo overlooking the main lawn, my mind wanders to the time Nathan and I visited Santa Barbara's Botanic Garden... Typically women swoon at the flowers men present to them but I was swooning at his interest in the flowers – it was like walking with a Jane Austen hero the way he would draw my attention to the shape of a bough or a tiny flower nestled amid the moss. I'd never been with anyone who really noticed these kinds of details before. It's strange to think he's been so far from dry land for so long. He must be due back any day now. My stomach churns at the thought. Not that it's any of my business any more. Still, I can't help but wonder if he's thought of me while he's been gone. Even if he'd had a sudden impulse to call me he wouldn't have been able to while on a mission. I suppose it makes for a cleaner break this way – no contact, no 'I was just in the neighbourhood' excuses. Just distance and silence.

Bodie extends his front paws in a long stretch and then looks expectantly at me.

'Is that my cue for lunch?' I ask.

A quick panini at the Salty Dog Coffee Bar and we're on our way.

I've barely settled into my seat when we pass a sign welcoming us to California. Just like that, *Oregon is gone!*

I feel instantly queasy – we're on the homestretch now, no new state to act as a buffer between us and reality. Suddenly I find myself pulling over, this time on to a grassy verge.

I'm not ready!

I step out of the car, release Bodie from the back and then shuffle us to the cliff edge. It's a stunning vantage point but then they all have been, for mile upon unspoiled mile.

While Bodie snuffles at the undergrowth I turn and look back at Oregon. Did I get everything I needed to get? Was I paying enough attention? Am I sufficiently changed? Or at the very least better equipped to keep moving forward…

Bodie continues to root around, pleasantly oblivious to my soul-searching, focused only on this gift of an unscheduled stop with all its accompanying smells. I nod to myself as I watch

Chapter 34

Trees of Mystery

Back in the car and bombing along Highway 101 we repeatedly pass billboards advertising the SkyTrail – a glass bubble winching you high amid the redwoods, creaking and swaying as it goes. Every time I see the image I think what a terrible situation that would be for a dog. I mean, they are low-lying earth-snufflers, not designed to be dangled mid-air. But when we actually find ourselves confronted with the option to board, I am the one who is nervous and reluctant...

It was never the plan to stop at the Trees of Mystery attraction. We were aiming for the Tour Thru Tree. (Dogs like to pee on trees, humans like to drive through them.) But then we spied the giant roadside statues of a bearded lumberjack and a blue ox and veered over to take a snap.

Bodie looks hamster-sized next to the looming 49-foot logger. This is Paul Bunyan – new to me but so famous in American folklore for his powerful brawn that he was immortalised and animated in a Disney musical in 1958.

Now that we're on foot it's easy for curiosity about the Trees of Mystery to lure us forward, through an archway and into the woodland.

Our initial progress up the slope is slowed by a group of enthusiastic Amish teenagers moving as a 30-strong pack. We pick up the pace to get ahead of them and then find ourselves 'pausing with reverent eye' beside the Cathedral Tree, which is actually a grouping of seven or so slender trunks, and a popular wedding setting.

> *Sink down, Oh traveler, on your knees,*
> *God stands before you in these trees.*

Although Bodie and I remain upright, we like the sentiment on the sign. Perhaps it's a newfound desire to ascend closer to heaven that has Bodie straining towards the boarding platform of the SkyTrail.

I look ruefully at the operator.

'I don't suppose you get too many dogs wanting to go on this?' I grimace. 'It's probably not wise, is it? Or safe?'

'Oh, it's perfectly fine,' he responds with cheer. 'They go on all the time.'

I feel queasy resistance. Are we seriously considering this?

I never thought of myself as someone who was afraid of heights until I went zip lining in Costa Rica and lost my nerve at the wobble of the towering platforms – I went to grab the tree trunk to steady myself and was told there was some kind of poisonous ant infestation so not to touch. I felt so faint I ended up having to 'taxi' the rest of the way attached to a pro. No more treetop swinging for me, I swore. And yet here we are.

Bodie looks pleadingly at me.

'How long does it take to get to the top?'

'Seven minutes.'

Not bad.

'And don't worry if it pauses on the way up – sometimes it takes a bit longer to load a family with a stroller.'

'Right,' I nod. 'So no need to panic if it stops. It will start again.'

'Yes.'

Still I hesitate. It's enclosed, I tell myself. It's seven minutes. Bodie asks for so little of me. And so we step aboard.

The second the door closes behind us, Bodie starts to look regretful. So now that's two of us. The higher we rise, the more he paces, and it's a very confined space – two bench seats and a patch of metal flooring between. But then we pass a cabin making its way down and the couple within are holding a Dachshund in their lap. The Dachshund looks at Bodie, Bodie looks at the Dachshund and it's almost like he conveys, 'It's cool, bro, no worries. Totally worth the view at the top.'

We hang on and then, oh the bliss of being released back on to solid ground. Climbing up on to the viewing platform we gaze out over layer upon layer of mountain greenery, reaching all the way to the sparkling sea.

America loves a lookout point. All across the country there are signs saying, 'Ooh you're going to love this – take the next left and have a good gawp.' They never disappoint.

But now what?

I hear a couple enquiring about the possibility of walking back down. Apparently it's doable but slippery after all the rain. Envisioning gloopy mud and twisted ankles we board again.

'Just seven minutes.'

This time Bodie has an expression close to wonder as he looks out of the glass at the sun-glow leaves.

'I suppose this is pretty amazing!' I sigh as he tries to climb on to my lap.

Once reunited with the soil, the most unique aspect of the attraction begins. Every corner we weave around reveals another wood sculpture – bold, rough-hewn and often comical designs mingling with the ridged bark and fern borders.

Max the Axe shows a muscular man about to hack steel into a tree trunk, his thighs and forearms highlighted with green moss. I tip my hat to Ol Redthumb Robbie with his big beard and Sawdust McPherson with his big boots, then Bodie sniffs around a carving of a giant floppy-eared dog chomping on a stick, his blunt nose larger than Bodie's entire head.

My brother would love all this. He's a genius wood carver and stone sculptor. It would be so great if you could beam in friends and family to share specific moments. My mum would have loved the Azalea Park, my dad the golf course we passed at Bandon Dunes. For the teeniest moment I feel homesick. I tend to only get this way when I'm feeling emotionally vulnerable and crave those most familiar of comforts. So why am I feeling this now? I check over my shoulder, as if foreboding is sneaking up on me, and then shake it off. *It's just nerves*, I decide. Just a harmless flutter of nerves.

As we exit through the gift shop, I resist the lure of fresh fudge and Bigfoot slippers and move us swiftly on to the Tour Thru Tree. (It has to be called Tour Thru rather than Drive-Thru as that name has already been taken by a rival attraction three hours further down the coast.)

I love quirky stops like this, even if you have to go miles out of your way and the actual activity takes but a minute or two.

We pay at the gate, wend our way into the forest and then reach a clearing with a few cars ahead of us. Each takes their turn – pulling midway through the tree, jumping out, taking pictures and moving on. It's amazing that so many of these roadside curiosities sprung up in the 1960s and 1970s when you'd think they were entirely devised for Facebook and Instagram.

While waiting our turn I scan the leaflet and am surprised to learn that the tree is still alive. This seems like an apt metaphor – you can have a great big chunk of yourself missing, even at root level, and you can survive! Even more than that, this seeming hole in your soul could be the very thing that makes you unique or special.

Perhaps I need to rethink the notion that, when someone leaves you, there is less of you than there was before you met.

I'm certainly pleased to look up and find all the other vehicles gone – we now have the place to ourselves. Less is indeed more.

Parking up, I let Bodie have a sniff around the base of the tree. Though it may sound odd, I thought he might get a kick out of having the opportunity to pee on such a big tree, as if it would offer some canine bragging rights, but he doesn't feel inclined. So together we walk through what is essentially a wooden tunnel – 7.4 feet wide and nearly 10 feet high. From this angle it's easy to see how the redwoods earned their name.

The damp wood is a lovely rusty red, dusted in green with a casing of scroll-like bark. It once had its top blown off in a mighty storm and bears the charred scars of a forest fire but still it stands, 725 years on – 725!

Before we leave I stare up and up at the tree and then out into the seemingly impenetrable forest, wondering how the first explorers ever found their way. And then it strikes me: it's not just those men who were pioneers – no one exactly like you has ever come this way before so if you want to create happiness that is a true custom-fit, you have to forge your own path.

As the Spanish poet Antonio Machado said, 'Travellers, there is no path, paths are made by walking.'

I think it's time I let go of the notion that I'm supposed to know what happens next. If I haven't been there already, how could I possibly know?

There was a time when I'd find it fascinating to see my life take an unexpected turn. If anything, that was the big thrill of it – anything but predictability! I wonder, could I relearn replacing worry with curiosity? Defeat with hope?

In the early days of being with Nathan, when he was training in Chicago, I went to see a hypnotherapist because I was having trouble sleeping, always fretting about the outcome of our long-distance relationship.

She said, 'You're a writer – can't you use your imagination for good instead of conjuring all these worst-case scenarios?'

She had a point. I was always 'awfulising' about him. Always visualising tears and heartache. It was like I was using the powers of *The Secret* in reverse.

Clearly it makes more sense to focus on what you want, rather than what you don't.

And now, more than anything, I want a cosy night's sleep.

Our stop-offs have got us behind schedule but I think it will be worth pushing through to our planned resting place, so on we go, past Big Lagoon, Fickle Hill and Eureka, where we spy a giant wall mural featuring a Husky in a Hawaiian shirt.

Just 10 miles beyond the entrance to the Avenue of the Giants we exit the freeway and feel our way through the darkness to the Benbow Historic Inn. Compared to our last miserable motel this feels like an enchanted castle. Or, more specifically, a Tudor-style mansion with a touch of Kellerman's resort from *Dirty Dancing*, on account of its verdant setting. Bodie and I hurry up the main staircase where we're greeted by a pair of stone hounds bearing baskets of fruit. I help myself to an imaginary grape and then cross the threshold into another world.

'Oh wow!'

Our hearts warm at the scene that greets us, and not just because there's a sooted stone hearth flickering beguiling yellow flames behind a medieval wrought-iron screen. Next to a set of wheezy bellows a court jester is captured mid-dance, complete with curly-toed satin shoes and tricorn hat dangling red baubles. Over by the chess set an enormous teddy bear slumps with a low-slung belly and off-kilter crown. I feel like we've come to stay at the home of some eccentric uncle with royal ancestry.

'I knew I should've worn my ermine-trimmed cape,' I tut, tugging at my fleece.

I may feel a little travel-worn and raggle-taggle as I approach the reception desk but I take this as a good sign – I've looked equally dishevelled the last two nights and still felt wildly overdressed while checking in.

The good news is that the Benbow Inn has a room for us – the bad news is that we've missed dinner. I must look sufficiently crestfallen because they offer to rustle up something to silence my growling tum. Frankly, I'd make a meal of the pillow mints if it spared us getting back into the car.

The usual chore of unloading and transferring our essentials is made infinitely more bearable by the room itself – we enter directly from our own private terrace, which overlooks sprawling lawns and the stoic arches of an old stone bridge. Inside, the colour scheme is a soothing array of sages, clarets and golds, offset with warm wood. There are Art Deco lamps, framed etchings and intriguing marble-topped bedside tables that look like they have been procured from an old pharmacy. There's even a gold B embroidered on the decorative pillow.

For one night at least, we're home.

My dinner of bread rolls and dessert cake is delivered on a heavy tray with linen napkins and I raise a glass of wine to Bodie as he crunches through his kibble.

'You know, I think we're going to be all right,' I decide. 'The worst is over.'

All we need to do is keep seeking out life's treasures and with Bodie's discerning nose and my ability to Google, I think we'll do very nicely.

When we wake in the morning, early but rested, there is none of the usual rush-tension. Motels offer little incentive to linger but this Egyptian cotton cocoon is something to savour.

Bodie and I enjoy a luxurious stretch and then lie there feeling safe and spoiled. It's moments like this that make me wish I had allowed for a little more flexibility in my schedule. I'd like to spend the whole day here. I don't know that we'd even stray further than our terrace. I just want to prolong this feeling – it's wonderful to see Bodie so relaxed. But then I remember our special afternoon appointment – a Graduation Ceremony at the Guide Dogs for the Blind facility three hours south in San Rafael.

'To breakfast and a-walking we go!'

Our exploration of the grounds takes us first to the trailer park with its own secure dog area and then down to the Eel River, a low-lying pebbly expanse lined with evergreens. There's no sign of modern life and I feel we're like a couple of prospectors about to start panning for gold. But first Bodie decides to make his deposit.

Midway through, my phone rings. Tangling with the leash, bag and my jacket pocket, I let the phone slip from my hand, sending it clattering on the rocks just millimetres from the water's edge.

'Oh for goodness' sake – hello?' I put it to my ear without checking the identity of the caller.

'Hello you.'

My faffing comes to an instant halt. It's Nathan.

Chapter 35
Guardian Angels

'Wh-where are you?' I falter, feeling suddenly light-headed.

'Russia,' he replies. 'I've just got a minute.'

'*Russia?*' My mind immediately summons the Facebook picture he posted with some fellow sailors and a stunning modelesque creature in some scenic square, and I hear myself say, 'Are the women there really as beautiful as they say?'

Because that's what I really want to know, with just a few precious seconds to communicate.

'They're all right.'

Great. Immediately I have come across jealous and needling.

'Where are you?' he asks.

'Northern California. I took a road trip—'

'I'm in the States.'

'What?' I frown in confusion.

'I'm not in Russia. I'm back in the US.'

I find myself looking around me like he might surprise me, even though there's barely a soul on earth who knows where I am right now. I don't even really know where I am.

'Wh-why did you say you were in Russia?' I question, disorientated.

'I was just teasing.' He's clearly smiling down the phone.

I am not. I feel like I'm being toyed with.

'I'm in Virginia,' he continues. 'But next week...'

'Yes?'

'I'm coming to LA.'

He may be expecting a whoop of joy from me but instead I feel backed into a corner, my mind in turmoil.

'I was thinking maybe you could pick me up at the airport...'

I feel faint. He's talking about an actual, specific meeting point. And choosing me to be the first person he sees. Is this a date? Are we back on? I go to speak but it's too late, his time is up.

'I'll call you Wednesday,' he says. 'I'll be able to talk more then.'

Wednesday. Two days.

'Gotta go!'

After ending all our phone calls with 'Love you', 'Love you too' it seems strange to hold back and say nothing affectionate, nothing relating to how I feel. All I manage is a snatched, 'Bye!'

For a while I stand in shock.

Eventually I notice Bodie looking up at me, as if to say, 'Well?'

'I don't know what to say,' I shrug. 'I don't know what just happened.'

I feel as if I drive the next 200 miles with a permanent frown on my face. Usually, I'm taking in every tree and roadside curiosity – today I'm weaving along the Redwood Highway in a state of distracted irritation, oblivious to its majesty.

Why does his call feel like such an intrusion? It's as if I was just beginning to feel the benefits of a detox and then wolfed a plate of junk food, doing myself a terrible disservice. It's typical, isn't it? When things were going swimmingly (in my mind) he wanted to break up. Now that I'm finally coming to terms with being apart, he's found a nifty way to spoil that. I feel all pouty and indignant – *and he thinks he can just call and I'll drop everything!* This is not who I want to be. I don't want to be the girl in a constant state of relationship rage. Suddenly the sadness I've been bearing for months is caught in the glare of reality – is this man really the 'dream guy' I present him as? Was it easy to call him that because he left? Is the truth more complicated? I mean, I'm sitting here, staring down the road, wishing he hadn't called when isn't that what I've been wanting all along – for him to reach for me again? I was missing all his tenderness but what I heard on the phone was cockiness. I didn't like it. But I used to. I used to laugh as I told people he had the Louisiana manners of a Southern gentleman and the arrogance of a Texan. (The places he was born and brought up.) Can I really have changed so much in these past days that I no longer want the same things? I'm certainly feeling more ambushed than adored right now. And irritated. So. Very. Irritated.

How much of that is with myself? With all my relationship choices over the years. I don't want to feel like this any more. I don't want to feel muddle-headed and jumble-hearted. There has to be a better way...

I take a deep breath and try to reconnect with Bodie and our road trip – getting sentimental around the Napa Valley recalling Bodie's carefree romp through Chappellet Vineyard. And then, as we pass Santa Rosa, I picture myself in the darkened screening room at the Snoopy Museum, watching the old footage of Charles M. Schulz.

'You have to drive your own way,' I murmur.

Suddenly I wish I could relive all our trip – take one more turn around, get the good feeling back again.

But that's the mixed blessing of travel: you get to have all these wonderful experiences but you can't hold on to any of them. All too soon they become drive-by memories. And all you can do is keep moving forward, on to the next.

Here we are now, in San Rafael – home to the late Tupac Shakur who, along with rapper Dr. Dre, created my all-time favourite hip-hop song 'California Love'. There are probably few things in life as ridiculous as me mouthing lyrics about tracks hitting my eardrum like a slug to my chest but it always conduces me to 'shake it' on the dancefloor. It's also what I tell Bodie to do when he emerges from a body of water.

After a thoroughly un-gangsta bite at Panera Bread, I drop Bodie at his daycare appointment and head to the Guide Dogs for the Blind facility on Los Ranchitos Road. I was not expecting to feel at odds with myself in this setting. I predicted abundant bonhomie (and bon-doggie) along with a renewed sense of determination to make a positive, meaningful contribution to the world. But instead I'm sitting in the car park, hands still on the steering wheel, trying to get myself sufficiently together to join the tour group.

Heartache seems such a trivial emotion compared to what these brave souls have endured and surmounted, yet you just need to look to the arts for acknowledgement of the pain of being rejected or trifled with in love – all your Heathcliffs and Cathys, Romeos and Juliets, Laras and Dr Zhivagos driven half-mad by their desires or separations. Of course it's all a terrible waste of time and it brings on too many tears and bad decisions, but there's no denying how disorientating a troubled heart can be.

I say all this to excuse in some way my distraction on the tour. I keep dipping in and out – taking in fragmented information as I come up for air and then the words become muffled as I sink back down again, lost to the swirl of anxiety about the impact of Nathan's return. Already I've lost the ability to be present. I feel as though I am divided into two: one person going through the motions in the real world (following the group, nodding at the guide) and the other fretting inside my head.

I do know this: Guide Dogs for the Blind receives no government funding – everything is made possible through the support of volunteers and donors. The services provided for clients are free of charge, including extensive post-graduation support and financial assistance for veterinary care, if needed. I find this amazing – that such a renowned institution as Guide Dogs for the Blind is run entirely on goodwill and generosity. And they're doing it in style: smart buildings set around a landscaped central area with plenty of sun-filtering trees and paw-pleasing grass. They breed from their own stock of Labrador Retrievers, Golden Retrievers and Lab/Golden crosses, chosen for their 'excellent temperament, intelligence and health'. The kennels are primarily concrete, which I wasn't expecting – I thought it was all going to be one big Andrex ad. But I must say I have great admiration for those raising the puppies: those people who bring home a cutesy furball, spend over 50 weeks transforming it into the ultimate assistance dog and then begin the process again with a new pup.

'Does it get any easier, saying goodbye each time?' I ask one of the trainers.

'No,' she shakes her head. 'But it's always worth it.'

Time to take a seat in the auditorium.

Before the ceremony begins, a video plays, showing a young woman's life before and after having a Guide Dog. I'm struck by her observation that she can now do everything so much faster – imagine inching your way along a street in the darkness compared to being able to pace confidently, knowing your dog can see a clear path ahead. And what a gap there is between feeling vulnerable and alone compared to being part of a team – always having someone by your side that has your best interests at heart.

Never has trust seemed a more vital component of a relationship. Do I have that with Nathan? Or am I walking with my arms outstretched, unable to see what lies ahead, trying not to bang my knee – or my heart. Even if it's an illusion that you and your partner will endure all odds, at the very least you want to feel like you are in it together. I used to find comfort in his presence but now even our impending phone call feels like a threat to my wellbeing.

And then the ceremony begins. I see the people who have lovingly trained their Guide Dog from puppyhood step forward and hand their charge over to the new owner with such grace and joy, knowing that they are doing the right thing – *even though their heart is simultaneously breaking.*

Each time they do a little speech, confirming that they feel this particular dog is the perfect match for the personality of the new owner. Because these things matter. A good match is what will determine the success of the duo.

I find myself nodding emphatically at this as I dab my eyes.

This ceremony concludes two weeks of 24/7 on-site training for the clients and dogs, who will now go home and start their new life together – a life with 'greater inclusion, opportunity and independence' all brought about by 'optimising the unique capabilities of people and dogs'.

I clap fervently and then heave a long sigh of admiration. This is such a humbling experience. I want to do something more to be of use in the world but for now I head to the gift shop to make my donation, pausing en route in the courtyard to count my blessings – always a smarter choice than listing what you haven't got.

I'm a little early to pick up Bodie from his play group so I take the opportunity to tap an email to Sam and catch up on her plans to move in with Marcus, renting out her Greenwich flat and relocating to his newer, bigger pad in Surrey. She seems to be speeding along – happily and doubt-free – in the fast lane. But when I update her on my situation, she's as conflicted as I am about how to proceed.

On the one hand she says, 'I just think it's all too bizarre that it didn't work out for you two. There's still heart-mileage in the relationship, don't you think? It was a huge shift in your life meeting such a wonderful man – it seems a shame not to get together and see if there is any possibility in making another go of it...'

When I detail my concerns she says, 'B, it's your life and you can be as happy as you want. You are worth millions to me and to yourself – be happy in everything you do, and if you don't feel happy about this then thank him for his time in your life and let him go. Then someone who you can be happy with will step up.'

Both things she says make sense. But pulling equally in two different directions leaves me at an impasse.

Of course, some things in life are splendidly straightforward.

'It always does my heart good to be reunited with you,' I tell Bodie as we head back to the car. 'And I want you to know that I'm always going to take as good care of you as you do of me.'

Which also means not putting him in any emotionally screwy situations. If ever I needed a reminder that dogs are in tune with the feelings of their owners, today has been it.

Chapter 36

Travels with Charley

We overnight at the sleek, spacious Aloft in the Silicon Valley town of Cupertino, aka Apple HQ. The iconic symbol appears on every street corner and, after such an emotionally charged day, it feels an appealingly neutral place to lay our heads.

But morning comes all too soon.

'Housekeeping!' There's a rattle at door.

I call out that we'll be leaving shortly but the housekeeper apparently doesn't hear because she barges in, causing Bodie to spring to his feet and bark in surprise, which prompts her to scream, 'Pit bull!' and start running down the hall. Bodie thinks this is some kind of fun 'chase me' game and takes off after her, with me hot on his heels. This is the closest I've ever got to starting the day with a jog and I'm clearer than ever on why I don't make that a habit.

After all this flustering hysteria, I end up leaving behind the very item this town is famous for: my Apple laptop, still charging by the bed. Worse yet, we're three hours down the road before I realise this.

'Oh my god – noooooo!'

I swerve over to the side of the road and call reception, heart yammering. After a reality TV-style pause they reveal that they have it safe and will forward it on to me in LA. It all seems rather dicey but what can I do? Turning back now would add six more hours' driving to the day and Bodie could not withstand that, even if I could.

If only I'd felt the loss when we'd stopped for lunch in Salinas.

Salinas has a population the same size as Slough but is nicknamed the Salad Bowl of the World on account of its grand contribution to the nation's lettuce production. It rates as the top city in California for air cleanliness but loses ground by having the highest youth homicide rates in the state, due to gang crime. So why come here? Well, Salinas is the birthplace (and burial place) of Pulitzer and Nobel prize-winning scribe John Steinbeck, author of *The Grapes of Wrath, Of Mice and Men* and, most relevant to Bodie and me, *Travels With Charley.*

This memoir of the all-American road trip he took with his Standard Poodle Charley was published in 1962 but, over 50 years on, how's this for poignancy: 'For all our interwoven breeds drawn from every part of the ethnic world, we are a nation, a new breed.'

American.

He believes that regardless of where you live in this vast country or what your country of origin may be, being 'American' overrides all else.

Interesting.

We had hoped to dine at Steinbeck's boyhood home – the prettily turreted, Victorian-style Steinbeck House. There's a chintzy dining room open to the public but, with no outdoor seating, we are obliged to divert to Elli's Great American Restaurant, which has a scaled-down Statue of Liberty in the front porch.

Stepping into the light-filled, dog-friendly conservatory, I half expect to see the Golden Girls eating cheesecake amid the white wicker and topiary. It seems a world away from the gritty realism of Steinbeck's stories but then again, we are just half an hour from Carmel. Talk about being *East of Eden*. What a difference a fork in the road makes – one route leads to a life of struggle, the other to extreme privilege. Be careful of the choices you make in haste – 'Yes' and 'No' are such little words but look what they can do. Yes to picking Nathan up at the airport and falling back into his beautiful arms? Or no, resisting his charms and continuing on this new path, not knowing where it will lead?

'What can I get you?'

I look up at the chirpy waiter. Oh to be able to order a portion of emotional clarity with a side of restraint! Instead I settle for a Zucchini Madness sandwich and an iced tea, and return to *Travels With Charley*.

Steinbeck undertook the 10,000-mile trip for two main reasons – one, to get back in touch with the American people so he could better write about them and two (according to his son) because, at 58 and with a heart condition, he wanted to see his homeland once more before he died.

When he asked his wife Elaine if he could take Charley with him on the trip she said, 'What a good idea. If you get into any kind of trouble, Charley can go get help.' To which he replied, 'Elaine, Charley isn't Lassie.'

He didn't plan his route around Charley as I have with Bodie, but the Poodle in question does get to bark at bears at Yellowstone, refuses to urinate on the redwood trees (ditto Bodie) and gives up a can of dog food for the coyotes of the Mojave Desert.

I reach for a pair of sweet potato fries – one for me, one for Bodie – and try to stifle the wish that he could talk because I want to read out so many lines to him and say, 'Doesn't this sound just like us?', especially when Steinbeck talks of 'a burning desire to go, to move, to get under way, any place away from any Here'.

Not to mention the futility of taking notes because 'if I do, I either lose them or can't read them'.

Every time, mate, every time!

Back on the 101 Freeway, I become aware that we're passing alongside so many of the highlights from our journey up – Big Sur, Moonstone Beach, Cambria – and I get the distinct feeling that I'm driving headlong into an either/or dilemma: either I choose Nathan or I choose all the natural wonders that Bodie has opened my eyes to. Which is strange – why can't I have Nathan *and* this newfound rapture? Why does it feel that if I open my heart to Nathan, I close it to everything else?

As I pass Santa Maria I recall my favourite celebrity life coach – Marie Forleo – recommending that, whenever you have a tricky decision to make, you should 'check in with your inner organs' to get some clarity.

'The screens, Nurse Jones!'

I take a deep breath, exhale and then picture being with Nathan. Immediately I feel constricted, on edge, uncertain, troubled, even nauseous. Hmmm...

And then I reflect back on how I felt driving Big Sur – expansive, zinging with optimism and feeling like I needed to up the ante, dream bigger, wilder, freer...

And so I have to ask myself, now that I've broken the cycle of being at the mercy of my own neediness, why on earth would I want to return to that state? Always waiting and pleading and reacting.

I look to Bodie for insight but he's out of sight – lying down and snoozing.

I turn the radio on and then off again. My insides are churning, as if something is processing and changing within me. The niggling question seems to be, 'Even if I know the right thing to do, have I changed enough to be able to do it?'

Just thinking of Nathan's call tomorrow, I feel a flurry of nerves as if I'm awaiting test results. How curious that even though the decision is in my hands, I still don't feel I can predict the outcome.

It comes to something when you can't trust yourself with your own wellbeing.

On the upside, there is no better place to postpone reality than Solvang, a Danish-themed village tucked away in the Santa Ynez Valley, brimming with so much hygge it feels like a toy town come to life.

Chapter 37
A Fairy-Tale Ending

We check into a motel strung with fairy lights and guarded by a chunky wooden Viking, then stroll past The Little Mermaid restaurant, a windmill with red sails and a cluster of cutesy boutiques that look like they should be run by the Elves and the Shoemaker.

Solvang was founded in 1911 by Danish immigrants fleeing the chill of the East Coast (most of them had settled in states like Minnesota and Iowa) and this home-from-home world has become a major tourist attraction, recently making the top-ten list of best historic small towns in America by *USA Today*. The name is Danish for 'sunny fields' and the weather is indeed glorious but that doesn't diminish the festive vibe. In fact, I'm just peering in the window of the Jule Hus ('Celebrating Christmas year-round since 1967!') and cooing over a wispy-bearded Nutcracker army when Bodie pulls me over to a grassy area with a bronze bust centrepiece.

'Hans Christian Andersen!' I smile, taking in the features of a man I always pictured as Danny Kaye, ever since he donned the storyteller's cap in the musical of the same name.

His best-known fairy tales include *The Ugly Duckling*, *Thumbelina* and *The Emperor's New Clothes* but I decide the most appropriate story for Bodie is *The Tinderbox*, telling of a soldier's encounter with three dogs, sitting on chests of copper, silver and gold...

'The first dog he meets has eyes as big as teacups, the second has eyes as big as mill wheels and the third has eyes as big as round towers!' I say, looking into Bodie's glossy brown marbles.

The way to summon them is to strike a match on the tinderbox and then, akin to Aladdin's lamp, a dog will appear and ask, 'What are my lord's commands?' I wonder what I would wish for, given the opportunity. Would it even be Nathan now? It seems such a horrible cliché – being the woman wishing for a man to love her. Perhaps it would be better to summon my true love rather than persuade a half-hearted soul? Or should I simply ask for acceptance of the situation?

I crouch down beside Bodie. Maybe my wish has already come true: this furry fella is everything I didn't know I wanted or needed. And so much more.

And just to prove the point, he then leads me to the most perfectly apt final dinner destination for our dog-themed road trip: the Wandering Dog Wine Bar.

A thorough sniff around the terracotta pots on the patio reveals a dog made of corks and straw with big, green wine bottle bases for eyes.

'Like something from *The Tinderbox*!' I gasp, and then usher Bodie under a burgundy awning and into the warm interior.

The other wine drinkers and tasters are perched on tall chairs at the bar but we make a beeline for the squishy sofa so I can be at the same level as Bodie. And he, in turn, level with my cheese and cracker selection.

As I sip my Syrah, I learn about how the Wandering Dog was named after a certain rescue pup named Mazzey: bar owners Jack and Susan Williams got her as a companion for their 'rambunctious' Newfoundland and initially she seemed content enough to relax at the family home. But then one night a wild storm blew down the garden fence and she got to meet the neighbours for the first time. Her bond was so instant with their two little boys that when the fence was mended, Mazzey nudged through some loose boards to get back to them. No sooner was that hole repaired than a second appeared. Jack fixed the fence a dozen times before giving in and installing a doggy door between the two yards. Over time Mazzey's social circle extended beyond the kiddiewinks to the entire neighbourhood and it is said locals could set their clocks by her daily visits.

I could see Bodie making house calls in a similar fashion, lapping up the extra attention, though I'm not quite sure how precise his timekeeping would be.

'Well, who's this handsome fella?'

Off he goes now, straining towards the outstretched hands of a young couple.

The three of us humans end up talking dogs for the rest of the evening and I find myself brimful of that buoyant contentment that comes from communing with strangers and thus feeling more connected to the world at large, as opposed to clinging to one person like a lifeline.

'So, buddy, are you ready to head home tomorrow?' I ask Bodie as we amble back to the motel.

'Home?' His ears prick up.

'That's right – one last drive and we'll have racked up over two thousand miles.'

No sooner are we in the door of our room than he's rolling on the floor in a seemingly delirious state.

'Are we celebrating?' I ask as I crouch down beside him.

He rolls over and offers up his tummy. I run my hands over its pale golden down, patting the arch of his chest and then grooving my nails on his rib area until his eyes close in sweet surrender.

'Come on, time for one last sleep.'

As we climb into our sixteenth bed of the trip, I recall another Hans Christian Andersen story from my childhood: *The Princess and the Pea*. No amount of mattresses could cushion the niggling lump of the pea. I know that feeling. And yet... tonight when Bodie and I cosy up, his body aligned with my leg conveying warmth and togetherness, I don't feel anxious about tomorrow being our last day or the fact that Nathan is due to call.

I very nearly feel all right.

One of the perks of staying at the Solvang Inn is that you get a little ticket for a complimentary pastry and hot beverage at Olsen's Bakery & Coffee Shop, just across the street.

I don't know if I can think of a nicer way to start the day than contemplating hundreds of flaky, twisty, puffy, strudely, sugar-dusted delights. I make my selection and then take my styrofoam cup of coffee and sit with Bodie at one of the dinky little tables where we bask in the new day sunshine.

I've just taken my second bite of Danish when my phone rings and I am compelled to press answer with sticky, cherry-jam fingers.

'Hello!'

'Hey!'

I find myself smiling – no, *beaming* – at the sound of Nathan's voice. Something has shifted. I don't feel threatened any more – there is a warmth and a playfulness to his tone that propels me straight back to our gleeful early days. Plus, how could anything bad happen in Solvang?

'So, do you want to pick me up at the airport?' I can hear the teasing confidence in his voice. He knows what I'm going to answer – how can I resist the man I love?

'Of course!' My heart whoops, all wariness and concern falling away. 'Just tell me the time and date and I'll be there.'

Suddenly, it seems so easy – all this angst for nothing, everything is going to be okay! What was I worried about? What a drama queen! And to think—

'Just to be clear...' he begins.

'Yes?'

'Nothing has changed. I still can't make you any promises. My commitment is to the Navy – I must keep myself fully available to them, first and foremost.'

My stomach plummets 50 floors. Even though I'm securely seated, I feel a disorientating thud.

'It would just be so nice to see you, to have some fun...'

So there we are: this is a booty call. A long-distance, plan-ahead booty call.

'If you're okay with that?' he asks.

That's when I notice Bodie nudging at my knee, tilting his head sideways to lap up the pastry flakes that have crumbled on to my leg.

Crumbs – here I am settling for crumbs again!

'Actually...' I falter, digging deep for the resolve to take the right turn. I have to do this... I have to say this. 'I'm sorry, Nathan. I was mistaken. I won't be able to pick you up after all.'

'You don't want to see me?'

'Of course I do, you know I do, but it would be too disruptive to go through it all again.' My heart wrenches at the mere thought. 'To see you and feel everything and then for you to leave...' My voice quavers. 'I truly appreciate your honesty and I think it's great that you can compartmentalise your feelings but I can't. I'm not made that way. I just can't do it.'

Silence.

And then, 'So that's your decision?'

'It is,' I say. 'I think it's the right one. I'm sure you understand?'

'Yes.' His voice is small now.

I want to reach down the phone and hug him. This is ridiculous! We should be together – we want to be together! What are we playing at, turning our backs on each other?

'Okay, well...'

We trail off with a goodbye that is equal parts uncertainty and finality.

As the line clicks off, my stomach lurches. '*What have I done?*'

I grab Bodie's leash, hurry us back to the room and brace myself for the tsunami flood of tears.

But it doesn't happen.

I remain beside the door, looking around as if I might find a clue amid the dated furnishings. Have I short-circuited emotionally? I look at my watch. It's getting close to check-out time – if I want to have a breakdown I need to do it pronto.

Still nothing.

Perhaps I'm in shock. This isn't like me not to cry. I always cry.

And then a possibility occurs to me – *is this what making a good decision feels like?*

Is this the great reward for forgoing instant gratification in favour of long-term wellbeing? I still feel a little swimmy but, oddly, not all at sea.

I didn't think I had it in me to say no. Not just to him but to the part of me that is always reaching for love, regardless of the painful consequences. Of course it's not a finite no to love. It's not a 'never again!' – just a no to this man making this offer. An offer that would make me feel worse. So now I don't have to feel worse. I can feel something else instead.

Wow.

'We've done it!' I turn and embrace Bodie. 'We've done exactly what we set out to do: we took a road trip to a better place!'

Suddenly, going home doesn't feel like a drag because now we've got a whole new life to live.

I give Bodie a sideways glance as we board the car.

'You know, there's actually a town called Bodie, up near Yosemite National Park.'

He cocks his head. 'Is that right?'

'It's a ghost town so you can't actually stay there but it's just a couple of hours from Lake Tahoe. I've always wanted to go there...'

He smiles. I smile.

'Just sayin'...'

Bodie and Belinda have since visited 30 US states together and now run a dog travel website called Bodie on the Road.

About the Author

Belinda Jones is a magazine journalist turned bestselling author and award-winning blogger.

Belinda has sold over half a million copies of her escapist, travel-themed novels, taking readers on romantic journeys from Italy to Tahiti. She especially loved the in-depth cake research for *The Travelling Tea Shop*, but her career highlight was appearing on the *Sunday Times* Top 10 non-fiction chart alongside her writing hero Bill Bryson, the man who inspired her first American road trip.

Belinda and Bodie are currently exploring the muddy wonders of Devon but their hearts belong to the paradise island of Coronado in California where they would often see dolphins and shirtless Navy SEALS on their morning walks.

Ultimately, Belinda's ambition is to open a Dog Ranch in Colorado where rescue pups can roam freely by day and then enjoy a campfire dinner before being lulled to sleep by a cowgirl singing Doris Day tunes under the stars.

About the Dog

Bodie was picked up as a stray in gangland Los Angeles, rescued by Pryor's Planet (run by Richard Pryor's widow Jennifer) and adopted by British writer Belinda Jones.

There is endless speculation about Bodie's breed heritage – he has the purple tongue of a Chow Chow, the underbite of a Bulldog, but most closely resembles a Carolina Dog aka the American Dingo.

Bodie loves romping on the beach, crunching carrots and dropping down in the middle of the street to wriggle and writhe on his back, ever hopeful of a tummy rub.

His ambition is to stay at the Dog Bark Park Inn in Cottonwood, Idaho – a 30-foot-high wooden guest-house in the shape of a Beagle.

About the Blog

The Bodie on the Road blog is your guide to tail-wagging travels.

As well as a multitude of photos from this California–Oregon road trip, Bodie on the Road offers:

- Dog-friendly Destination Guides – to scenic spots in the US and the UK.
- Dog-Walking Fashion – including dog-motif sweaters and matching looks for pups and people.
- Bodie's Bookshelf – dog-themed reads ranging from novels to memoirs to travel guides.
- On The Road with… – insightful interviews with Instagram dog stars and pet industry celebrities.
- Dog Treats – pet travel mutt-haves!
- Dog Tips – including car travel with canines and how to take the best holiday snaps of your four-legged friend.
- Plus lots of surprise fun posts like The 10 Cutest St Bernard Gifts at Geneva Airport and The 12 Most Scenic Poop Bag Dispensers in America.

www.bodieontheroad.com
Instagram: @bodieontheroad

Top Tips for Tail-Wagging Travels

Ten of Bodie's travel-savvy pals offer their best tips for trips:

Lucy Postins, founder of The Honest Kitchen
Smaller and more frequent meals can lessen the risk of travel sickness. Adding a small amount of dried ginger or ginger tea to a light meal before you depart can also be beneficial for pets who are prone to sickness in the car. Some dogs do better if they fast right before hitting the road.

Dr Roger Mugford, animal psychologist, author, trainer to the Queen's Corgis and founder of The Company of Animals
Chose the right make of car – a Porsche or Lamborghini is not dog-friendly! Be sure there is good air-con with plenty of space for the dog to lay out. Start early with training a puppy and teach them that car travel (usually) has a happy ending. Finally, be sure to restrain your dog tightly with either crash-tested crates or, for larger dogs, a tight fitting and robust harness, such as the CLIX CarSafe.

Nikki Star of @wtfrenchie
Always have a water bottle and portable water bowl handy, because dogs can get especially thirsty in cars. I also always pack a couple Nylabones for the Frenchies to chew on in the backseat when they get bored.

Carol Bryant of Fidose of Reality & BlogPaws
Make a temporary identification tag with hotel information and your mobile phone number to help reunite Fido with you quickly, thus avoiding checking with out-of-area vets/shelters to find your lost pooch. You can create a homemade tag with an easily replaceable insert using materials from a craft store. Change the destination with each trip you and your canine pal take. How much fun would it be to later scrapbook these tags representing all the places Fido has been with you?

Teresa J. Rhyne, bestselling author of *The Dog Lived (and So Will I)*
If it's going to be a long trip, we map out where the dog parks are so we can make regular stops. This is particularly important for Percival and his carsickness issues, but Daphne appreciates being able to run about and sniff new things – very important to a Beagle!

Rachel Oates, photographer @winnythecorgi
My camera is always kept around my neck on a strap. Dogs can be adorably unpredictable and it can be heart-breaking if you miss documenting it! I also recommend getting on your dog's level rather than shooting down at them – this will help to include more of your surroundings!

Crusoe the Celebrity Dachshund
I have three main carriers I bring on every trip: a carry-on pet carrier for the plane, a sling bag for carrying me around on hikes or long walks when I get tired, and a little shoulder bag that I can be concealed in if we need to sneak into someplace that's maybe not *totally* dog-friendly!

Seth Casteel, *Underwater Dogs* photographer

Take your time and stop along the way to enjoy the scenery and adventures. Also, I always think it's fun to ask a bunch of people you don't know to pose in a picture with your dog – having that photo on display in your home makes for a great conversation piece!

Monique G. Nerman, author of *King Tommy*

A way to help hotels maintain their faith in dog owners is to show how well-behaved our pooches are! If your dog wants to sleep on the bed or lie on the couch then bring a spare blanket to cover the bed or sofa. I also always bring a small towel to place under the water and food bowl to avoid stains on the floor. And if it's raining (or you are coming back from a day at the beach) do dry off paws before entering the lobby and your room to avoid leaving marks on the carpets.

Maria Himmich of The Tropical Dog blog

The key word is PLAN. Obviously travelling with a dog is not as easy as travelling solo. We need to check out pet-friendly transportation, accommodation, places to visit... My dog has changed my way of travelling but in a very good way. Thanks to her, I now look for places off the beaten track. I prefer nature to cities because she does. At the end of the day, what really matters is the satisfaction of having shared an unforgettable adventure!

The Dog Suitcase

Bodie's doggie dozen of travel essentials:

1. Pet Travel Organiser Bag

A dedicated dog bag really helps streamline road tripping – everything in one place, ready to go. The best and most comprehensive we've found is the Solvit HomeAway Pet Travel Organiser Kit which has an over-the-shoulder strap and comes complete with a secure pouch for dry dog food, two foldable dog bowls, a large water bottle, mesh sides ideal for holding toys and tennis balls, and even a front dispenser for poo bags (we rate Earth Rated as the best quality). It really is the next best thing to a Louis Vuitton steamer trunk and can hold all these goodies:

2. Kong and Peanut Butter

Natural rubber Kongs filled with peanut butter are fantastic for getting your dog into a Treat Trance, thus forgetting the unfamiliarity of his/her surroundings. I opt for the plastic jars of PB: just remember to pack a plastic knife or two – peanut butter is not something you want to be scooping out with your toothbrush handle. Trust me.

3. Dog Wash Shampoo Miniatures

Just as you decant your shampoo into travel-size bottles, you can do the same with your dog's favourite cleaning potion. Bodie's fur gets all soft and gleamy with Earthbath's Eucalyptus and Peppermint shampoo, until he rolls in the dirt two seconds later.

4. Dog Robe

This sounds like a joke but Bodie's towelling Dog Robe has proved indispensable – say he's taken a dip in the sea or a stream and then needs to get straight in the car, just wrap him up and in half an hour he's dry. Also great for containing a mucky or moulting pup in a posh hotel.

5. Dog Brush

If your dog likes to be brushed this is another comforting activity that can help settle him/her. Bodie is a big fan of the bristle and metal prong combo and now obediently turns around when I say, 'Other side!'

6. Dog Aromatherapy

I tried vet-prescribed calmers on Bodie but it was too disturbing watching him try to battle the sedating effects. As you'll know from the book, Ajne's lavender-infused Tro DaBone works a treat on Bodie and we also like Pet Remedy's De-Stress and Calming range, which uses natural essential oils and even includes a plug-in diffuser option for hotel stays.

7. Medication

Bodie gets his dose of flea medication on the nineteenth of the month so if this falls while we're away I make sure to take his vial along. We also pack anti-itch sprays for when he's gone foraging where he shouldn't. Any special pills for your dog, zip them in a secure spot!

8. Favourite Dog Toy

Out of consideration for your hotel neighbors it's best to opt for something non-squeaky!

9. Chuckit and Extra Balls

I never learned to throw with any skill or force so a Chuckit is vital for getting Bodie to run at full tilt. I definitely recommend packing an extra ball or two because if your dog is anything like Bodie he'll occasionally decide not to retrieve it and you'll have to watch it bobbing slowly out to sea.

10. Dog Bowls

Obviously you want to leave your heavy chinaware at home and opt for something light and non-breakable. Other than the ones that come with the Solvit bag, PetsPyjamas do a neat collapsible silicone dog bowl for travel.

11. Mini Dog Treats

Training treats like Zuke's Mini Naturals are handy for incentivising your dog to stay in position and pose for a holiday snap, as well as a handy reward when your dog hops back in the car after an all-too-brief pit-stop on a long journey. Happy tum, happy chum.

12. Dog Bed

Unless you have an itsy-bitsy dog this isn't going to fit in the dog suitcase, but you definitely want to bring your dog's foam favourite, even if he/she will inevitably end up sleeping on the bed with you...

Bone Appetit!

Belinda's Tips for Dining Out with Your Dog

1. Look for a dog bowl and/or treat jar outside the restaurant – these are surefire signs that the place is especially accommodating of canine customers, as they are actively luring them over!

2. Before you enter the restaurant, check the spacing of the tables on the patio. If they are packed too tightly and another dog arrives, it can become a little fractious and stressful. Plus Bodie always tries to rear up and sniff passing plates so it's best if the waiter isn't having to constantly step over him. Nobody wants a lapful of linguine.

3. If you are lucky enough to find a restaurant with a dog menu, my tip is not to actually set the bowl down on the floor as the entire meal will be wolfed in a microsecond. Better to help pace your pup by hand-feeding him one piece at a time. It will help hold his attention and keep him sitting nicely. When the last piece is done I make an 'All gone' motion with my hands so Bodie knows that he can lie down and relax with his full tum.

4. Bring your own water bowl. We have a foldable fabric one from Outward Hound that fits in my smallest bag. It means Bodie can have a drink as soon as we are seated and there's no chance of him turning his nose up at a water bowl other dogs have supped at. (Or flies have dropped into.)

5. Make sure your dog is properly secured. Nine times out of ten it's just me and Bodie stopping for a snack and if I have to step inside to order he's typically good as gold, waiting patiently for my return. However... There was this one time outside Starbucks in Virginia when a cat scooted by and Bodie took off in hot pursuit, dragging the hefty metal chair with him. I now favour a railing or a sturdy table post where possible. Better to be safe than chasing furniture down the street, as I always say.

6. Introduce your dog to the waiter and any concerned onlookers. If I catch a glimmer of wariness I try to make a cheery announcement that he's very friendly and won't be any trouble. Either that or I'll take out a tiny training treat so they can see that he takes it from me oh-so-gently (as opposed to savaging my arm) and then a sense of peace and happy dining is restored!

Acknowledgements

Although this entire book is a gratitude-filled love letter to Bodie, I must begin by thanking my furry muse – he was the beginning, middle and happy ending to this book. And the ultimate road trip companion.

Were it not for Jennifer Pryor and the team at Pryor's Planet, Bodie would not have lived to have this adventure and I shall always be profoundly thankful to her and every rescue group, animal shelter, humane society and foster volunteer on the planet.

Molly Hayden paved the way to Portland and was an exemplary example of a woman-and-dog team. Although dear Winnie (to whom this book is dedicated) has since passed on, we feel your eternal love for her.

I'd also like to thank Leslie Melvin for introducing me to Molly and for being the dream Los Feliz neighbour.

Other California-based thank yous include all Bodie's playmates (human and canine) at Camp Bow Wow and Camp Run-A-Mutt in San Diego and my dearest lunch-and-chat pal Tony Horkins who, rather like Bodie, always makes me smile. (Thanks for snapping us in the Honda.)

In the UK we have love match Sam and Marcus, now happily Mr & Mrs, always such generous hosts and supportive, encouraging friends. And James, a confirmed cat man who turned out to be a total dog whisperer when it comes to Bodie.

Instant mutual adoration. James is, and always has been, my rock (Hudson).

Which leads us to Doris Day – an inspirational animal advocate radiating pure sunshine. You drew us to Carmel and the most scenic dog beach in the land. (Bodie thanks you.)

From sunshine to Summersdale, my exceptional publishers – so caring, receptive and enthusiastic, every single step of the way. First there was my wonderful and warm-hearted editor Debbie Chapman, then kind and conscientious copy-editor Daniela Nava, super savvy publicist Lizzie Curtin and, overseeing the whole process, the meticulous and wise Robert Drew. What a pleasure it is to work with such a diligent and harmonious team.

Cover designer Jarmila Takač – one of the loveliest and most talented people in the world. Thank you for always going the extra mile across the miles – your designs make my heart so happy!

Finally, thanks as always to my mother Pamela who cheered this project on year in, year out. And who, despite claiming not to be an animal lover, I often find lying on the carpet whispering sweet nothings to Bodie...

Bodie on the Road
Fuelled by Forthglade!

When Bodie and I moved from the West Coast (USA) to the West Country (UK) we had a lot of new things to explore – beaches with pink sand, woods with bluebells and, most importantly to Bodie, the food aisles at our local pet stores...

While I was busily studying the ingredients and cooing over the pretty packaging, Bodie decided to go one step further and consult with an expert in the field – key dog food taster at Forthglade: a Yellow Lab named Bo.

I have a suspicion Bodie was swayed by her name but for me it was the fact that the majority of the food was produced in a country village under an hour from our new home! Forthglade have been making delicious doggie dinners for over forty years – free from from junk and fillers, their recipes use only 100% natural ingredients.

The wet meals were an instant hit – Bodie's favourite is the lamb (much licking of chops in anticipation) but he also loves the turkey with sweet potato. We switch between the complementary range called Just 90% (containing 90% high-quality meat to be served with a mixer) and the Forthglade Complete range which is a fully balanced meal in itself. These packs are especially good for travel and, if need be, Bodie can enjoy them straight from the tray!

Seeing as Bodie now eats every last morsel from his dog bowl and his coat has never been so soft and shiny, we can't wait to try Forthglade's new 'cold-pressed' range of dry dog food – meaning that the ingredients are gently pressed at low temperatures to preserve all the natural fibre, vitamins and enzymes. (It is also incredibly easy for pets to digest as it breaks down without absorbing water from the dog!) Available in duck or chicken options, the recipes also contain brown rice, vegetables, fruit, omega-3 oils, vitamins, minerals and botanicals. If only I had such a healthy diet!

So now when you see Bodie bobbing along on the Shaldon Ferry or strolling the Torquay seafront, you'll know he's exploring Devon fuelled by Forthglade!

Forthglade is available at Waitrose, Tesco, Pets at Home, Ocado, Morrisons, SPAR, independent pet retailers and online at www.forthglade.com.

EST.1971
Forthglade®
NATURAL PET FOOD   FROM DEVON

Have you enjoyed this book?
If so, why not write a review on your favourite website?

If you're interested in finding out more about our books, find us on Facebook at **Summersdale Publishers** and follow us on Twitter at **@Summersdale**.

Thanks very much for buying this Summersdale book.

www.summersdale.com